DATE DUE

Bestsellers

John Sutherland

Department of English, University of London

Bestsellers

Popular fiction of the 1970s

Routledge & Kegan Paul
London, Boston and Henley

First published in 1981
by Routledge & Kegan Paul Ltd
39 Store Street,
London WC1E 7DD,
9 Park Street,
Boston, Mass. 02108, USA, and
Broadway House,
Newtown Road,
Henley-on-Thames,
Oxon RG9 1BN

Set in 11/12pt IBM Journal
and printed in Great Britain by
Biddles Ltd, Guildford, Surrey

British Library Cataloguing in Publication Data

Sutherland, John Andrew
Bestsellers.
1. Bestsellers
I. Title
823.914   PR881   80-41390

ISBN 0-7100-0750-7

Mickey Spillane, one of the world's top mystery writers, is read in fourteen languages every minute of every day. Since *I, the Jury*, published in 1947, his books have sold more than 55,000,000 copies throughout the world. People like them.

(1970s blurb to Spillane's paperbacks. Spillane himself claims to have sold over 150,000,000 copies of his work.)

For some literary critics writing a book that is popular and commercially successful rates very high on the list of white-collar crime.

(Bestselling author Irwin Shaw reviewing superselling author Mario Puzo's *Fools Die*.)

Contents

Acknowledgments

The author and publisher would like to thank the following for their kind permission to reprint copyright material:

George G. Harrap & Co, Unesco and Robert Escarpit for use of the table on p. 7; New English Library for the illustration on p. 128. Stephen Brook has been very helpful at every stage of writing. I am grateful to University College London for sabbatical leave, during which I had time to work on this project.

Preface

When I tell my colleagues that I am 'working' on bestsellers I have detected behind their polite interest the unstated question, 'Why bother?' Such scepticism, and even a mild rebuke, is understandable enough. Since one third of my salary as a university teacher is designed as a stipend for research, I (and my colleagues) can estimate that some £10,000 of UGC cash has gone into this exercise in reading less than good books. Most academic teachers of English become adept over the years at parrying the familiar accusation, 'You lucky sods, you get *paid* for reading fun books. We have to do it in our own time after a *real* day's work.' (To which the standard reply is, 'So you think reading the *Pisan Cantos* and *Finnegans Wake* is fun, do you?') It is harder to parry when the literature in question is universally disdained by one's own profession.

I don't pretend to be adept in explaining it, but I have satisfied myself as to the value of spending my time and the state's cash on 'seriously' reading the likes of Frederick Forsyth and Harold Robbins. As I have argued in a previous book, it seems evident to me that the literary or 'quality' novel is much more closely tied to the mass-consumption article (James's 'novel of commerce') than our educational syllabus customarily allows. 'Tied' does not necessarily imply bondage. The thinking behind this study is not alarmist. I do not think the serious novel to be, as one slogan of 1975 put it, 'an endangered species' — endangered, that is, by mass-produced *Trivialliteratur*. But I do think that the dominant mode of commercial production of fiction brings all sorts of formative and deforming pressures to bear on the best novels and novelists of our age. I would not go so far as to say that unless we understand *Jaws* we shall not fully understand Naipaul, but the fact that Benchley and Naipaul are both published (in Britain) by André Deutsch suggests, if not a congenital, at least a place-of-work relationship between bestseller and Booker Prize winner.

There is also, in my opinion, a usefully corrective aspect to the study of bestsellers. These novels deny us the luxury of clear cut, autonomous authorship and achieved 'texts'. The lamentable decline of bibliography as a subject in recent years has confirmed among its students an attitude to literature which is both mystical and lazy. Even undergraduates now seem to assume that books are produced magically, effortlessly wished into existence by their artistically independent authors. One of the useful aspects of bestsellers is that we cannot see them as isolated texts with single minds behind them. We have to see them as books: things which are made and are successful in so far as they sell, not just things which are composed and are successful in so far as they are critically evaluated. Nor are bestsellers entirely made by their 'authors'; a whole string of agents, editors and salesmen could − if copyright law and literary convention allowed − claim 'credits' in an essentially corporate venture.

Wherever possible I have used blurbs and publishers' synopses − not just out of idleness (though they are very convenient) but because such material bears an impress from the producers of the commodity and is thus often doubly demonstrative.

Annotation

A Checklist of the fiction works mentioned in the text will be found appended, with author and date of first publication. Since different forms and places of publication are involved I have not attempted to give the various British and American publishers. An exception is made where I have quoted. In such cases the edition used is indicated parenthetically after the Checklist entry. For non-fiction I have used the Harvard system of notation. Full details will be found in the Bibliography of non-fiction works appended.

Introduction

What, Henry James asked in 1899, would the novel of the twentieth century be like? That there would be a future for the form he was certain: 'till the world is an unpeopled void,' he prophesied, 'there will be an image in the mirror.' But the quality of that image, the 'art' which he had laboured to raise, James saw as threatened by fiction's spectacular success as a market commodity. There had been 'monstrous multiplications':

> The published statistics are extraordinary, and of a sort to engender many kinds of uneasiness. The sort of taste that used to be called 'good' has nothing to do with the matter: we are so demonstrably in presence of millions for whom taste is but an obscure, confused, immediate instinct. In the flare of railway bookstalls, in the shop-fronts of most booksellers, especially the provincial, in the advertisements of the weekly newspapers, and in fifty places besides, this testimony to the general preference triumphs (James, 1962, pp. 48-9).

The great novelist's overture to the new century finishes on an uplifting note. But the essay as a whole is haunted by James's 'uneasiness' at the perceived 'triumph' of the 'general preference' of the 'millions'. Trampling through the neat parterres of the House of Fiction is Demos, emancipated by the Common Schools Act of 1870 and sodden with an excess of those low novels that George Eliot memorably called 'spiritual gin'. The Hogarthian allusion is not quite right, however, for it was the newness and, in an obscure way, the new technology which alarmed the nineteenth-century clerisy. Matthew Arnold, for example, picked on the same associations of 'flaring' gaslight and steam engines in his description of 'the tawdry novels which flare in the book-shelves of our railway stations, and which seem designed, as so much else that is produced for the use of our middle class seems designed, for people with a low standard of life' (Williams, 1961, p. 169).

It was a couple of years before James wrote 'The future of the novel', but it was in his other home, America, that the term 'bestseller' originated. And clearly enough it is the now familiar glossy bestseller and bestsellerdom that he foresaw. It is noteworthy, however, that although it alarmed him as a portent, James — who almost single-handedly made his kind of fiction *discutable* — does not discuss the 'English novel of commerce'. To do so is 'impossible, I think . . . without bringing into the field many illustrations drawn from individuals — without pointing the moral with names both conspicuous and obscure. Such a freedom would carry us, here, quite too far, and would moreover only encumber the path' (James, 1962, p. 54). The task is declined by James, not only 'here' but elsewhere. The taste of the millions in novels — their fiction factory, to adapt the Jamesian metaphor — is glimpsed only fleetingly in stall displays, through shop windows and in advertisements.

The majority of critics of the twentieth century follow James's practice. Anthony Burgess, for example, writing a study comprehensively entitled *The Novel Now* ('now' being 1945-71) confidently discards much of what is, ostensibly, his subject matter:

Very occasionally the best book and the bestseller
coincide, but generally the books that make the most
money are those which lack both style and subtlety and
present a grossly over-simplified picture of life. Such books
are poor art, and life is too short to bother with any art
that is not the best of its kind (Burgess, 1971, p. 20).

Embodied in this bluff dismissal notice served on a large slice of Anglo-American fiction are a familiar set of interlocking prejudices, all confirming Burgess's critical triage. First, there is the *prédilection d'artiste* for the 'aristocratic', the stronger since Burgess, like Lawrence who elaborated the theory, is a major novelist ('style and subtlety' opposed to 'poor art' — the class attributes transpose clearly enough). This hauteur is buttressed by an appeal to the select canon of 'real' and 'classic' art which transcends the flux of time; of the many maxims he could have chosen, Burgess chooses to cue us with Hippocrates' *ars longa, vita brevis* ('life is too short to bother . . .'). Finally, underpinning the whole is Arnold's notion of the 'culture' of the highly educated minority, 'the best that has been thought and said' (Burgess's gloss: 'the best of its kind'). The bestness which is not respected is that of selling.

Burgess's is one book, and within its self-imposed restriction a good one. But around us, every week, we see the same prejudice at work. An alien, with nothing but the back ends of our weeklies or the Friday and Sunday supplements to go on, would hardly infer that the fiction industry depends preponderantly on a handful of current bestsellers and a mass of genre productions, largely brought out in paperback (a form generally ignored by reviewers, though for twenty years the majority of novels have been bought as reprints in soft covers). This flattering misapprehension of a reading public abuzz with interest in the week's 'quality' hardback novels is quickly dispelled by a visit to any of W.H. Smith's eighty or so station bookshops. In their 'flare' (brighter even than that which appalled James and Arnold) one is bombarded by 'W.H. SMITH'S TOP TEN PAPERBACKS' (predominantly fiction), a 'bestsellers' section (paperback novels) and rank upon rank of sf (science fiction), gothic, thriller and romance volumes — all paperback. What one does not find are the £5 apiece novels earnestly evaluated in this week's *New Statesman*, *Spectator* or *TLS*.

One can cite other examples of the bestseller's invisibility at the level where literature is seriously discussed. In 1976 a comprehensive guide to British and American *Contemporary Novelists* was prepared by St James Press, London, and St Martin's Press, New York. It is a massive volume, more like a building block than a book. Some 1,650 pages long, it represents the efforts of two Editors, twenty-nine Advisers (all distinguished academics or otherwise literary dignitaries) and 194 Contributors. Between them this critical regiment have produced entries on nearly 700 novelists, arranged alphabetically from Ahmad Abbas to Sol Yurick. The comprehensiveness of the work is astonishing; everyone will find authors whom he has never heard of, but whose contribution to contemporary fiction is clearly substantial. And equally astonishing is the cyclopaedia's omission of novelists one cannot but have heard of, but whom the Advisers regard as beneath notice. Even a reference work of this extensiveness can find no room for Harold Robbins (with an estimated 200 m. sales), Alistair MacLean (with an estimated 150 m. sales), Frederick Forsyth (with an estimated 50 m. sales), Mickey Spillane (with an estimated 150 m. sales), Barbara Cartland (with an estimated 100 m. sales), Jacqueline Susann (whose bestselling novel has sold over 6 m. in the US) or Peter Benchley (whose bestselling novel has sold over 10 m. in the US).

There are good reasons for this quite typical neglect. Academic and higher-journalism approaches habitually establish a critic/subject to literary/object relationship, which the bestseller slips out of. The bestseller is never static or sufficiently complete in itself for criticism either to get to work on it, or to make the work worthwhile. (Thinking along these lines Colin Watson observes, in his entertaining *Snobbery With Violence*, that looking for literary qualities in Edgar Wallace is as futile as applying canons of sculpture to a pile of gravel.) We have no critical vocabulary for applauding the ingenious, polymorphic tie-ins of an otherwise poor novel (its media adaptability), or for congratulating a novelist who writes indifferently — or even appallingly — but promotes his or her book with genius (Jacqueline Susann is a prime example). Above all, criticism has great difficulty in coming to terms with the ephemeral product; there is no good criticism of the bestseller for the same reason that there is no good criticism of television; the thing is never around long enough to be engaged with. Denied his customary durable object, the reviewer/critic falls back on a kind of Podsnappery ('Not literature!') and saves his time for more worthwhile activities. Bestsellers are left to the mock-critical assessments of the advertising man.

Traditionally, then, 'bestseller' is not a term which has figured much in literary-critical discussion, other than as a pejorative for an outlying area of books which literary criticism prefers not to discuss. Yet, for some purposes, the utility of bestsellers lies in the very fact that they often have no literary merit to distract us. We are not therefore detained by any respect for their sanctity as 'texts'. Nor are we automatically led to think of them as finished products in their own right; instead we can view them as integrated and dependent parts of a frankly commercial machinery, itself the product of a particular society at a particular period of history. Seen in this way, the bestselling novel may be reckoned as subordinate to other parts of the manufacturing and consuming system — such as the publicity which helps sell it, the author's 'image' or the public's 'needs'. One is rarely tempted to detach the bestseller from the specific conditions of its typically brief bestselling existence. And what is useful about such culturally embedded works is what they tell us about the book trade, the market place, the reading public and society generally at the time they have done well. As a German critic neatly puts it: 'the bestseller indicates a successful sociological experiment' (Peters, 1976, p. 139). There is a hand-in-glove relationship between the bestseller, its time and its productive apparatus. Withdrawn from this relationship they perplex us: why, one wonders, should close on two million otherwise sensible Americans in 1972 have wanted to buy *Jonathan Livingston Seagull*? Answers can only be found by looking at the historical and book trade circumstances in which Bach's book 'made it'. In this way the bestseller forces us to think, as Raymond Williams, for example, would have us always think, of 'Literature in Society' rather than 'Literature and Society' (Williams, 1977, p. 24). There are other reasons for reading bestsellers — not least that they are often fun to read. But it is the inextricability of bestsellers from their host culture and productive machinery that directs the attempt to read them critically in the following pages.

On the use of the term

The word 'bestseller' and its derivatives (bestsellerism, bestsellerdom) are not governed by any agreed definitions. In the book trade the many usages are casual, and often abused by the advertising industry's version of poetic licence and suggestive indefiniteness. 'Bestseller' can refer to books, a style of books or an author of books (Sidney Sheldon, for example, is proclaimed as 'Mr Bestseller'). One regularly encounters such illogicalities as still unpublished (and therefore entirely unsold) novels being described as 'surefire bestsellers'. And indeed, so many works in the course of a year are put forward as *best*sellers as to make the superlative meaningless. (Once achieved, of course, the true bestseller would mean the end of bestsellerdom.)

Commentators on bestsellers have adopted various definitions of convenience. Simplest is Alice P. Hackett's taxonomic approach, in her various books on the American bestseller. For these surveys Hackett merely summarizes the works which have figured in the New York lists and makes up an annual 'ten bestsellers of the year' (fiction and non-fiction) aggregate. For Hackett, bestsellers are books which have had the honour of appearing in American bestseller lists. Slightly more analytic is F.L. Mott, in his 1947 study *Golden Multitudes*. Mott employs a quantitative threshold to identify the books which are his subject. His test for bestselling status is that a book shall sell a quantity equal to 1 per cent of the population of the US for the decade in which it was published. The advantage of Mott's calculus is that he can include in his discussion long-term steady-sellers which move too slowly to figure on weekly, monthly and annual lists, or which are too unglamorous to be included, since the essence of bestsellerism, as with pop music, is that there should be hectic change and turnover. The disadvantage of Mott's approach is that for him the bestseller is not a distinct genus but an ordinary book which succeeds to an extraordinary degree. Whereas for the book trade, of course, the bestseller stands in the same relation to other books as does a star to a supporting player. It is importantly *different* from the run of merchandise.

Robert Escarpit, in his works on the sociology of literature, confronts this question of how the successful book is different in kind, not just degree. For him the bestseller is typified by a distinctive selling curve; and the graphs which he sets up record not just a volume (which is what Mott does) but pace of sale (which Mott doesn't). Using this bi-axial measurement

Escarpit discriminates between three forms of sales success: fastseller, steadyseller and bestseller (see table).

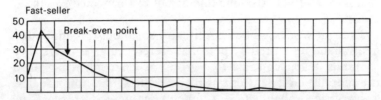

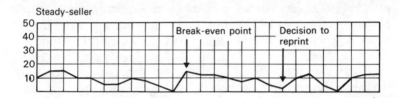

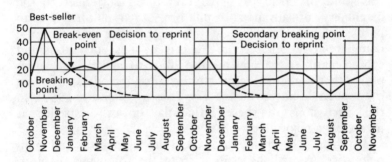

Source: Escarpit, 1966, p.117.

For Escarpit the bestseller is one of a very small number of books (some 2-3 per cent, as he reckons) which combine characteristics of the other two kinds of successful book: 'a best-seller is in fact a fast-seller which, at a certain point, develops into a steady-seller' (Escarpit, 1966, p. 118).

Escarpit's definition is precise and satisfyingly technical. Its disadvantage is, it seems to me, that it does not always do justice to the bestseller as 'an American kind of book'. Nor does Escarpit's method allow him to deal easily with the bestselling *author* (for example, Barbara Cartland, who has sold over 100 m. copies of her romances, yet rarely if ever has any single title on a list at any particular time) or *genre*, that is to say the bestselling line of books ('romance', 'gothics' etc.).

Escarpit's work, as befits a literary sociologist, is admirably neutral and untainted by personal preference. In its neutrality it stands in flat contrast to a group of what might be called the morally indignant critics of bestsellers, of whom the best known are probably O.H. Cheney (*Economic Survey of the Book Industry*, 1932), Q.D. Leavis (*Fiction and the Reading Public*, 1932), and, most recently, Per Gedin (*Literature in the Market Place*, 1977). For these commentators the bestseller is, primarily, the product of a debased cultural ethos — bestsellerdom. Their studies, all of them highly eloquent, are suffused with pessimism, or at best a depressed sense that whatever hope there is lies in the resistant power of 'an armed and conscious minority'. The bestseller is conceived by this kind of critic to signal literature's surrender to the machinery of advanced capitalism. As a cultural system bestsellerdom is marked by an internal drive towards total commercial rationalization. So driven, it is portentous and symptomatic of general malaise (it is to make these larger points that Richard Hoggart, for instance, introduces a survey of popular literature in his *The Uses of Literacy*, 1957). In the discussions of these influential critics 'bestseller' is invariably a pejorative.

My own use of the term is, I hope, neutral and non-pejorative. As will be evident from the following chapters, I would contend that bestsellers are usefully approached by an examination of the apparatus which produces them (bestseller lists, the publishing industry, publicity), an apparatus which is called here, for convenience, 'bestsellerism'. In the following pages I do not make Escarpit's fine distinction between 'fastsellers' and 'bestsellers'. Nor, of course, do the American and British book trades. For me (and them) the contemporary fiction bestseller is, more often than not, a fastselling book which never achieves the respectable middle-age of steady demand. And the main form in which this fastseller/bestseller retails is now the paperback. (Arguably in the UK, where titles get on what bestseller lists there are with sales of 20,000 or less, there is no such thing as a 'hardback bestseller'.)

In the 1970s the production of paperback bestsellers has rationalized around two poles: that of the blockbuster (whose sales, in the US alone, can achieve 10 m. in a couple of years) and genre (one of the striking features of the period has been the growth of traditional genre lines, like sf, and the innovation of bestselling new lines such as the 'bodice ripper', or soft-porn historical romance designed for the women's market). In the main section of this study I have concentrated on the more spectacular blockbusters and supersellers of the 1970s, especially those which have benefited from being tied in to films and television.

Chapter One

An American kind of book?

To begin with the most obvious and important point:
America is, in my experience, the only country in the
world which is, for better and for worse, squarely, uncom-
promisingly in the twentieth century.

(A. Alvarez)

I

A vast number of new novels are published every year.
Probably no ordinary reader gets through more than 1 per
cent of the 2,000 or so new titles which are put out annually
in the British and American markets. Even extraordinary
readers — regular reviewers, for example — are unlikely to
take in as much as 10 per cent of the whole. One year's wave
washes over the last, and in a decade hosts of literary aspirations, small achievements and potboilers are irretrievably
gone. Few categories of book can be less disturbed in the
six copyright libraries than the unmemorable bulk of this
century's 100,000 novels.

In the flux of new products which the book trade churns
out, a minority of works achieve some more or less permanent
existence and stay in view for longer than the moment
granted to most novels. A very few — certainly less than one
a year — enter the canon of literature, the hoped-for destiny
of any self-respecting work. These touchstones will eventually
be studied in schools and universities. Their author's working
materials and literary remains will be sought out and carefully
archived; for in all probability there will follow a biography,
critical monographs, theses, scholarly editions and exegesis

in learned journals. Lay readers will deferentially buy or borrow the endorsed 'classic', whose worth they largely take on trust. There are, in fact, few better preservatives of a novel and its author's fame than to be set for examination, to be judged as suitable research material by the committees which approve PhD topics, or to be approached by an American university offering the curatorship of manuscript materials.

Permanence of a less absolute kind is achieved by bestsellers. For a season, extending usually from a few weeks to a year, these novels withstand the forces which push most fiction into speedy oblivion. But even supersellers cannot reckon on staying in the lists for much more than a year, and most will do well to last a couple of months. And to gain this moderate lease of life a novel will have to sell enormously: between 100,000 and 800,000 in hardback, and between one and six millions in paperback (these American figures can be scaled down to about a fifth for the UK market).

Unlike the candidates for literary canonization, the number of bestsellers is quite predictable. From week to week there will be ten in the two main book forms. By the end of the year some forty new novels, and newly paperbacked novels, will have made the lists. Given this even-paced turnover, the superlative 'bestseller' is something of a confidence trick. It should correctly be 'better-than-average seller' or 'top-bracket seller'. But it is, of course, unthinkable that the book trade in the interest of semantic precision should ever sacrifice the salesworthy implication that the bestseller is *the* book of books. 'Hype' (trade lies) is the first language of bestsellerdom.

One of the most striking features of the bestseller, compared to the 'literary' novel, is the all-or-nothing nature of its achievement. It is commonly the book that everyone is reading now, or that no one is reading anymore. Once a bestseller is spent, or its formula is spent, no residue is left. This partly explains why popular fiction has no generic sense of sustained progress or tradition. It is always 'new' but never an advance; *Airport '75* is ahead of *Airport*, *Airport '79* ahead of *Airport '77*, only in date. *Jaws 2* is a sequel, but in no sense an advance on *Jaws*. And no more than popular fiction is the bestselling author registered in the public mind as developing from novel to novel. He has no *oeuvre*, merely a rate of production and a brand-named, standardized product. The 'latest Harold Robbins' is a very different formulation from 'Lawrence's later novels'.

It is also, one might argue, a fundamentally un-English formulation, alien to cisatlantic cultural traditions and book trade customs. The OED gives an American origin for the term bestseller, an etymology which one instinctively feels to be right. The word still sounds American, like 'movie star', 'hit parade', or baseball's 'hall of fame'. It is, however, earlier in origin than these three coinages. The first recorded use of the term 'bestseller' is in the last decade of the nineteenth century, and we can trace the system ('bestsellerism') to preverbal origins in the practice of American publishing and bookselling before the Act of 1891 which enforced the observance of international copyright. As a business in the nineteenth century largely dependent on systematic piracy, the American book trade had much more interest in the sale of books than their origination. Until 1891 the raw material was always readily available to be stolen from (notably) British sources — how to merchandise it was the problem. Competitive price cutting, mail order, paperbound editions, high-pressure publicity, gimmickry, mass production economies of scale, sales in nonbookstore outlets were all force grown in the hot-house atmosphere of American book retailing. And so too was bestsellerism.

Historically, bestseller lists have been a part of American literary life since February 1895, when the *Bookman* began recording titles of novels 'in the order of demand' (piratical habits died hard; eight out of the ten novels listed were British). In 1897 this information was digested as 'Best Selling Books' and has been available to the American public ever since. (In 1912 *Publishers Weekly* extended coverage to non-fiction — but, true to its first formulation, the term bestseller still largely evokes the novel.) Various American journals and trade journals now not only list over-all country-wide successes from week to week, but also provide specialist lists for cities, regions, various categories of book and groups of readers. Thus, for example, it could be verified that the 1975 bestseller *Looking for Mr Goodbar* (the tragic story of

a school teacher given to pick-ups in singles' bars) headed lists
in northern and southern California, New York and Boston —
that is to say, areas where mores were relaxed and women's
liberation well organized. The feedback from bestseller lists
concentrated publicity for the follow-up paperback where it
would do most good. Campus bestseller lists inform the book
trade how the student body, with its 20 per cent or so of the
American book market, is behaving. Children's books,
religious books, cookery books, DIY books, all have their
sales charted and provide simultaneous publicity and market
research. Every year since 1911, *Publishers Weekly* has had a
special issue analyzing the leading sales of the past twelve
months based on publishers' figures. And over the decades
this information has been gathered by Alice P. Hackett into
a series of regularly updated reports, of which the latest is
entitled *80 Years of Bestsellers: 1895-1975*.

Anyone attempting Miss Hackett's comprehensive and
numerically informative account for British bestsellers would
face a Herculean task. There were no widely publicized or
systematic lists in Britain until the *Sunday Times* began its
weekly survey amid some controversy in the 1970s, decades
after the *New York Times*. The *Bookseller* is similarly over
half a century behind its opposite book trade organ in
America, having begun its bestseller list only with the last
change of editorship in the mid-1970s. The *Evening Standard*
runs a modest paragraph at the foot of its Tuesday review
page, indicating a few books doing well in London that week.
It is based on telephone reports from six metropolitan
bookshops. The recently introduced, and conservatively
sub-titled, *Sunday Telegraph* 'Bestsellers in demand this
month' is also based on information from six outlets, all
older-fashioned, stockholding bookshops. The half-hearted
conviction behind the *Sunday Telegraph* exercise is witnessed
by the compromise of monthly rather than weekly reports
and the fact that it gives five or six titles (not, apparently, in
order) rather than the conventional 'top ten'. All of which
seems very amateurish when the *New York Times* informs us
that *its* hardback listings 'are based on computer-processed
sales figures from 1,400 bookstores in every region of the
US' and its mass-market paperback listings 'on computer

processed reports from bookstores and representative wholesalers with more than 40,000 outlets across the US'. This
extraordinarily conscientious census is clearly trusted by the
American book trade and its public. Escalator clauses can be
built into contracts with additional payments for every week
a novel features in the *NYT* or other lists. And the *NYT* #1
symbol is a supreme award, and when earned is flaunted and
prominently advertised. (It is, incidentally, quite meaningless
to the British public, for whom it has to be glossed as 'number
one international bestseller' — never, of course, 'number one
bestseller in America', which would inflame a national
inferiority complex.) As well as promoting individual titles
for publishers, the bestsellers lists in America add sparkle to
the bookclubs, which have in the past been much less reprint
affairs than in the UK. The Literary Guild, for example,
advertises itself as 'the Bestseller Bookclub' with huge double
centre spreads in the *New York Times Book Review*, usually
featuring the same titles that appear creditably in the journal's
back-end bestseller lists.

The British book trade issues formidably precise statistical
material when it wants to (witness the quarterly gross figures
published in the *Bookseller*). British amateurishness, when it
comes to recording what books are currently doing well, and
just how well, goes with what seems to be a general luke-
warmness about the value or decency of such exercises. (It is
well known, for example, that the West End, unlike Broadway,
does not publish box-office takings.) The British are not
really sure they want that kind of thing — though American
success with it constantly tempts them into thinking that it
might be worth trying. The result is something that looks
rather like timidity; a series of half-hearted and often abortive
experiments. When the *Observer* began a list to rival the
Sunday Times it was dropped after a short time. *Paperback
and Popular Hardback Buyer*, which was launched in 1977
as a new-style trade journal (i.e. modelled on *Publishers
Weekly* rather than the *Bookseller*) dropped its domestic
bestseller charts in June 1979 (according to its editor, Brian
Levy, he 'had not been happy for some time with them').
The decision, declared in a high-sounding editorial, was
publicized, and given sympathetic comment in another new

trade organ, *Publishing News*. The *Bookseller* somewhat stuffily stuck to its recently acquired list, but was noticeably shaken under the fire directed at the practice. Similar shakiness was evident elsewhere. When in 1979 it returned after a year's stoppage, the *Sunday Times* enlarged its survey of bestsellers to include records, films and television as well as books. In the first issue of the newspaper this 'Complete best-sellers list' was brought forward to p. 2 of the main news section of the paper. After a while it was relegated to the penultimate page of the 'Weekly review'. Meanwhile *Paperback and Popular Hardback Buyer* — now retitled *Paperback and Hardback BOOK BUYER* — had gone back on its June 1979 stand, and by January 1980 was offering domestic bestseller charts once again. All this, taken against the Book Marketing Council's pious contention that 'the industry must have an effective and credible bestseller list' (which 'the industry', manifestly, had no immediate intention of setting up), indicated the inability of the British book trade to make its mind up, one way or the other.

British objections to the bestseller lists fall under several heads. In the first place, the lists are suspected of being inherently spurious in their attention to quick, rather than real, bestsellers. Their week-to-week attention singles out sensational books of the moment, at the expense of longer-lived titles or groups of books which might eventually have the larger if less dramatic sale. Anthony Blond convincingly demonstrates what are the 'real bestsellers' in the supplement to his 1971 book, *The Publishing Game*. They are in the main a very drab selection of cookery books, educational texts etc. When *Now!* was launched in 1979 it carried, true to its *Time/Newsweek* inspiration, a bestseller list; predictably it was attacked by British book trade commentators as capricious and inaccurate. But worse than any likely inaccuracy, what British lists we have are alleged to carry a taint of corruption about them. Speaking while still the literary editor of the then silenced *Times*, Ion Trewin, in the Summer 1979 British controversy on the subject, made an outright accusation that 'some booksellers are being tempted to feed in titles which are not moving but to which they are oversubscribed'. Lists thus cooked, Trewin concluded, were not worth the paper they were printed on. His outburst could be taken to support the criticism, common enough in Britain, that the American book trade, by institutionalizing bestsellerdom, has sold out to its basest commercial element.

Suspicion as to the integrity of the bestseller list is confirmed by regular scandals to do with pop record charts (also an American innovation — but one to which there has been no comparable British resistance). Notoriously these charts do not merely record success, they are methodically used to generate it; that is to say a record sells because it is number one, as much as it is number one because it has sold well. The number one record in fact gains its top position by rate of sale over a week in some 300 selected stores all over Britain. Once placed, it only then achieves the bulk of its sales. Despite their pseudo-objectivity the charts are thus a potent and invitingly accessible instrument for maximizing profit and minimizing risk. Not surprisingly they are regularly suspected, and sometimes convicted, of being rigged by big business interests in the music industry. At the very least the lists and their effect on radio's weekly 'playlists' condition consumers into thinking that there are only a very few records which matter at any moment — perhaps only one. In America, pop record charts and bestseller lists have much in common; as with hit records the number of copies a book has already sold, or its 'place', is used to bludgeon other readers into buying their copy, if not immediately, then when the book comes up in paperback or book club form. 'Do we want to sell books like gramophone records?' was one question posed in the Trewin controversy (*Publishing News*, 4 May 1979). The questioner's anticipated answer was a horrified 'No!'.

Given British dissatisfaction at the inevitable inaccuracy and possible venality of weekly lists based on 'outlets' it is conceivable that publishers might release their figures, along the lines of the annual *Publishers Weekly* roundup. But it is a well known feature of the British book trade that it is always coyer about giving such information than its American counterpart. No American publisher, apparently, feels it necessary to veil the successful side of the firm's annual dealings. In Britain figures are occasionally winkled out (the *Evening Standard* makes an incomplete and impressionistic survey every Christmas), and paperback publishers are more forthcoming than hardback; but generally sales remain a trade secret, 'a confidential matter between author and publisher and never divulged to outsiders', as one famous British publishing house once told me. (Another publicity manager, who actually did divulge sales figures for a novel, requested that they not be specifically cited in print, that his name not be revealed and waggishly signed himself 'industrial spy'.)

There are doubtless snobbish reasons mixed up in the British book trade's customary reticence about letting 'outsiders' know what is going on. But it is largely founded on a traditional and worthy resistance to spotlighting the bestseller on the grounds that it diverts attention from the whole range of books available at any time. Books, it is felt, do not naturally compete against each other or do each other down in fighting for top places; rather they complement and supplement each other. The rationale of 'general trade publishing' adhered to by most major firms endorses a healthy mix of ingredients, with minority and specialist readerships catered for. It is the well balanced publisher's list, not the bestseller, that matters. The value of a book lies not in how well it sells against a competitor just like itself (how, for example, Sheldon outsells Robbins, or vice versa), but in what the best critics make of it, how well it stands the various tests of time and how usefully it fits into the general pattern of books in print. There is of course a place in this for the widely-read new novel; but it must not be the cynosure.

Not to take too lofty a view, this British prejudice in favour of a low level of competitiveness in the retail book trade may be seen to derive from a European tradition, going back at least as far as the Renaissance and its ideals of cultural wholeness. Sharing the tradition, continental neighbours have also fought shy of American bestsellerism. Systematic lists did not begin in West Germany until 1961. Eloquent critics objected that the aim of such lists was merely to induce a *Bestseller Bewusstsein* — bestseller consciousness. The fact that no sufficient German word existed was in itself proof of the barbarism of the enterprise. Protestors predicted the dire consequence of bestsellerism on the justly renowned service offered by the Geman retail trade. The stockholding bookshop would be sacrificed to the bookstand in the supermarket, whose wares are sold by publicity, eye-catching covers and an excited awareness that here are the bestsellers of the week. In both Germany and France in the 1960s there was a connected revulsion against the 'American' mass-market paperback and its 'outlets' because, as Hans Magnus Enzensberger put it in 1962: 'there the role of the bookseller is reduced to that of a mere cashier. These businesses are literary supermarkets' (Enzensberger, 1973, p. 135. The German has a wonderfully indignant resonance to it: 'Diese Geschäfte sind literarische Supermarkets'). This national resentment has simmered on. In November 1978, a few months before the Trewin-led attack on the British bestseller lists, there was a flare-up again in Germany when for the first time *Der Spiegel* began to print paperback bestseller lists. Again the indignant cry was 'Americanization'.

The issue here can be focused on a crucial ambiguity in the current usage of the verb 'sell'. In business expression the term has two distinct meanings. First is the neutral commercial transaction of exchanging a product for an agreed sum of money. Traditional bookshops sell largely in this uncoercive way; one browses in them as one would in a library with little oppression from display, advertisement or intrusive sales assistance. But the common American usage of sell is that of 'persuaded to buy'. This meaning is evident in the aggressive policy declaration by Peter Mayer, the young American publisher hired to head Penguin Books in 1978, after their worrying profit slump: 'We have . . . to go out and *sell* books. People must read what we publish, otherwise what is the point of doing it?' (*The Times*, 27 September 1978). This dynamic sense of selling by crashing through sales resistance ('People must buy . . .'), as opposed to the passive sense of booksellers offering a service in a civilized spirit of invitation, is inherent in the bestseller system.

In line with his notion of what bookselling meant, the first thing that Mayer did was to concentrate much of Penguin's effort into a sales drive for a single title, M.M. Kaye's *The Far Pavilions* — a book which evoked, but which was of a higher quality than, the women's romances for which Mayer had

helped make Avon famous. This had done well as a hardback
(250,000 reportedly sold in hardcover worldwide, six months
on UK and US bestseller lists), and Penguin/Mayer packaged
it as 'The Great Bestseller!' and 'A *Gone With the Wind* of
the North-West Frontier'. The sales campaign was outlined in
a four page pull-out supplement in the spring 1979 *Bookseller*.
On the first page stood a simple, immodest message:

> On 17 May, there will appear a Penguin that will be backed
> by the most ambitious promotion ever. It will be a unique
> event in Penguin publishing, in paperback publishing and,
> quite conceivably, in the history of publishing.

In fact the 'unprecedented advertising and promotion budget'
(£40,000), the initial print run (450,000) and the battery of
merchandising apparatus struck one as far from unique if one
subscribed to *Publishers Weekly* as well as the organ of the
British book trade. What Mayer had done was to market a
Penguin book *à la mode Americaine*. If it worked, the un-
English advertising blitz (give-away chapters and posters on
tube station walls, for example) would circulate the novel
well beyond the traditional range of Penguin's 'bookshops
within bookshops'. *The Far Pavilions* was to be a practical
demonstration of what was meant by 'going out and *selling*
books'.

The campaign probably did not immediately deliver all
that was hoped for, and there must have been some anxious
conferences at Harmondsworth. Apparently the unusually
high £2.50 price created an initial sales resistance which undid
some of the promotion. But there was a clear commercial
logic behind this atypical Penguin effort. The biggest sellers
of the 1970s — the half-dozen American novels which have
sold 10 m. plus in the home market — circumvented the old-
fashioned bookshop to a large degree. Ubiquitous self-service
paperback racks in drugstores, supermarkets and newsstands
cleared most copies of *Jaws*, *Love Story*, *The Exorcist* and
The Godfather, aided by the publicity pressures of 'all time
record breaking' movies and general 'hype'. (It is significant,
for example, that neither *Jaws*, *The Exorcist* nor *The Godfather* were the bestselling novels of their year in hardcovers —
the form in which bookstores mostly deal. *Jaws* sold just over
200,000 copies in 1974 as a hardback, close on 10 m. copies

between 1975 and 1976 as a paperback.) If Penguin wanted to have 'blockbuster' titles on this scale it would have to follow the American lead and colonize new selling territories. *The Far Pavilions* could be thought to express a clear intention to go American – not just in Penguin's chief personnel, but in the firm's way of doing things.

The American book trade, like other booming areas of big business, is not typically harrowed by self-doubt. Every year the previous years' records are broken, and complacency is the keynote of company reports. An industry which turns over four billion dollars a year and shows 10 per cent profit or more cannot think ill of itself. Nevertheless there have been longstanding objections by American commentators to the celebration of books for nothing nobler than the number of copies they can be made to sell in the shortest space of time. In his monumental study of the American book trade in 1930-1, O.H. Cheney associated the modern rage for bestsellers with the weakening of the 'civilized' bookshop system by the widely bankrupting 1929 crash. (He calculated that a mere 500 'real' bookstores survived nationwide.) Cheney foresaw a book industry on the way to suicide in its wilful surrender of professional codes and skills to short-term market imperatives:

Bestsellerism shows how far the inertia of an industry can carry it in ignorance and self-delusion. . . . Discouraging as are the ethics of bestsellerism, the light it throws on the commonsense of the industry is even more discouraging. If ever an industry needed to know the truth about its operations, it is the book industry – and all it gives itself is bestsellerism (Cheney, 1932, p. 128).

Cheney coined a vivid phrase for the hectic coming and going of titles in a bestseller-dominated book trade: 'book murder'. Books, traditionally things of permanence, are rendered as transient as newspapers or magazines by bestsellerist marketing methods, each monthly batch ruthlessly blotting out its predecessor: 'the life of a book', Cheney observed, 'is one of the most terrifying phenomena of publishing, – and it will continue to be so as long as the industry works on the spawning theory' (*ibid.*, p. 85).

Cheney's outrage was echoed in the later observation of

A.D. Van Nostrand, who perceived a 'denaturing' of the American novel, directly connected with such twentieth-century practices as the merchandising of books in department stores and the goldrush for bestsellers. Coming closer to the present day, a similar line of analysis is offered by Charles Madison (like Van Nostrand, a publisher) in his *Irving to Irving*. This book traces the decline of American book trade ethics from Washington Irving (who supplied his publishers with cash when they were in financial trouble) to Clifford Irving (who coolly attempted to embezzle *his* publishers out of a million dollars). These events record a completed cycle for Madison from 'bookworld' to 'industry'. *Irving to Irving* is a lament at the industrialization of the American book trade and the surrender of old 'genteel' codes of practice in the new ethos of brutal materialism, an ethos recently summed up in 'success' theorist Michael Korda's dictum that 'there's no such thing as a good book that doesn't sell' (*New York*, 16 January 1978). The corollary being that the book which sells best *is* best.

Of all literary forms, fiction is most vulnerable to commercial rationalization of Korda's kind. Because of its length, its need to be marketed in bulk as a new ('novel') commodity and the large, speculative investment it requires, the novel is necessarily tied to the wheels of progressive technology, commercial management and the dictatorship of the consumer. Fiction cannot adapt to the cottage-industry scale of poetry's little magazine nor, for any length of time, to the democratic regime of the underground-press publishing collective. For the novel there is no such facility as a fringe, or off-Broadway alternative. If it comes to the Blakean dilemma of making his own system or being enslaved by the other man's, the novelist has little option but slavery.

There are good historical reasons for seeing the bestseller as the logical end-product of the nineteenth- and twentieth-century American book trade. Bestsellers and big publishers make natural partners. The best bestsellers and the biggest publishing giants in the world are now American. Following the Wall Street interest in publishing in the 1960s, many firms have gradually become incorporated into conglomerates whose annual turnover and diverse operations beggar the imagination. The pattern is still shifting (the *Bowker Annual*'s review of the American book trade now has a special section on 'Takeovers and mergers'), but among the best-known fiction publishers Random House, Ballantine and Knopf are (or recently were) affiliates of RCA: Simon & Schuster and Pocket Books of Gulf & Western; Putnams of MCA; Holt, Rinehart & Winston, Popular Library and Fawcett (for a short while) of CBS. Bantam — the biggest paperback publisher in the world — has belonged successively to IFI and RCA, and now is attached to the German multinational Bertelsmann. Expansion, merger and takeover has, over the same period, made giants of the surviving 'independents' like HBJ and Doubleday.

Any time since the Second World War one can find American authors complaining about the increasing materialism of the American book trade. (English authors, by contrast, have tended to complain more about the grudging indifference or sheer philistinism of their reading public.) American authors are understandably alarmed at such grandiose statements as that of Richard Snyder, tycoon president of Simon & Schuster:

> I was the voice that said many years ago that there was going to be a consolidation in this industry before it even started to consolidate [since Snyder is in his forties it can scarcely have been so very long ago]. However it has gone well beyond what I ever thought it could go to. What we are going to see now, if this trend continues, is that like the seven sisters of the oil business, we will have seven giant publishing companies (*Publishers Weekly*, 11 April 1977).

Snyder might as well have said, 'like the five majors who dominate the world record industry'. Three of these giants also have major interests in publishing, and/or TV and movies.

American authors have naturally been less sanguine than Snyder about this massive concentration of publishing power, and its tie-in with a nucleus of dominant media corporations. The novelist John Hersey, chairman of one of the committees of the 7,500 strong Authors' Guild, observed, as one of the worst effects of the corporate nature of the 1970s American book world, that 'publishers are now going for the big book;

it is more and more a choice of *whether a book will sell*, not whether or not it will contribute to our culture' (*American Book Review*, December 1977). Indeed, to aggressive publishers of Snyder's stamp the notion of 'our culture' seems to inspire Goering-like twitches towards the revolver: 'we [at S & S] *never* use the word "literary". . . . We say "It's a good solid commercial work" ' (*New York*, 16 January 1978).

Apprehension among American authors as to the growing commercial ruthlessness and bestseller consciousness of their paymasters was heightened by the announcement in July 1979 that the venerable National Book Awards (funded by the Association of American Publishers) were to be abolished in favour of a new set of 'American Book Awards'. The main effect of the change was, briefly, to shift selection from panels on which authors and critics were predominant. The enlargement of the awards from seven to twenty-five also bestowed new prizeworthiness on paperbacks and well-merchandised books in addition to those that could merely claim to be well written. Fifty of the country's best-known authors and critics (headed by Nobel Prize winner Saul Bellow) collectively protested and called for a scornful boycott of the new awards. In a statement delivered to the APP and the *New York Times* simultaneously, the protestors claimed that

the main purpose of the new program would be 'to transfer decision-making from those who write books to those who sell and buy them' and that the program was designed 'to make sure that no more shockingly non-commercial choices are made in the future.' They argued that the new awards would be 'a rubber-stamp prize for bestsellers' (*New York Times*, 9 August 1979).

II

Despite a shared language and a common literary heritage, the British way of publishing has marked differences from the American. Famously, in Britain it has survived longer as a 'profession for gentlemen' than for salesmen or tycoons. There is an honoured tradition of disinterested and often unremunerative patronage of literature – flimsy, uncommercial work in Snyder's definition; good books that don't sell in Korda's. The creative sector of British publishing has consistently been, and to some extent still is, the middle- and smaller-sized houses – Cape, Calder, Chatto, Faber, Secker & Warburg, Deutsch, etc. – each with their carefully nurtured house character. These relatively small firms have ingeniously come to terms with the huge British overseas market (protected as an imperial domain for far longer than with non-book products), the institutional purchaser (notably public libraries) and paperback reprinters (such as Penguin). This accommodation has typically been achieved without sacrificing a 'human' scale of operation.

It is a truism to observe that in publishing, as in other areas of business, British practice has come nearer the American in the last thirty years. Some publishers have approved, arguing that an American size liberates. The late Tony Godwin gave publicity to this theory, scorning, at the same time, the British mystique of distinct house personality. A more traditional body of publishers have witnessed the drift Americawards with trepidation or despair. Such was Victor Gollancz's response in the early 1960s, after a distinguished lifetime in the profession:

> What beastly changes I have seen in my thirty-three years
> of publishing [he wrote in a private letter]. The only thing
> I am finally concerned about, professionally, is getting
> ideas over to the public. But the whole economic situation
> is developing in such a way that it is becoming
> progressively difficult, and may soon become impossible,
> to do this. The British publishing business is rapidly going
> the way of the American: it is becoming impossible,
> without the certainty of bankruptcy, to publish really
> good work by young people or books of social and
> political importance of the 'non-popular' kind. Everything
> is becoming canalised into a few huge sellers: because, with
> costs of production as they are, and the drying up of
> middle-class incomes, small sellers involve a loss which
> can't be faced (Hodges, 1978, pp. 204-5).

Old men, when their time is almost played out, are prone to see a general end in their own. But Gollancz's is an interesting complaint. He was no aesthete with an innate distaste for the bestseller or the razzmatazz that gets if off the ground. It was his firm in the 1920s which displayed a new flair in publicity, with imaginative 'stunts', bold advertising and the famous eyecatching yellow covers. His list always included such surefire bestselling authors as Daphne du Maurier, Dorothy Sayers, or A.J. Cronin. Gollancz pioneered the respectable publishing of popular genres, such as the detective story and, in the postwar period, sf. In the 1940s, Gollancz was among the first British publishers to cross the Atlantic in search of rights, thus initiating the postwar interchanges of property by which the two great English-speaking markets consolidated round the same books.

Yet for all his commercial flair and flamboyance, Gollancz seems to have held the optimistic belief that a healthy expansive commercialism can be contained by a set of literary and (in his case) political values. He was interested in bestsellers, he once said in happier days, 'because I don't believe in publishing propaganda on a shoestring'. Bestsellers, that is, were a subsidiary not a primary aspect of his book publishing philosophy. A healthy, pluralistic approach could find a place and an auxiliary use for them; but they remained·a lesser kind of book.

Gollancz fits into a typically British tradition of what might be called decent compromise. He held the very civilized belief that one can make money without surrendering principle; indeed, mammon can be enlisted in the service of publishing good books. It was a similar belief, presumably, which led a high-minded firm like Cape to take on the biggest of postwar British bestsellers, Ian Fleming. As Michael Howard notes in *Jonathan Cape, Publisher*, the annual profits from the Bond books in the 1960s were suspiciously equivalent to the firm's general surplus, with which it was able to continue its good work publishing more adventurous fiction.

A group of British novelists have also achieved their ends within a tradition of British compromise. Writers such as Iris Murdoch, C.P. Snow and Margaret Drabble regularly make, and sometimes head, British hardback bestseller lists, selling, one surmises, between 20,000 and 80,000. They may be suspected of a certain middlebrow infection; nonetheless some adventurous academic will always be found to provide a critical monograph, attesting to their intellectual worthiness. And the award of Booker and James Tait Black prizes bestow an establishment certificate of literary respectability.

There are, of course, American writers of literary distinction who make a modest, and sometimes a spectacular showing in American bestseller lists. One thinks of Mailer, Roth, Vidal and other writers as likely to have been found in NBA short-lists as among the bestsellers. But often one senses an ulterior purpose in their publishers' motives, an itch to convert quality into cashable, mass-market quantity. The following advertisement from *Publishers Weekly* (23 July 1973) illustrates it nakedly:

> With this extraordinary novel about a girl who frees herself
> through adulterous love Joyce Carol Oates has written a
> story destined to be a bestseller. *Do with me what you will*
> is the breakthrough booksellers have long known Joyce
> Carol Oates would write, a novel of bestseller caliber as
> well as of literary brilliance.

It is hard to imagine her British publisher making the same vulgar-sounding claim for Doris Lessing or Muriel Spark. It is as though for the American trade an author, whatever the literary brilliance, is only fully realized with the 'novel of bestselling caliber'. This publisher's anxiety to harness literary talent to the demands of the mass market is almost ingenuously displayed in a more recent advertisement for Jerzy Kosinski's *Passion Play*, again in *Publishers Weekly*: 'The "breakout" book by one of the world's major writers! In his first truly commercial work of fiction . . .' (*Publishers Weekly*, 2 July 1979). At last, one feels, Kosinski has got his head straight and done his duty by the book trade.

III

Differences, and important differences, remain. But in general the British book trade has increasingly followed the American example, especially where bestsellers are concerned. As Mark Goulden, of W.H. Allen, observes:

> There is little doubt most books which achieve

'bestsellerdom' in America will travel to Britain and win similar acclaim. . . . The reverse is not always the case. Many of our bestsellers do not automatically hit the jackpot in America and I attribute the cause of this to the simple fact that Americans are by no means as 'Anglicised' as we are 'Americanised' (Goulden, 1978, p. 96).

Surprisingly, perhaps, this Americanization has not entailed financial takeover (indeed, British publishers have made resourceful raids on the American book trade). What has happened, however, is an assimilation to modern American practice, with a general acceptance of this as standard, and Britain when it does not conform as lagging behind the times. With authors, this sometimes manifests itself as an impatience with the pettiness of the British scale of doing things. On being offered a paltry £1,000 by a British house for one of his recent novels, for example, Anthony Burgess refused: 'I'm fed up with being humble when Mario Puzo can get two and a half million dollars for 500 pages and characters saying things like "I knew he was full of shit" ' (*Guardian*, 29 September 1978). Burgess, like other Britons capable of producing 'international bestsellers', now thinks of the US as a primary market and its stars as his peers. It is interesting to note in this respect that Frederick Forsyth was reported to be gloomy that his *The Devil's Alternative* was to be published first in the UK; his great rival, Harry Patterson's *To Catch a King*, was more rationally published first in America with the UK as an overseas market. Both Patterson and Forsyth are, of course, 'British' authors and in these specific cases with British themes to their novels.

Taking a larger view, one can see systematic movements towards American styles of business in key institutions. W.H. Smith and Penguin provide usefully clear-cut instances. As they have for a century, Smith's dominate the retail bookselling trade in Britain, with their chains of High Street and station shops. In the late 1970s, book materials took up about 30 per cent of their floor space, and accounted for some 25 per cent of the firm's profits (their turnover is a massive £400 m. plus annually — which puts them not far behind the whole British book trade, whose money turnover is reckoned at £500 m. a year). Smith's have always been in the forefront of bookselling to the public. In the 1850s they pioneered mass marketing of the 'railway novel' — cheap reprint fiction aiming to exploit the new middle-class crowds at stations where Smith's have had a monopoly since the 1840s. In the 1860s they went into the circulating library business — based originally on their station outlets. Although this side of their operation shifted to High Street sites in the twentieth century, they continued to dominate the rental library trade until the postwar period. Smith's clearly made a realistic assessment of public library growth in the 1950s, and closed their commercial library branches in 1960. Their attention switched to two progressive modes of book mer-chandising — the book club and the mass-market paperback. With the American giant Doubleday they set up what is now known as Book Club Associates. By the mid-1970s it was the biggest book club chain in Britain, and was run on lines directly imitative of the American BOMC and Literary Guild. Smith's style of selling paperbacks is similarly American. They *do* want to sell books like records. They would like to have a bestseller list with which to scale out distribution as the pop charts are used in commercial radio and BBC 1 to draw up the week's playlist. In 1975 W.H. Smith's launched their 'top ten paperbacks' strategy. This partners 'W.H. Smith's top twenty records' and 'top ten albums'. The bestseller list (albeit an internal one) is now installed at the centre of W.H. Smith's book operation.

The changes in Penguin Books' style of business have been more subtle, but no less towards an American model of trading. Milestones have been the surrender of the uniform cover in the 1960s; the adoption of more dramatic blurb and advertising; the takeover of Viking in 1975 to create an Anglo-American axis and in 1978 the appointment of Peter Mayer, formerly with Pocket Books and Avon, as the London-based chief executive. As one commentator put it: 'Mayer is expected to introduce to Penguin the revolutionary style of publishing for which he is known in America' (*Evening Standard*, 27 September 1978. So much, incidentally, for Allen Lane's earlier 'revolution' whose evangelical aim was, as the defence counsel at the *Chatterley* trial proudly declared, 'to republish, in a form and at a price which the ordinary people could afford to buy, all the great books of our culture'). Mayer inaugurated his rule at Penguin by declaring that he at least was not overawed by 'institutions'. His personal style of management was promptly marked by *The Far Pavilions* campaign, discussed earlier.

Smith's and Penguin are not the whole book trade; but they are, indisputably, bell-wethers. Both are now distinctly Anglo-American; not primarily in terms of ownership, personnel and national territory, but in terms of their style of business and book promotion. In both cases a move towards bestsellerism is clearly evident. And it would seem to presage a general relocation of the bestseller to a more central position in the British book trade. Predicting the future of the book trade is notoriously hazardous, but I would guess that Smith's and Penguin's commercial instinct is right. It also seems a fair guess that in a few years we shall have more of the apparatus of bestsellerism in Britain — notably an authoritative list of the *NYT* kind. (On the other hand it might be thought that the hardback sale of books in the UK — where 20,000 can qualify a book for bestseller status — will mean that any such list will be something of a contradiction in terms, at least where the expensive first form of fiction is concerned.)

In the following survey I have made the assumption — perhaps prematurely — that in the 1970s one can discuss the bestseller as something supranational. The machinery which produces a Frederick Forsyth winner or an Ira Levin winner are no longer distinctly English or American machineries, but the same machinery operating in different countries. (In the nature of things the Americans, of course, are usually a few years ahead.) The bestseller is, by definition, a novel which maximizes sales and in so doing sets itself — with striking success — to override national differences. Returning to the distinction with which this chapter started, 'world literature' is demonstrably a less sure category than 'international bestseller'. Witness the fact that *The Godfather* was a number one bestseller in Japan and France, Forsyth earns 80 per cent of his income outside the UK, and *The Eagle Has Landed*, written by a Briton and set in Britain, was first published in America and was estimated to have sold 18 m. copies by

1979 in forty-two languages. Such examples could be multiplied to support the view that from its origins as an American kind of book, the bestseller is now established everywhere in the western world.

The decade's top ten

The following are the fiction bestsellers of the 1970s in the United States, as determined by the *New York Times Book Review*, 30 December 1979 (hardcover figures represent copies sold, paperback figures represent copies in print).

1 The Godfather, by *Mario Puzo* (published 1969). Hardcover, 292,765; paperback, 13,225,000.
2 The Exorcist, by *William Blatty* (published 1979). Hardcover, 205,265; paperback, 11,948,000.
3 Jonathan Livingston Seagull, by *Richard Bach* (published 1970). Hardcover, 3,192,000; paperback, 7,250,000.
4 Love Story, by *Erich Segal* (published 1970). Hardcover, 431,976; paperback, 9,778,000.
5 Jaws, by *Peter Benchley* (published 1974). Hardcover, 204,281; paperback, 9,210,000.
6 The Thorn Birds, by *Colleen McCullough* (published 1977). Hardcover, 646,503; paperback, 7,450,000.
7 Rich Man, Poor Man, by *Irwin Shaw* (published 1970). Hardcover, 99,610; paperback, 6,550,000.
8 The Other Side of Midnight, by *Sidney Sheldon* (published 1973). Hardcover, 85,000; paperback, 6,500,000.
9 Centennial, by *James A. Michener* (published 1974). Hardcover, 458,788; paperback, 5,715,000.
10 Fear of Flying, by *Erica Jong* (published 1973). Hardcover, 100,000; paperback, 5,700,000.

Chapter Two

The bestseller machine and its diverse products

I

Typically, the bestseller shares a productive and marketing apparatus with other kinds of fiction and other kinds of book. General trade publishers will have bestsellers and 'quality' fiction cohabiting on their lists. Paperback houses will put their imprint on both kinds of book. Both quality novels and bestsellers will wholesale and sell through the same trade chains and (in many cases) reach the public via the same retail outlets. Until posterity sorts the matter out, there may even be some doubt as to a novel's true character. 'Literary' works have taken off and become bestsellers, and books cynically designed as down-market bestsellers have eventually made a mark as 'literature'. Some critics have plausibly argued that the qualitative opposition of 'literature' and 'mass-produced fiction' is a historically specific phenomenon which will mutate or wither away with future sociohistorical change. The distinction as to whether a work is literary or commercial will then be as anachronistic as the test of religious orthodoxy or heterodoxy is to contemporary book production.

It is clearly unwise to be artificially precise. But within the book trade as it worked in the 1970s one can identify a number of features which mark the bestseller off from other kinds of novel. It is not just that it sells more; the bestseller is more likely, for example, to have been subjected to negotiation and commercial interference at the 'idea' stage of its existence. It is less likely than the literary novel to have been 'original' (*Women in Love* is not *Rainbow 2* after the manner of *Jaws 2*); it is more likely to be fashionable (the 'follow up' or 'me too' kind of novel is qualitatively different from literary *hommage* or 'influence'). As commodities, contemporary bestsellers are very often pre-sold. Huge advances and subsidiary-rights sales can be obtained on the strength of a draft or a synopsis. Forsyth's *The Devil's Alternative* got its British record £250,000 while still a synopsis; Judith Krantz secured her corresponding American record $3.2 m. with a summary of *Princess Daisy*. James Michener gets his huge advances in return for one small piece of information — the location or theme of the future novel.

Partly because of the vast sums involved and the need to fit works so heavily invested in to the present tastes of the market, agents and editors play a large part in modern bestsellerdom. And in their search for the maximum sale, supersellers of the 1970s have come to depend more than ever before on the tie-in (which again requires the specialist intervention of brokers and agents). In this reciprocal tie-in arrangement, alternative media versions of the original work (or patented 'idea' — see *Star Wars*, Chapter 8) support each other in creating a publicity bandwaggon and a universal sales mania. A notable development in the mid-1970s was the emergence from the tie-in business of the 'novelization' as a superselling form of novel in its own right, thus reversing traditional ideas of text originality. For the first time, film spin-offs like *The Omen* headed American lists.

In the commercial sphere there are analogies to the tie-ins in the new 'conglomerate' business organizations into which, by the end of the 1970s, much of American publishing had become incorporated. Since these diversified giants might simultaneously own hardback houses, paperback firms, television networks, recording companies and film studios, 'vertical' or 'synergistic' sequences became possible and will certainly figure more prominently as features of the entertainment industry in the future. One recent example: Judith Rossner's *Looking for Mr Goodbar* was published as a hardback by Simon & Schuster, as a paperback by Pocket Books and produced as a film by Paramount; all three belong to the conglomerate Gulf & Western.

The contemporary bestseller in its book form has in the 1970s spectacularly enlarged its sales prospects in the paperback form, typically selling a bulk of its copies via the sales-rack or dump-bin in non-bookstore outlets. The figures for the top ten titles of the 1970s, quoted earlier from the *New York Times Book Review*, are, in every case, fully twice what any bestseller would have achieved as paperback in the 1960s. (Hardback figures were, in some cases, slightly higher in the 1960s.) These statistics are more striking than the much publicized record-breaking box-office receipts of the top ten blockbuster films of the 1970s, which were reckoned not in terms of seats sold, but money taken over a period when cinema tickets doubled and trebled in price. The term is often used loosely, but the 1970s would seem to have witnessed a genuine paperback revolution.

Especially in its paperback version the popular novel is likely to be pre-categorized as a 'lead' title, a 'filler', a 'blockbuster' or a 'genre' product. These categories correlate to the conventional racking hierarchy, which permit the paperback to be product-merchandized like convenience or 'fast' foods ('a quick read'). And since paperbacks are as subject to the calendar as perishables, their shelf life is likely to be measured in a set number of weeks rather than indeterminate years. For obvious reasons the trade has found it convenient to synchronize paperback fiction issue with that of the magazines which pulse out monthly from the same wholesalers. The bestseller therefore is typically a frontlist rather than a backlist item, and if later reissued will probably need a 'facelift' to make it 'new' again.

The bestseller is nowadays associated with a high degree of hype and gimmickry. Great attention will be given to its launch; promotional activity may well include such things as an author's tour. Advertising is a main concern of publishers aiming at bestselling success, and will take in everything from pre-publication 'leaks' to cover artwork (increasingly sophisticated in the 1970s) and point-of-sale apparatus.

One has to use the term guardedly, but it is feasible to take this ensemble of productive and sales activities as a 'bestseller machine' operating powerfully within the general book trade. It is likely that this machine will emerge more distinctly in the future and may well come to dominate the production of fiction. Not that its workings are yet entirely streamlined, one should note. The tie-in procedure, for example, is still in its early experimental days and there have been some perplexing setbacks for the masterminds behind the biggest multi-media campaigns. *Jaws 2* for instance, did well as a novelization until the film it novelized was released; the *Superman* tie-in circus, which included a range of trademarked products from comics to novels, log books, records and T-shirts, seems to have fallen far short of what its originators at Warner's intended. Synergistic lines of production have not been as vigorously exploited as one might have expected. It is usual, for example, for a paperback company to bid at auction against rival companies for rights to a book which its parent owns through another hardback affiliate. Publicity remains a blunt instrument, and the book trade is unsure how the mass media (particularly TV) can best be used. Bearing all this in mind – and with the proviso that book trade prophecy is a hazardous business – one expects the 1980s to be a decade which tests, consolidates and rationalizes the breakthroughs and innovations of the 1970s.

II

Very largely speaking, the bestseller has two functions. The first is economic. It exists to sell the best and make money for its producers and merchandisers. The second, more flexible function is ideological. The bestseller expresses and feeds certain needs in the reading public. It consolidates prejudice, provides comfort, is therapy, offers vicarious reward or stimulus. In some socially controlled circumstances it may also indoctrinate or control a population's ideas on politically sensitive subjects. In other circumstances, especially where sexual mores are concerned, it may play a subversive social role, introducing new codes and licence. (Post-1960 popular fiction is constantly jostling against the standards of conventional decency, as the familiar 'makes *Lady Chatterley's Lover* look like a vicarage tea party' line of advertising suggests.)

It is quite in order to discuss the workings of the economic and productive aspects of bestsellerism as a machine whose end product is money. But one cannot talk of a single 'ideology', or even a coherent ideological function performed by the myriad intermediate products of the popular fiction industry. In some ways it makes better sense to go to the other extreme and assume a distinct ideology for each separate bestseller.

As a working principle I would maintain that any generalization about the ideological or social function of bestsellers, or their literary quality, is as risky as the book trade's search for the Eldorado of the 'bestselling formula'. Take — as an example of invalid generalization — Ernst Fischer's Marxist presumption in lumping together all western popular art and literature as 'barbaric trash' (Fischer, 1978, p. 101). It is true that one can find an answering assortment of bad bestsellers to confirm this blanket denigration (my candidate for trash would be *Jonathan Livingston Seagull*, and for barbarism the novels of Mickey Spillane). On the other hand it would be possible to put together a very decent higher-educational syllabus from American superselling novels of the 1970s (Solzhenitsyn, Updike, Roth, Bellow, Vonnegut, Burgess, Greene etc). One can represent the extreme range of fiction bestsellers as a conundrum:

Q. What do Spillane and Orwell have in common? A. They have both sold 6 m. copies of an individual work.

Q. Where would one find *August 1914* and *Jonathan Livingston Seagull* side by side? A. On the 1973 bestsellers' list as the two top titles.

Q. What achievement brings *The Godfather* and *Lady Chatterley's Lover* together? A. They are the bestselling novels ever in the US and UK respectively.

This rather frivolous game could be extended to make all sorts of nonsense of stock responses to popular fiction. But what it boils down to is the truism that the bestseller is a very unpredictable thing. Anything can be on the list — even 'literature', so long as it sells. And with a change in market conditions the most stereotyped forms of popular literature can perform remarkable *volte faces*. Thus woman's romance, against all its aspirin traditions, becomes articulate, radical and sexually aggressive in the 1970s: its assumed generic motto changing from Mills & Boons's 'Books that please' to Marilyn French's 'This novel changes lives' (this threat-cum-promise figured prominently on the paperback cover of *The Woman's Room*). The square-jawed doctor fantasies of traditional romance are invaded by Isadora Wing's quest for the 'zipless fuck' (she too, incidentally, has a thing about doctors). This drastic turnabout in the nature of women's fiction is attributable, I think, to the female reading public — or its trendsetting vanguard — becoming more like the male market for science fiction: that is to say, younger, college-educated and susceptible to 'ideas'.

A structural explanation for the ideological shiftlessness, the mixed literary quality and year-to-year unpredictability of bestsellers can be found in the book trade's production methods as they have evolved in the twentieth century. Fiction has built into it a huge redundancy of supply at every stage of its making. Authors have lots of 'ideas' for novels (Harold Robbins, for example, is reported always to have the ideas for his next three novels firm in his mind). Multitudes of these ideas reach written, but not printed completion. Publishers reliably report that they receive up to a hundred times as many unsolicited manuscript novels as they could ever hope to publish. Slurping around the book trade, then, is a huge, irreducible 'slushpile'. Publishers themselves saturate the market — 2,000 new works and as many new editions of old works are churned out every year. Not all these are candidates for bestsellerdom: but many must be conceived in hope. Since only forty or fifty a year make it into the lists, the hopes of most are ill-founded. And if most cannot hope to be bestsellers, some will not even be, in the literal sense, 'sellers'. Up to 50 per cent of all American paperbacks are reported to die on the shelf after an average of two weeks' display life.

In this redundancy, fiction is quite different from TV, pop music and film, whose production money and manufacturing effort is customarily wrapped up in a relatively small number of expensive market-researched ventures. It is cheap to devise a novel — after all, they come flooding in, fully formed, with every day's post. A small edition is still a relatively inexpensive investment; failures can be written off without any great worry as 'overhead' or as helping make elbow room on the racks for the firm's frontrunners. A broad range of titles also helps keep the producer 'in touch' with the consumer. Feedback is immediate, and resupply in the form of quickly reprinted editions, or follow-up novels on the same lines, is a routine business. Fiction is therefore constantly testing response and itself responding to the market. Its supply-demand-supply cycle is rapid, pulsating, constantly adapting. In this cycle the novel is a product in its own right, but it is also a test-run for its successors (i.e. more of itself, subsequent novels like itself, or — negatively, where it has flopped — novels unlike itself).

This saturation of the production system and market place coexists with a relative lack of coercion or persuasion. Bestsellers are, item for item, less advertised than films, and reviews count for less; they are rarely, if ever, prescribed by institutions as 'set reading'. The result is that the public can drift here or there, propelled by whim, habit, prejudice, collective anxiety or transient mania. Add to this that popular fiction is read for diversion, even craving at times diversion from the staleness of its own familiar forms, and one has a recipe for bafflingly random patterns of reader preference.

There follow a number of readings of novels and novelists' output. All the books which are discussed have one thing in common — they have been bestsellers or belong to bestselling lines of fiction. Economically they form a category, but as texts they have markedly different ways of working with the reader and defy general categorization. It is the individuality of these selected bestsellers, their specific literary achievements and ideological functions, which is the primary focus of the following discussions. At the same time I have tried to indicate as much of the underlying productive machinery as is compatible with a literary-critical exercise.

Chapter Three

The Godfather

> I wrote it to make money. . . . How come you people never
> ask writers about money?

The background to *The Godfather* is well known and blatantly
self-proclaimed. Puzo wrote two 'literary' novels which were
well received (*The New York Times*'s 'small classic' is a
phrase which stuck in the proud author's mind), but which
netted only $6,500 between them. 'I was forty-five years old
and tired of being an artist. . . . It was time to grow up and
sell out' (Puzo, 1972, p. 34). Publishers had shown some
interest in 'that Mafia stuff' in his second novel, which dealt
principally with the struggle of an Italian immigrant family.
So Puzo drew up the outline of a full-blown gangster saga
set in the 1940s New York, and loosely based on folk demons
like 'Uncle Frank' Costello. Those ten pages earned him
$5,000 advance from Putnam. This was 1965; Puzo, who
seems by his own account to be a hand-to-mouth sort of
writer, finally delivered the manuscript in 1968, spurred by
the need for some money to take his family on holiday.
While he was away, paperback rights were auctioned to
Bantam for a then record $410,000. Once published *The
Godfather* assumed the #1 spot on the *New York Times* list,
and held a place in the top ten titles for sixty-seven weeks.
It was also number one in England, France and Germany;
countries where, perhaps, interest in 'gangster' America was
heightened by the Vietnam war. 'They tell me', Puzo wrote
in 1972, 'it's the fastest and bestselling fiction paperback of
all times' (Puzo, 1972, p. 40). By 1978 it was one of the
select half-dozen novels to have broken the 10 m. sales
barrier in the US, and is credited by Hackett as being the

bestselling novel ever. By the end of the decade *The God-father*'s publishers were claiming worldwide sales of over 15 m. Puzo's only mistake in an otherwise triumphant 'selling out' was to release the film rights for $12,500 while he was between agents, and at a time when a few thousand still 'looked like Fort Knox'. Altogether the novelist's connection with the movie industry was unhappy. He was hired by Paramount at $500 a week to co-author the *Godfather* script with another 2.5 per cent 'points' in the profits. But the self-effacing nature of the work offended his aggressively free-lancing instincts. It particularly upset him that he was not consulted on the final cut − that last and most influential stage of editorial revision. 'It was not MY movie', he concluded, and vowed never to work in Hollywood again 'unless I have complete control' − a stipulation which he was realistic enough to acknowledge might disbar him from further serious film work.

None the less the film, starring Marlon Brando, James Caan and Al Pacino, was judged by most critics to have been better of its kind than the novel. As New York critic Pauline Kael saw it, Puzo's *Godfather* was a clumsy performance, 'all itch and hype and juicy *roman à clef*', but 'Puzo provided what Coppola needed: a story teller's outpouring of incidents and details to choose from, the folklore behind the headlines, heat and immediacy, the richly familiar' (Kael, 1973, p. 420). Swollen with this kind of praise, Coppola became overnight a cult director reputedly able to make silk purses even out of rehashed *Little Caesar*. But to hear Puzo tell it, Coppola's motives were not much different from his own; both were working calculatedly 'below their gifts' so as to bankroll better things:

> One interview I have to admit depressed me. Francis Coppola explained he was directing *The Godfather* so that he could get the capital to make pictures he really wanted to make. What depressed me was that he was smart enough to do this at the age of thirty-two when it took me forty-five years to figure out I had to write *The Godfather* so that I could do the other books I really wanted to do (Puzo, 1972, pp. 65-6).

It is a reflection on author/auteur vanity that neither the

enriched Puzo nor Coppola have, in the event, done anything surpassingly good after the dizzy success of their *Godfathers*. Puzo's *Fools Die* earned, in its turn, a record advance paperback sale of $2.2 m. and was proclaimed '*The* publishing event of the decade', yet only someone addicted to gambling could have read this rambling, painfully autobiographical Las Vegas melodrama without embarrassment, and one learned with gratitude that Puzo's next commission was as consultant to *Godfather III*. For his part Coppola weighed in with the $30 m. epic *Apocalypse Now*.

The germ of *The Godfather* is an exuberantly paradoxical essay which Puzo wrote for *Cavalier* (a girly mag) in 1966: 'How crime keeps America healthy, wealthy, cleaner and more beautiful.' Puzo has elsewhere written 'A modest proposal', and evidently feels an affinity with Swift. In his panegyric to American crime he puts forward a 'logical' argument for abolishing conventional civic virtue:

> How are we to adjust to a society that drafts human beings
> to fight a war, yet permits its businessmen to make a profit
> from the shedding of blood? . . . as society becomes more
> and more criminal, the well-adjusted citizen, by definition,
> must become more criminal. So let us now dare to take the
> final step (*ibid.*, p. 79).

In the spirit of this final step the best adjusted citizen of all is taken to be the most powerful criminal in America, Don Corleone, the Godfather. And as the essay applauds the social achievements of crime, so the novel insinuates a warm commendation of Mafia 'family life', of the military virtues of the family's 'soldiers' and the efficiency and high business ethics of the 'organization'. These are the *true* Americans; 'are we not better men', the modestly murderous Don asks, 'than those *pezzonovanti* who have killed countless millions of men in our lifetimes?' (*The Godfather*, 1977, p. 297.)

Puzo complains that readers fail to register 'the casual irony in my books'. But he confesses that this quality in *The Godfather* was not just casual but oblique: 'so oblique in fact, that most of the critics missed the irony in the novel and attacked me for glorifying the Mafia' (Puzo, 1972, p. 70). A disservice was done to Puzo in this respect by Brando's superbly leonine interpretation of the Don, and the self-justifying speeches which Coppola added to make a decent-sized 'part' for his star — especially the role the script assigns to Corleone in the treaty meeting with Sollozzo. This scene also stresses that the Corleone family will have nothing to do with the 'dirty' crimes of narcotics, a special plea which sets up a facile opposition of good-guy gangsters and bad-guy gangsters. Watching the film it is only too easy to believe the canard that Puzo and Paramount were paid a million dollars to do an advertising job on the Mafia. But the novel, while not exactly a modern *Jonathan Wild the Great*, insists on being read ironically if one reads it at all carefully. Take the following description of the Don's funeral. He has died, it will be remembered, of natural causes, cultivating his garden. By a stroke of acting genius, Brando improvised the famous business in which grandad cuts out orange-peel fangs with which playfully to terrify the children, just before having a massive heart attack. As with the whole creation of the part it is magnificent, but fatally humanizes Puzo's consummate businessman:

> It was time for the cemetery. It was time to bury the great Don. Michael linked his arm with Kay's and went out into the garden to join the host of mourners. Behind him came the *caporegimes* followed by their soldiers and then all the humble people the Godfather had blessed during his lifetime. The baker Nazorine, the widow Colombo and her sons and all the countless others of his world he had ruled so firmly but justly. There were even some who had been his enemies, come to do him honour. Michael observed all this with a tight, polite smile. . . . He would follow his father. He would care for his children, his family, his world. But his children would grow in a different world. They would be doctors, artists, scientists. Governors. Presidents. Anything at all (*The Godfather*, 1977, pp. 413-14).

The epigraph which Puzo chose for *The Godfather* is Balzac's 'Behind every great fortune there lies a crime'. It may be that he is *au courant* with nineteenth-century French fiction. But it seems more likely that he borrowed Balzac's apt sarcasm from C. Wright Mills's *The Power Elite*, which makes the same epigraphic use of it. In the mordant description of the new Don's funeral musings, Puzo gives his own social theory of the formation of America's *pezzonovanti*/power elite, and the barely hidden criminal power on which governors and presidents build their 'legitimate' authority.

Irony, especially anti-American irony, never sold 15 m. novels, and Puzo was wise to keep it so oblique as to be invisible to most critics and virtually all lay readers, for whom it would fatally have interrupted the pleasures of the quick read. Ignoring any literary sophistication, popular reception of *The Godfather* ran along two well-grooved channels. There was the shocked response, which found in the novel a naturalistic exposure of American vice almost too horrible to contemplate: 'This is the hard, chilling, incredible, brutal reality of the vice that this nation tolerates' (from a Chicago newspaper, appropriately enough). And there was the thrilled reading which found the novel, in Kael's phrase, 'a juicy *roman à clef*' (Kael, 1973, p. 420). The ubiquitously reported scene of Sinatra balling Puzo out in a Hollywood restaurant fuelled the sales-promoting conviction that here was a novel/film which spilled some interesting beans.

Whether it was read for the inside story of American crime, or the inside story of show business scandal, *The Godfather* was universally taken as a novel whose author knew what he was writing about. Since Mario Puzo was himself of Sicilian extraction it was only too easy to see the work as a rare violation of ten centuries of *omerta* (silence) — the work of a once-in-a-lifetime canary like Joe Valachi. (Puzo, incidentally, strenuously affirms that his novel is based solely on 'research' — but he would, wouldn't he?) And yet the novel's cleverest trick is to go through an elaborate ritual of apparently disclosing while actually giving no hard information for the reader's $1.95. Like Valachi, Puzo shapes as if to tell all. But since, unlike Valachi, he has no privilege against libel law and no FBI protection against assassination, his 'revelations' are folded back into fiction. Of course, the reader quite understands the necessity for this. Did not Sinatra successfully sue a British newspaper which injudiciously slandered him by falsely suggesting that he might have mob-associations along the lines of Johnny Fontane? Did not the Italian-American Anti Defamation

League lean on Paramount so that the names 'Mafia' and 'Cosa Nostra' could not be mentioned in a film, which if it is not about the Mafia and Cosa Nostra is about nothing?

By drawing the audience/reader into a conspiratorial acquiescence with its prudent vagueness — the omissions of reference, misnamings and distortions — *The Godfather* contrives to suggest indiscretion while in fact giving nothing away. And in this pleasantly tantalizing game with the reader, Puzo is helped by the paradoxical nature of the mythological (and historical?) Mafia. In the popular mind, it is an institution which is invisible — yet all-powerful. It is omnipresent, but no one in authority acknowledges its existence (for most of his career, for example, J. Edgar Hoover apparently denied the existence of any significant organized crime in America). It is a force about which one knows nothing — except that it affects and possibly controls every department of one's life.

Since a totally 'secret' organization can only be constituted and tested against the reader's fantasy of it, Puzo can pull off yet another spectacular trick in *The Godfather*. This is to suggest that Cosa Nostra is so powerfully influential as to have rendered the rest of American life a mere accessory to itself. Where other institutions appear in the novel they are either shams or secretly controlled by the family. Anything can be fixed. Union co-operation, for example, can be turned off and on like a tap by Don Corleone; this it is, together with limitless finance and violence against prominent persons that makes him a power in Hollywood. Among his minor fixes is to speed up Michael's demobilization — had his son so wished he could, of course, have arranged promotion or release from military service altogether. The omnipotence and omnipresence of the Mafia explain why in a novel of gangster life there is no opposing law enforcement by society at large. The two policemen we encounter in the novel are Mafia place men in uniform — McCluskey and Neri. Neri, the fearless executioner, is particularly interesting since the narrative contrives to suggest that he serves Don Michael Corleone as the *real* NYPD police chief:

And now, finally, Albert Neri, alone in his Bronx
apartment, was going to put on his police uniform again.
He brushed it carefully. Polishing the holster would be

next. And his policeman's cap too, the visor had to be cleaned, the stout black shoes shined. Neri worked with a will. He had found his place in the world, Michael Corleone had placed his absolute trust in him, and today he would not fail that trust (*The Godfather*, 1977, p. 429). He is not, as one might think, preparing for a mayor's parade. Properly turned out, Neri puts three bullets in rival Don Barzini's chest with his service .38 for the honour of his own Don.

Similarly, there is no justice in the novel save what the Mafia buys or what the Godfather administers. The first scene in which the distraught undertaker, Amerigo Bonasera, sees the defilers of his daughter set free by a tainted judge establishes the hollowness of 'legitimate' institutions. 'For justice we must go Don Corleone,' he resolves. The few 'outsiders' in the novel, like Jules Segal, Tom Hagen and Kay Adams, have the status of refugees who, by an extraordinary stroke of luck, have managed to struggle into the 'real' world. All three are 'adopted'. Segal, the struck-off doctor, becomes the family physician. Hagen, the former Irish waif, becomes the family lawyer. Kay, the blonde girl whose ancestors came across with the founding fathers, becomes family *tout court*. She is converted to Catholicism and as Mrs Corleone becomes *plus Sicilienne que les Siciliennes*. The novel ends with this patrician young WASP preparing to take communion, herself transubstantiated more than any wafer could be:

She emptied her mind of all thought of herself, of her children, of all anger, of all rebellion, of all questions. Then with a profound and deeply willed desire to believe, to be heard, as she had done every day since the murder of Carlo Rizzi, she said the necessary prayers for the soul of Michael Corleone (*ibid.*, p. 448).

The Mafia and the Godfather possess everything and everybody. The fabric of American life — its institutions, political, legislative and judicial, its law enforcement, its entertainment industries, its commerce are reduced to filmy insubstantiality. The Mafia has hollowed out America, and filled what remains with itself.

Puzo's vision of secret yet irresistibly extensive Mafia

omnipotence has clear elements of solipsism and maniac self-aggrandizement in it. And to indulge a vein of speculation, one may note that immediately after the Second World War was a significant period in which to have set *The Godfather*. Historically the two years 1946-8, in which the novel's main action occurs, cover the only moment in history when one man — the President of the United States — enjoyed global omnipotence. The US's sole possession of nuclear weapons, and the presidential structure which put one man's finger on the button, gave a new dimension to the idea of absolute power. For a moment, Nero's fantasy about the world having but one neck to cut came true. Yet this climax of American potency was also a period of national shame for Italian Americans. Italy as wartime enemy had made a notoriously poor showing in the recent war; revealed herself as militarily incompetent and cowardly. The Duce was universally regarded as a poltroon. It is possible, I suspect, that these contrary facts are somehow condensed into the 'dreamwork' of *The Godfather* — a novel which fantasizes about the private possession of irresistible power, and whose chronicle reasserts Italian military prowess as displayed in the savage, but highly disciplined, wars of the families. Puzo, incidentally, was in his mid-twenties at the time of *The Godfather*'s main action, and served in the Army Air Corps in Europe.

As a bestseller *The Godfather* is more like *Love Story* than *Jaws*. That is to say it renovates old material rather than introducing new. Any moderately practised cultural consumer of the 1960s would come to Puzo's novel more of an expert on the Mafia than sharks. American TV, films and paperback fiction have been obsessed with gangsters, mobsters, urban banditti for most of the twentieth century. And their images of the arch-criminal — the *capo di tutti capi* — have traditionally been both morally ambiguous and emotionally extravagant. Orwell, for example, noted with astonishment the perverse hero-worship that a Neapolitan crook like Capone inspired: 'Books have been written about Al Capone that are hardly different in tone from the books written about Henry Ford, Stalin, Lord Northcliffe and all the rest of the log cabin to White House brigade' (Orwell, 1968, p. 220). Against this one can put a hysterical, hostile depiction of

the Godfather genus from Spillane's *Kiss Me, Deadly*:
The Mafia. The stinking, slimy Mafia. An oversize mob of
ignorant, lunkheaded jerks. . . . Someplace at the top of
the heap was a person. From him the fear radiated like
from the centre of a spiderweb. He sat on his throne and
made a motion of his hand and somebody died. He made
another motion and somebody was twisted until they
screamed. A nod of his head did something that sent a guy
leaping from a roof because he couldn't take it any more.
      Just one person did that (*Kiss Me, Deadly*, 1967,
pp. 34-5).

The achievement of Puzo's *Godfather* is to have made a
stale cliché fresh again, and to have brought the pervasive
American ambivalence about stylish crime under a new artistic
control. He managed this by an injection of 'researched'
historicity and ethnic inwardness; by a cool, deadpan natural-
ism which works against the melodramatic and sensationally
charged subject matter; and by an irony which permits us to
read (and Puzo to own) the work as 'critique'. At the same
time the irony is so oblique as to be virtually private; 'unso-
phisticated' readings of the novel are also permitted. Frank,
vicarious thrill-seeking approaches are not turned away. As a
result 15 m. copies are sold and *The Godfather* takes its place
as the bestseller of bestsellers.

Chapter Four

The novels of Arthur Hailey

Hailey gives readers their money's worth.

(New York Times)

I

Arthur Hailey's writing career began in 1956, with the TV play later filmed and novelized as *Flight Into Danger*. It ends with *Overload* (1979), an appropriately apocalyptic chronicle of continental power failure that Hailey announced as his farewell to fiction. If true, he is retiring while still champion. Each of his last five novels (*Hotel, Airport, Wheels, The Moneychangers*, and *Overload* itself) have been international supersellers.

Hailey did not start writing until he was thirty-five, after careers as a serviceman, a real-estate salesman, a business-paper editor (where he seems to have gained his respect for factual detail) and as a sales and advertising executive. Originally *echt* English working class (outside-lavatory, fourteen-year-old school leaver) Hailey rose through RAF ranks in the Second World War, immediately after which he emigrated to Canada. He became a Canadian citizen in 1952, moved to California in 1965 and — as his fortunes continued to prosper — left there for the Bahamas in 1969 where he now enjoys the life of a millionaire tax-exile. (It was fully to enjoy his millions that he gave up writing.) Since the early 1960s his work has been directed towards the American reading public and to Hollywood, which has prudently taken options on all his fiction and produced blockbuster movies of *Hotel* and *Airport*. *The Moneychangers* was rendered into high-class soap as one of the most successful of the 'bestseller' TV mini-series that the American networks went in for in the 1970s. Hailey's big five novels are all set in the US, and the US is the market in which they were first launched and into which he consistently puts the major promotion-tour effort that is one of his specialities.

Understandably, for a writer who has changed his nationality and his place of residence so drastically, Hailey has a keen sense of the international literary market. And like most Canadians of his generation, he frankly acknowledges US cultural ascendancy. *In High Places* actually fantasizes an Act of Union which will weld the two North American neighbours into one superstate in the face of Russian aggression and waning European energy. (There is a nice palace scene in which the Prime Minister of Canada fends off the tea-time attentions of the Queen and the Duke of Edinburgh – both of whom are desperate to keep the Dominion in their 'shaky' Commonwealth.)

It was clearly formative in Hailey's development that his first work should have been for television. American prime-time TV entertainment aims at a broad, undifferentiated and nationally diverse public. Something for everyone, everywhere, has correspondingly been the trademark of all Hailey's subsequent work. He aims to satisfy the broadest possible band of readers – overriding any specific market areas or genre boundaries.

The TV *Flight Into Danger* is, in fact, one of the best things Hailey has ever done. It is a tight, count-down-to-disaster melodrama. A charterload of passengers and their pilots are stricken by botulism from an in-flight meal. An ex-wartime pilot (like Hailey) is called to take over in the cockpit and perform heroically. The play's gimmick (less successful in the film and novel) is simple and gripping; it also expresses one of Hailey's religiously held beliefs – that people have a latent heroism which can be evoked by crisis.

The British publisher with whom Hailey's career is linked, Ernest Hecht of Souvenir Press, had the professional wit to persuade the writer to novelize his TV drama. Hailey in the first instance refused, preferring the cash-in-hand quick sale which television offered (he has always been impatient of the publication delays and professional collaborations novels entail). But when he read the proofs of the stodgy novelization of *Flight Into Danger* by the ghost writing team 'John Castle', Hailey confided to his wife that he should have done the novel after all: 'most of my dialogue is here and the plot was already worked out' (Sheila Hailey, 1978, p. 63). There was also the fact that the market for the one-off TV play was shrinking as the American TV industry evolved, and Hailey has always been fanatically independent; co-writing a series would not suit him. He therefore converted the TV play he was working on into his first proper novel, the hospital melodrama *The Final Diagnosis*, which appeared in 1959. This first novel carries a full load of the famous Hailey 'research' ('He watched an amputation, open-heart surgery; listened to radiologists, pathologists, anaesthetists; talked with nurses, interns, and hospital directors', Sheila Hailey, 1978, p. 63). *The Final Diagnosis* also offers the Hailey *mélange* of concurrent plots together with the familiar passport to an inner sanctum: 'It takes you', as the advertisement put it, 'into a world no patient ever sees.' Privileged insight is a main ware of Hailey's fiction.

Hailey's next novel, *In High Places* (1962), is an oddity and seems to have had something to do with a temporary crisis of national identity. The theme (Canadian surrender of sovereignty to the US, and the ethics of selective immigration policy) made it a bestseller in Canada, but the Canadian market was too small to contain Hailey, who had seen the vast possibilities beyond the forty-ninth parallel with the success of his NBC television plays. Indeed Canada could not contain Hailey himself, who was soon to move on to California.

The mature Hailey formula emerged with his first block-buster novel, *Hotel* (1965), and has varied very little since. The foundation of his superselling fiction is to fix on a contemporary 'universal experience' — something which everyone who can afford $2 for a paperback has, does, wants or is likely to be affected by. Vast numbers of 'ordinary' people now travel by air and congregate in airports (often they beguile dreary hours reading Hailey's novels); few escape hospital; in America everyone of minimal economic competence drives a Detroit-made car, frequently stays at a hotel, uses banks and carries credit cards. Everyone in the civilized, novel-reading world uses electricity, and will be affected by a total energy blackout. Folk wisdom has it that the New York blackout, together with the Kennedy assassination, are the only simultaneous mass experiences which Americans have had in the modern era. At the same time, each of these universal experiences involves a mystery for most of us: doors marked private, areas sectioned off for staff only.

Hailey has shown great skill in locating major social vortices into which the mass of his readers will have been sucked at some time, without fully knowing how the machinery which processes them actually works. At the same time his fiction makes a brave show of engaging with 'big' social questions that his readers know all about, but feel impotent to answer — racial discrimination, pollution, inequitable distribution of wealth. Hailey's publishers are canny enough to highlight this 'muckraking' aspect of their author and to align him with the fearless tradition of American crusading (and frequently radical, or leftist) journalism: 'He contrasts Detroit's slums with the auto industry's tremendous wealth and covers problems experienced in hiring the hard-core unemployed and with militant blacks on the assembly line' (Pan blurb for *Wheels*).

It is tenable that there is something substantial behind Hailey's muckraking pose. He has always stressed the need for modern man to 'keep up to date' and — superficially at least — a Hailey novel puts the reader in touch with the issues of the day and elucidates some of the complex machinery of contemporary society. But the primary appeal of Hailey's formula is, quite clearly, old-fashioned 'human interest'. His novels feature a carefully assembled medley of largely melodramatic plots, designed to maximize this interest and to vary it for different reader-groups. Invariably, for example, these subplots are strung out vertically in a line which extends all the way from the top to the bottom of society, with an even distribution of heroes and heroines. In *Airport*, typically, the narrative ranges between a top stratum which chronicles the decision dilemmas of the airport management, through the love lives of pilots and stewardesses, to a baseline narrative centred on the escapades of a little old lady stowaway. She, inevitably, is instrumental in foiling the male plane-bomber, whose desperate attempt makes up the suspense element of *Airport*. *Wheels* switches in its first two chapters from the bedroom of the president of General Motors to the car assembly line. The first scene-change in *The Moneychangers* similarly oscillates from boardroom to bank floor dealings. In Hailey's fiction these initially discordant juxtapositions are gradually harmonized to reveal organic interconnectedness. Thus in *Hotel* the manager's main problem (how to expose the penthoused Duke and Duchess of Croydon as the criminals they are) is finally solved by a conscientious 'negro' garbage man sifting refuse in the basement of the building. In *The Moneychangers* the outcast criminal bank-teller reforms and, by double-agent work, fingers the counterfeiters whom the heroic vice president of the bank has been pursuing throughout the novel.

This vertical range creates an 'all human life is there' plenitude, a feature which Hailey's publishers plug as a main selling point: 'Once again [in *Wheels*] Arthur Hailey puts a whole world in your hands — from the crime and toil of a Detroit assembly line through top-secret design studios to executive bedrooms and boardrooms.' Hailey's characteristic range is, of course, something more than neutral 'coverage'. It makes the political point that 'we're all in this together', 'we've got a job to get done'. There are no *single* centres to Hailey's multiplot novels. Society's large unit is made up of numerous but vitally important small lives, each with their small novel to be told. The therapeutic function of Hailey's fiction (which must be part of its phenomenal selling appeal) is its reconstruction of the 'average citizen' as centrally important in the context of the institutions of modern life which, he fears, really dwarf him. I suspect no passenger feels important in an airport; he knows he is just so much self-loading freight. In a hospital one is stripped not just of one's own clothing, but of personality and autonomy (one has to ask to go to the bathroom, as one did as a child, for instance). Banks are, for the average account holder, vaguely humiliating places where one's secret poverty and true financial insignificance are recorded. The computerized bill from the public utility is one of the most belittling communications modern society has evolved. Hailey reassures us that a full melodramatic range of experience is possible, even for the ego diminished and disenfranchized by the vast new units and technologies of modern existence. 'All these things have one reason for existence,' says a character in *The Final Diagnosis*, pointing to the hospital's elaborate equipment: 'people.' Hailey makes the same populist assertion that in the vast apparatus of modern urban life people, ultimately, matter most. In this way Hailey's 'rich tapestry' contradicts a pervasive anxiety that modern life reduces us to dehumanized components of the social machine: passengers, patients, accounts, 'guests', consumers. He emphasizes the drama, the fullness, the violent emotion which seethes beneath the familiar social surfaces of everyday life:

> The scene is the St Gregory Hotel, New Orleans. Through Arthur Hailey's totally fascinating novel move vividly drawn characters — the tycoons of the hotel industry, the guests, the staff, men and women, young and old, the dedicated and the amoral — sealing their own destinies in five days of dramatic change (Pan blurb to *Hotel*).

Hailey's fiction flatters us by returning our diminished image of ourselves melodramatically enhanced. Everyone in his novels is taken seriously, has 'star' status; there are no *ficelles*, no Rosencrantzes and Guildensterns leading merely auxiliary existences. For the same reason every Hailey novel displays a careful mix of romance, suspense, violence, technicality, each ingredient appropriate for a different kind of reader in the mixed Hailey reading public:

> The genius of Arthur Hailey combines Money, People and Banking into a suspenseful, totally absorbing story of the financial and personal crises behind the dignified bronze doors of a major US bank. Interwoven with the dreams, passions, rivalries and guilty secrets of its employees are currency and credit card frauds, embezzlement, a prison-gang rape, Mafia torture, and the call girl sex that sweetens irregular business deals (Pan blurb to *The Moneychangers*).

Writing over twenty years Hailey has had to vary the condiments, if not the stock ingredients of his mix. In his early novels, he seems to have had a hangover from the inhibitions laid on the peak-viewing TV writer. He went through the 'bullshit' barrier at about the same time as *Love Story* (Sheila Hailey tells us there were complaints at his slipping standards from the little old ladies who have always been faithful readers). Up to *The Moneychangers* his sex had always been decently vague. (According to *Penthouse*, a typical Hailey love scene required only three words — 'they made love'.) But Hailey sloughed off his decorousness with his 1975 novel which featured a prison gang rape of Miles Eastin ('a searing of membrane, the fiery abrasion of a thousand nerve ends . . .') followed by a protracted Mafia torture (six inch nails are driven through the luckless Eastin's fingers and etching acid thrown in his eyes). It was not easy for Hailey to come into line with the increasingly violent fiction mores of the 1970s in this way, though as always public taste (now a younger and harder-boiled public's taste) was sovereign. As his wife reports:

Arthur received much comment — oral and written — about his homosexual rape scene in prison, and the torture of Miles Eastin that became known as 'the crucifixion scene'. . . . It was a personal breakthrough for him to write about homosexuality at all. A strong heterosexual, he had always been uncomfortable when the subject of homosexuality came up. . . . In fact he almost liked to pretend that homosexuality did not exist (Sheila Hailey, 1978, pp. 140-1).

Having made the breakthrough, Hailey let his imagination rip with *Overload* which features, among other things, copulation between a beautiful quadriplegic and a senior executive sexual athlete (his company's failure to produce electricity eventually kills the girl) and an unfortunate character who has his penis charred off by the electrocution and later replaced by sophisticated cosmetic surgery. Were *Overload* not his swan song it would be piquant to guess how much further an emancipated Hailey might go.

II

Hailey discloses that his novels each take him four years: one year for planning, one for research, one for writing and one for production. And the second stage, grandly called 'research' is the one on which he most prides himself. Hailey's novels, famously, have a high information content, and he takes an ingenuous pleasure in the fact, for example, that *Hotel* is a prescribed book at Cornell — not in the English department but on the hotel administration course (from which, incidentally, *Hotel*'s hero, Peter McDermott, has graduated). Pride of place in the Hailey study is given to a plaque from the Professional Air Traffic Controllers Organization 'In Appreciation for RECOGNIZING UNDERSTANDING COMMUNICATING The Problems of Modern Aviation Through the Novel AIRPORT' (Sheila Hailey, 1978, p. 233). It is a tribute the novelist would particularly value, coming as it does from 'experts' who know what they are talking about.

Hailey has a naturally pedagogic bent, and his novels are thick with lecturettes and informative asides. One becomes wearily apprehensive of the clunking prefixes by which he changes from narrative to expository gear: 'Few people are aware that . . .', 'In fact . . .', and there follows some such nugget as that Detroit insiders avoid Monday and Friday cars 'like the plague', leaving it to suckers like the reader to buy those lemons assembled just before the workforce goes off for the weekend, or just after it returns with the weekend hangover. Often characters will lecture other less knowledgeable but insatiably curious characters for what seems like hours on end. Thus McDermott breaks off from conducting hotel business to explain at length to a straight man how 'Hotel law in fact goes back to the English inns, beginning with the fourteenth century.' The ingenuous auditor is a frequent device. Frequently, too, Hailey stages seminars in his fiction: set-piece arguments and controversies are arranged in order that researched information can be plausibly introduced with some lively give and take.

In their totality, Hailey's novels often present themselves as a debate between a number of informed and articulate points of view. This 'debate' structure is evident from the publisher's synopsis of *Overload* given on the hardback dust jacket:

Angry critics of Golden State Power & Light accuse the giant corporation of being a heartless monster, piling up profits at the expense of its hapless customers — the users of electricity and gas.

True or false?

False! — argues Nim Goldman of GSP and L, dedicated and aggressive, who believes a devastating electrical famine is alarmingly near.

True! — charges Davey Birdsong, colourful, dynamic leader of p & lfp (power and light for people), an activist engaged in his version of a holy war.

Maybe! — broods Laura Bo Carmichael, ex-atomic scientist and prominent environmentalist.

These conflicts and others pit the men and women of OVERLOAD against each other.

(Only Hailey, incidentally, would call an environmentalist 'Davey Birdsong'.)

Hailey is conscientious as regards giving opposite viewpoints fair exposure. He was annoyed, for instance, by the imbalance which he felt that Ross Hunter's televisation brought to *The Moneychangers*. Too much implicit approval, he felt, was accorded to the views of 'left wing activist' Margot Bracken, and not enough to those of the right wing, Friedmanite economist, Lewis D'Orsey. This thumb in the pan was particularly painful since, as Sheila Hailey observes: 'Arthur's [private] financial views parallel those of Lewis D'Orsey — he is pro-free enterprise and strongly anti-socialist' (Sheila Hailey, 1978, p. 178). Hailey himself is also on record as thinking that, even in America, 'there is too much government'. In *Overload* a utopian future is envisaged in which a reconstructed US government goes back on the gold standard.

Hailey does his conscientious best to impersonalize his fiction, but given his prejudices it is humanly impossible for him to be fair to the group whom he refers to as 'the critics'. Emerson Vale in *Wheels*, for example, is clearly based on Ralph Nader. In case we miss the connection, Hailey has Vale the author of a book ludicrously entitled: *The American Car: Unsure in Any Need*. Hailey caricatures the careful criticism of *Unsafe at Any Speed*:

He presented charges based on no more than his own mail from disgruntled car users. While excoriating the auto industry for bad design, poor workmanship, and lack of safety features, Vale acknowledged none of the industry's problems nor recent genuine attempts to improve its ways. He failed to see anything good in auto manufacturers, and their people, only indifference, neglect, and villainy (*Wheels*, 1973, p. 50).

As the hero, Adam Trent, puts it a few pages later:

the critics have done their job . . . we're consumer oriented. For a while, we weren't. Looking back, it seems as if we got careless and indifferent to consumers without realizing it. Right now, though, we're neither, which is why the Emerson Vales have become shrill and sometimes silly (*ibid.*, p. 60).

Hailey's essential confidence in the American way assumes that criticism can always be usefully absorbed without dismantling old hierarchies or radically disturbing things as they are. Nothing more is required of the leaders of society than an ethical readjustment. In the traditional symbolism of fiction, for instance, the new president of *The Moneychangers'* First Mercantile Bank of America and its main 'activist' civil rights opponent, Margot, finally marry. The lion lies down with the lamb. The radical critic is tamed and the hard-nosed manager liberalized.

Hailey's life and work expresses the convert's fanatic belief in the American dream (his comments about class-ridden Mother Britain are scathing). A main article of this dream is a firm commitment to the necessity of technology-led progress. 'Keeping up to date' with progress is essential to social and personal survival in Hailey's world, and he clearly regards his 'researched' fiction as helping the public themselves to keep up to date with their advancing society. Progress, however, is not won without struggle and has its vexatious, even tragic, aspects. Each of Hailey's novels centres on a renewal crisis, an interregnum, a succession struggle — those tricky historical moments when the present jerks into the future. *The Final Diagnosis* thus takes as its main theme 'the engrossing story of a young pathologist and his efforts to restore the standards of a hospital controlled by a once brilliant doctor'. The old 'washed up' generation of medical experts is swept out by the super-efficient, stream-lined young men with their up-to-date knowhow. Hailey reserves considerable sympathy for the plight of the irascible senior surgeon in this, his most sentimental work − but go the patriarch must. There is no room for any Gillespie-Kildare cosiness in Hailey's social-Darwinist universe. *In High Places* pivots on the historically decisive moment in Canadian history: will she retain the traditional British link or forge a new forward-looking American union? The novel ends with the Prime Minister rising to give his key speech from a front bench, most of whose members have deserted him. Formally the novel is open ended, but there is little doubt that for Hailey the Canadian future lies in the young republican south rather than the old monarchical east. In *Wheels*, the progress problem is whether Detroit should continue volume production − environment be damned − or go into a new 'responsible' auto concept (smaller, energy-efficient cars with lower exhaust emission). *The Moneychangers* opens with the patriarchal president of the First Mercantile Bank of America announcing his retirement. Which of the young vice presidents will succeed him − Roscoe Heyward (old family, committed to profitability and massive, high-risk industrial loans) or Alex Vandervoort (new man, committed to corporate social responsibility, new store-front banks for 'little people' and thrift). The novel ends with the vindication of Vandervoort's faith in 'the little investor', and new-style banking, after Heyward is ripped off for $50 m. by a Vesco-style embezzler and jumps off the bank skyscraper.

The 'dawning new era' of *The Moneychangers'* ending is one of the more clearcut of Hailey's affirmations about US progress. The most ambiguous conclusion to a renewal crisis is found in *Hotel*. The New Orleans St Gregory of the title is an old 'personal' hotel; as its owner (another patriarch) approaches the end of his life it is threatened with takeover by a Conrad Hilton-like tycoon who methodically reduces all his establishments to 'chain management conformity'. Curtis O'Keefe believes that modern American society has no place for the 'first class concept'. What is required is uniform, classless efficiency. The St Gregory, as it approaches the crucial historical moment, cannot in economic logic survive as a 'Grand Hotel'. It must become a Hilton or a superior Holiday Inn. There is a transparent symbolism in, for example, the lift, whose worn-out equipment gives way at the climax of the novel. Yet survive the St Gregory does; an eccentric millionaire turns up at the eleventh hour to buy the hotel from under O'Keefe's nose. An 'old timer' who struck it rich in the Northern territories, this improbable sugardaddy insists that the new St Gregory carry on its old traditions – he appoints the young Cornell graduate as the manager.

The historical sentimentalism of *Hotel* seems to have been an aberration. In his latest (and allegedly last) novel, *Overload*, Hailey expresses a ferocious malevolence towards 'conservationists' whose hypocritical concern for the environment and resistance to industrial 'progress' is nothing but a mask for Baader-Meinhof or Weathermen-type violence. As he has grown older it would seem that his views have moved ever rightwards.

Chapter Five

Frighteners of the 1970s: *Children of the Dark*

They are children just like your own. Except for one murderous moment when they become CHILDREN OF THE DARK. Suddenly they are transformed into killers of unnatural strength and power — killing the adults around them.

(Advertisement for *Children of the Dark*, by Charles Veley)

I

At the moment of decision in Herzog's 1978 film *Nosferatu the Vampyr*, Lucy finally turns on the prating Dr Van Helsing and declares: 'Genug von ihrer Wissenschaft!' — *Enough of your science!* As I observed it, the cinema audience experiences Lucy's unusual assertiveness as a relief. Van Helsing's 'science' can never understand or combat the Dracula and his rat hordes who have mysteriously come to plague Wismar. Freed from the rationalism which has hitherto paralysed her, Lucy is free to follow the good old folkloric remedies for killing the undead — in this case by offering her chaste body for seduction and so trapping the adulterous ghoul in morning sunlight.

The 1970s entertainment vogue for occultism, fantasy, ufology and horror clearly exploits a popular disfavour with orthodox science and an urge to escape its disciplines and authority. Films, books and television series like *The Exorcist*, *Lord of the Rings*, *Close Encounters of the Third Kind* or *Star Trek* offer a welcome holiday from rationalism; less dangerous certainly than the lifetime's commitment (and sometimes savings) demanded by Moon, Hubbard or Maharaji, but a small taste of the same kind of escape that these cults offer the thoughtsick. It is, for obvious reasons, a vogue which has alarmed some social commentators friendly to the US, while giving gloomy satisfaction to the Kremlin, who see in the epidemic irrationalism and pornography of western culture evidence of the final spasms of 'unscientific' and immoral capitalism.

Whatever their significance as a historical portent, the fashionable irrationalisms of the 1970s have charged the gothic novel with new life and vast sales potential. The trendsetting works are, by general agreement, *Rosemary's Baby* by Ira Levin and, most spectacularly, *The Exorcist* by Peter Blatty. In fact neither of these novels can claim much in the way of originality. The diabolic or demonic possession of children has been a horror-fiction standby since *The Turn of the Screw* at least; and the related idea of the changeling can be pursued as far back as one cares in pre- or sub-literary folklore. At any time in the postwar period one could have found pulp novels similar to Blatty and Levin's being published (as, presumably, one could have found hole-in-corner sects like the Moonies); what made *The Exorcist* and *Rosemary's Baby* remarkable was that they appealed beyond the genre circuit and made the mass-market bestseller lists (as, to complete the analogy, the Moonies grew from lunatic fringe to multi-million dollar industry). Before *Rosemary's Baby* no novel of the supernatural had figured in the postwar lists of the ten bestselling novels of the year. Since then it is rare for some such novel not to have made the lists, especially in paperback form, and *The Exorcist* is now credited with worldwide sales of over 12 m.

The book trade is not always good at spotting the coming thing, and Blatty originally had great difficulty in placing his novel with a hardback publisher, all of whom must have seen it as low-grade schlock unworthy of their stiff covers. Very unusually it was accepted first by Bantam Books, who reversed standard procedure by commissioning the novel from Blatty's synopsis and leasing out hardback rights. (Blatty's dedication is to Bantam's Marc Jaffe for his 'singular and lonely' faith in the novel.) The paperback publisher's faith in Blatty was very astute; it is now the firm's best-ever selling novel, and is second only to *The Godfather* in all-time American fiction sales. In 1973 *The Exorcist* was made into a box office record-breaking film, efficiently directed by William Friedkin (of *French Connection* fame). Blatty, who had a long writing association with the film world, produced. This too was trendsetting. For like the shorter-lived disaster vogue of the 1970s, horror has forged close and lucrative links with Hollywood. Most of the market leaders in the fiction field have inspired big-budget, wide-appeal movies and so set up the reciprocating tie-in boosts by which film sells book and vice versa. In one famous case, that of *The Omen*, the film came first, and from its Hollywood-originated screenplay David Seltzer wrote, to order, the bestselling novelization of all time. It had sold getting on for 5 m. in the US, around 7 m. worldwide by the late 1970s and made the #1 spot in America as a paperback. Since *The Omen* the previously despised novelization and its hack novelizer have acquired new dignity – at least in the eyes of the moneymen who run the film and publishing industries.

Unlike the generally mediocre disaster movies, and the gimmicky sf epics, many of the horror blockbusters of the 1970s have been the work of distinguished or at least competent directors, who have managed to defy the tyranny of their special effects department and create films which should last. In drawing up a roll of something less than artistic dishonour one could add to Friedkin's *Exorcist*: Polanski's *Rosemary's Baby*, de Palma's *Carrie* and *The Fury*, Richard Donner's *The Omen*, Kubrick's *The Shining* and *If You Could See Me Now*, Michael Winner's *The Sentinel*, Richard Loncraine's *Full Circle*. These are names to conjure with, even if the films are not directors' masterpieces.

II

Horror, sf and fantasy have all done well in the 1970s. But so spectacular was the success of *The Exorcist* (and to a lesser extent *Rosemary's Baby*) that their main plot gimmick – the diabolic or demonically possessed child or adolescent – has been widely imitated and elaborated upon. It is the usual process by which lucky strikes become goldrushes in popular fiction. Monstrous children were suddenly found everywhere in the racks. Typically these unnatural offspring victimized and often sexually abused their perfectly decent parents and elders. In *The Exorcist*, for example, the demon in eleven-year-old Regan drives her to twist the head off her single-parent mother's lover and impale him on a spiked railing. For most of the book and film she launches vomit projectiles in the face of any adult who comes within range and, in one peculiarly distasteful episode, she devirginates herself with a crucifix and, applying demonic strength, rubs her mother's nose in the hymenal gore. In *Damon* the possessed four-year-old hero ('the mind of a genius − the body of a man') incestuously rapes his mother and drives her to suicide; he also sodomizes his night nurse and murders a little girl nearer his own age after sexually assaulting her. In *The Shining* a rather more amiable five-year-old with 'powers' drives his academic father to alcoholism, arson, child battering and attempted wife-murder. In *The Fury* (whose film and novel versions differ considerably) the young hero uses his telekinetic powers to bring about the death of, among others, his father; the similarly endowed heroine crowns a violent career by shaking the blood out of her would be father figure, a CIA 'control' who wants to use her against the Russians. In *The Omen* Damien, 'an imp of Satan', embarks on a homicidal orgy in which he hangs his nanny, induces a miscarriage in his mother, later drives her to suicide and polishes off the remaining family by murdering his father, the American ambassador to London. At the end of the novel the orphan is seen at the funeral, holding hands with the President of the United States. In *Holocaust 2000* a somewhat older imp of Satan, called perversely 'Angel', arranges his mother's murder and nearly does his father in by throwing him strait-jacketed into a ward full of homicidal psychopaths. His aim in all this is to fulfil the Book of Revelation with the aid of the family's nuclear power plant in Israel. *Sentinel I* and *Sentinel II* take as their subject the young girl who in every generation becomes 'the living guardian of the gates of hell . . . the sole barrier between humanity and the forces of satanic evil pent up since the Fall from Grace.' (Konvitz's two novels, incidentally, make great play with the swish New York apartment milieu which Levin and Polanski had used brilliantly in *Rosemary's Baby*.) The sentinels' guardianship naturally involves widespread slaughter of those who get in their way. Carrie is the most murderous of all these violent prodigies. With the aroused exercise of her telekinetic powers she wipes out no less than 450 of the inhabitants of her New England home town, so revenging herself for being drenched in pig's blood at a high school dance. For the elimination of her mother (one of the few unpleasant mothers in a field where parents are typically nice and utterly mystified by their prodigies) Carrie devises the refined technique of squeezing her heart dry of blood. As the paperback cover puts it — somewhat redundantly, I think — 'Carrie White was no ordinary girl'.

A whole gallery of parents are haunted by revenant children. In *Audrey Rose*, for example, a little reincarnated girl (born 1959, died 1964, born 1964) wreaks havoc on her parents and foster parents. This novel climaxes on a bizarre child-custody trial where two sets of parents argue their respective rights in the US courts. Assisted by 'powerhouse advertising', *Audrey Rose* made the #1 spot on the *Publishers Weekly* paperback lists in January 1977. (It was made into an equally feeble film.) In Straub's much superior *Julia*, a bereaved American mother is driven to suicide by the return of a sadistic stepchild long dead but reincarnated to haunt Holland Park (following *The Omen* English settings behind American protagonists were clearly modish). Straub's work is a distant homage to James as well as a self-confessed imitation of Blatty. In its Blattyesque aspect it features an unpleasant digital rape of mother by stepdaughter. This novel — perhaps the best of its kind — made an unfortunately poor film, though it did star Mia Farrow of 'Rosemary' fame. In William Katz's *Death Dreams* a drowned daughter's ghost returns, night after night, voicelessly tormenting her mother and drawing her towards the fatal lake.

A desperately ingenious twist on the haunting and reincarnation idea was devised by Terry Cline in *Death Knell*, where a teenage American girl begins taking a grim interest in SS memorabilia. She is, it emerges, intermittently a reincarnation

of a Polish Jewish victim of Auschwitz. She revenges herself
on six former Nazis, one of whom, inevitably, is her father.
Echoes here of Sylvia Plath. The father in *Death Knell*, as
is common in these 'Nazism-resurgent' fantasies, occupies a
position of great power; he is the head of the US computer
industry.

These are a sampling of the top drawer of fiction and
novels thrown up by the 1970s horror boom. There were, of
course, the usual crop of 'most terrifying stories since *The
Omen*, *The Exorcist*, etc. . .' Not least, naked self-imitations
like *Omen II*, *Sentinel II* and *Exorcist II*. A typical chip off
the block is Bernard Taylor's *The Godsend*:

> The Marlowes took the beautiful, abandoned baby to their
> hearts. And when their own new baby died, golden haired,
> blue eyed little Bonnie was a godsend, a comfort in their
> grief, a wonderful new sister for their three happy
> children. THEN THE NEXT CHILD DIED.

Kenneth McKenney's *The Moonchild* presents a similar
parental crisis:

> On a carefree Xmas holiday in the snow-capped Bavarian
> Alps, tragedy struck Anne and Edmund Blackstone.
> Simon, their beloved son, fell mysteriously ill and died.
> OR DID HE? The brutal slaying of his governess revealed
> that Simon was THE MOONCHILD, a creature out of
> legend, from beyond the realms of nightmare.

John Saul's *Suffer the Children* made the paperback best-
seller lists in 1978 (like *The Exorcist* it was a paperback
original), taking the by now clichéd plot of two supernaturally
endowed young girls wreaking mayhem in a small community.
Jessica Hamilton's *Elizabeth* was a female Damien/Damon
('She could be the girl next door — if next door was Hell!').
In David Ferran's *Mendaga's Morning* an innocent child wakes
the devil and becomes a Satanic vessel. Dean Koontz's *Demon
Seed*, Graham Masterton's *The Manitou* and C.K. Chandler's
God Told Me To pick up the diabolic violation and conception
gimmick of *Rosemary's Baby*. Richard Woodley's *It's Alive*
and Gene Thompson's *Lupe* ('strange, obscene manchild')
take the subject into a post-natal, or perhaps one should
say post-spawned, phase of the Satanic/monstrous child's
existence. Lupe, as a spirit impersonating a child, has, however,

to rape his future mother in order to incarnate himself. The demonology of some of these tales becomes very intricate. In Terrel Miedaner's *The Soul of Anna Klane* a ten-year-old girl loses her soul after a brain tumour operation. Her scientist father, perceiving this, orders her to kill herself and in a climax reminiscent both of *The Omen* (offspring slaughter) and *Audrey Rose* he is put on trial for murder — 'his only defence, to prove the existence of the soul'.

It would be wearying to go through a complete catalogue of the multitudinous novels and films there have been on or around this theme. More interesting perhaps is to note briefly the ways in which it has slopped over to colour other areas and sub-genres of fiction and film. For example, an indirect connection can be traced in Craig Jones's impressive *Blood Secrets*. Much of this novel's narrative centres around an 'impossible' (that is to say badly behaved) daughter who torments her middle-class academic parents. For most of its length *Blood Secrets* shapes in the usual way as an unhappy-families novel. Finally and most effectively the secret is revealed that the father comes from a coven of incest — there follows the obligatory gothic bloodbath. In *Magic*, where a young ventriloquist is driven schizophrenic by his child-like dummy, one catches definite echoes; and one can even discover them, with a little ingenuity, in *Alien*, where the larval or infant parasite destroys the adults on the spaceship Nostromo. At the end of *CE3K* (*Close Encounters*) the aliens are revealed as 'children' — at least in appearance. (Science fiction is, as any fan will know, rich in stories based on supernaturally endowed children: freaks, mutations, child geniuses, star children etc.) The unnatural conception of the hero in *The World According to Garp* (his mother seduces a brain-damaged airman) is arguably connected. Perhaps the oddest meandering of the *Exorcist* stream is into Walt Disney's *Return From Witch Mountain*, which features a gang of kids possessed of 'the power' which they use to charmingly comic purposes.

Another well-established area of fiction which finds a common frontier with the demonic-child gothics is that dealing with the disturbed or mixed-up adolescent. Burt Hirschfeld's *Father Pig* has as its subject a group of teenagers who dedicate themselves to the murder of their parents. ('Charles Livingston was rich, famous . . . and scared. His son was coming to kill him'.) More a *roman à clef* is Max Ehrlich's *The Cult*, in which teenagers are brainwashed to turn against their parents. ('Jeff was a loving son to Mr and Mrs Reed. But when he went to Ashtaroth, they lost him. He took a new name. He cursed his parents and spurned their love'.) William H. Hallahan's *Keeper of the Children* gives this topical theme an occult twist; the parent is obliged to struggle for his teenage daughter, alienated by a quasi-religious sect, on the astral plane. ('If Edward Benson wants his daughter back, he will have to fight a battle no human has ever fought before'.) A trendy feminist flavour is given to the 'nasty teenager' gimmick in Bari Wood's *The Killing Gift*. The heroine of this well-written thriller is a girl with the power to crush any male chauvinist to death, simply by willing it. (The novel starts and finishes with the same killing, seen from different viewpoints, as did Rossner's *Looking for Mr Goodbar*.)

On the whole there seems a lot of life left in the 'nasty child' idea which was still throwing up new works and adaptations after eight fully exploited years. In terms of stamina it long outlasted the nasty fish, nice love story and nice-nasty godfather fashions in popular fiction.

III

There were other formulas thrown up in the boom of 1970s frighteners: adult reincarnation (*The Reincarnation of Peter Proud*), variations on Shirley Jackson's *The Haunting of Hill House* (*Hell House*, *The Amityville Horror*) and old favourites like vampirism (*Salem's Lot*) and the Faustian contract (*Falling Angel*) all made a mark on the lists or at the box office. But the diabolic, possessed or supernaturally powerful child clearly hit the public fancy most often and most lucratively between 1971 and 1979.

A number of explanations can be put forward for the popularity of this theme, especially its popularity in America. The possessed child, notably the girl at the sexual threshold of childhood and womanhood (like eleven-year-old Regan or sixteen-year-old Carrie) is a legacy of Salem which American popular fiction has frequently returned to. But in order to understand its extraordinary florescence in the 1970s one has, I think, to concentrate on the Hollywood connection. Given the economics of the film and publishing industries the movies involved here have, in almost every case, been more important financially than the novels. *The Exorcist*, for example, has sold at least 10 m. copies in America; but the film was seen by a likely 100 m. Americans — each of whom paid twice as much as the paperback cost. *The Omen* — which was, for a while, the top box-office grossing film of all time, only exists in print as an afterthought novelization. What is most striking about these films is that they are centrally 'about' children and teenagers, but not *for* children and teenagers. No child, for example, could legally go and see R- or X-rated *Omen*, *Exorcist*, *Fury* or *Carrie*. When *Rosemary's Baby* was shown in the late 1970s on British TV the Viewers' and Listeners' Association wrote in, predictably, to complain of children being exposed to it — it's a fair guess that while Mrs Whitehouse has breath in her body we shall never see an unedited *Exorcist* on our screens. Scenes in the films such as the eleven-year-old Regan masturbating with a crucifix, or sixteen-year-old Carrie White menstruating for the first time in a communal shower, are, then, for adults only.

This exclusion is relatively rare in our 'open' culture, where the majority of bestselling books and top-grossing films are accessible to a broad range of the literate and financially solvent population. An analogy for what one has with these films (and presumably with the tied-in novels, most of whose sales depend on being the book of the film) is found in what used to be called the 'smoking room story': that is to say the dirty joke — invariably about women — told on premises (the smoking room) which women are strictly prohibited from entering. It is not entirely uncon- nected, I think, that the *Exorcist* style of films came into its own at the same period as the 'Family Viewing Policy' adopted by the major American networks in 1974; this set up 'the children's hour' — in fact the two hours between seven and nine — during which only material suitable for

whole-family viewing was permissible. The smoking room
story licenses one to fantasize about women without the
control of women being present. The *Exorcist*-style film
allows one to fantasize about kids, without kids being present
to inhibit the fantasy. It creates a 'parents' viewing hour'.

With a little statistical investigation — and an awareness
of film licensing regulations — one can reconstruct the
likely audiences for these films. Only 15 per cent of adults
apparently go to movies by themselves, and another survey
suggests that over 60 per cent of all movie-goers are in the
fifteen to thirty-five, or 'young adult', age group. (An older
age group, incidentally, makes up the main market for
novels.) From which one deduces that a large proportion of
the hundreds of millions of Americans who have flocked to
see these films are young marrieds, probably, in the demo-
graphic nature of things, with children of their own at home.

It is therefore not surprising to find that the narratives of
these films and novels centre on routine situations familiar
to parents with young families. A typical scene, for example,
is that between the well meaning but 'desperate' parent, who
doesn't know what to do, and a doctor, psychiatrist or child
guidance expert. The tone of such episodes is often strikingly
reminiscent of everyday parent-counsellor dealings. Take this
description of the mother in the psychiatrist's office in
The Exorcist:

> For a time, no one spoke. Chris was on the sofa. Klein and
> the psychiatrist sat near her in facing chairs. The
> psychiatrist was pensive, pinching at his lip as he stared at
> the coffee table; then he sighed and looked up at Chris.
> She turned her burned-out gaze to his. 'What the hell's
> going on?' she asked in a mournful, haggard whisper
> (*The Exorcist*, 1977, p. 126).

Out of context this could fit into a 'parent worried about
child's progress' scene. In fact, Regan has just been speaking
in tongues, has psychokinetically lowered the temperature of
the room and exuded an overpowering smell of corpse.

Other scenes, such as the absurd child-custody trial at the
centre of *Audrey Rose*, have painful overtones for many
American parents — some third of whom are now scarred by
divorce. Many — possibly most — of these novels and films

feature one-parent families, broken or breaking marriages. *Julia* begins with the recently divorced heroine experiencing a shock familiar to all parents – that of seeing a child uncannily like one's own (in this case the look-alike is a peculiarly sadistic demon). The dramas are typically parental dilemmas which parallel – in their grotesque way – everyday parental dilemmas. It is a chord often struck in publicity. 'These are children just like your own,' runs the advertisement to Charles Veley's *Children of the Dark*. 'In one moment [these] children are transformed into killers of unnatural strength and power. Just as suddenly, they become ordinary children again.' Ordinary parents with ordinary children (who are sometimes extraordinarily naughty) have clearly been identified as the main reading public for these books.

It is striking how often these gothic stories contrive situations in which 'decent' parents are licensed, indeed *required*, to batter their children – in *Damon*, for example, when the little brat ('his enormous penis projecting upward, the hair on his chest and abdomen matted with perspiration') attempts to rape his mother:

He grabbed at her, his aim being her pubic area. Melba brought up her knee with every ounce of strength she could muster. She heard his nose crunch and she held the back of his head and brought her knee up again, a sick thud and a gush of blood spewed from his nostrils. Again! Damon sank to his knees and with a final, furious blow, Melba knocked him flat. The penis began to ebb as she stood over him. Melba looked around the room, eyes darting, and she ran to the closet. Edward's golf bag was there. She grabbed one of the irons and moved towards Damon, club raised. He was gasping, reeling, struggling to his knees. Melba lifted the club for the decisive, killing blow and he met her eyes.

'Mummy!' Damon screamed.

Why did she halt? Why didn't she drive that steel shaft down on his skull? One well-placed blow and he would fall dead at her feet. Kill him. Hit the beast and kill him!
(*Damon*, 1976, p. 213.)

The climactic section of *The Omen* presents at length, and with sympathy, the dilemma of a nice-guy father, who must — for the wellbeing of the human race — slice up his little six-year-old boy with a set of ritual knives. In *The Soul of Anna Klane* the father is morally obliged to exterminate his daughter, for her own good (rather like those apocryphal Victorian schoolmasters who prayed with their pupils before flogging them to death). The only extended and at all sympathetic account of child battering which I have read in contemporary bestsellers occurs in Stephen King's otherwise clichéd *The Shining*. The adult hero of this novel is a likeable academic with a drink problem, who has an occasionally explosive temper. One day he comes into his study and finds his three-year-old son (who has strange and disquieting paranormal faculties) emptying a can of beer over his papers. He breaks the child's arm. In the context of the novel we do not blame him — we'd do likewise if we had a three-year-old 'shiner' instead of an 'ordinary' child. This legitimation of child beating is again evidently motivating the 'discovery' scene in *The Killing Gift* where the mother (as usual very likeable) sees for the first time a demonstration of her daughter's telekinetic powers. A falling vase is plucked out of the air and restored, unbroken to its shelf:

> Kate straightened up, looked again at the vase, and back at the smiling child.
> 'Jennifer?' she whispered.
> Jennifer's smile wavered.
> Kate went to her daughter slowly. She put her hand under Jennifer's chin, tilted her head back, looked at her intently. The smile was gone.
> One last time Kate looked back at the little unbroken vase glinting in the sun streaming through the window.
> And then she drew back her hand and slapped Jennifer ¡ across the face as hard as she could. The little head jerked to the side and while it was still turned, Kate whipped the back of her hand against the other cheek (*The Killing Gift*, 1977, pp. 23-4).

Only a thin fictional membrane separates this from the classic child battering situation (child breaks vase, affectionate but overwrought mother impulsively lashes out at child). But the effect of that fictional membrane is to make the hideous act normal, a natural response in the unnatural circumstances.

One could multiply evidence that these works are directed at the parent as reader or audience; and that these works' function is — in the largest sense — therapeutic. They allow the playing out of common parental frustrations in the absence of the children who cause those frustrations. Gothicism's extravagant recasting and patent unlikelihood has the added benefit of permitting the parent adept in doublethink not to recognize, or own, his disgraceful feelings, embodied as they are in such manifest hokum. Superhuman parental control discharges itself in fantasies of superhuman infant possession.

All this is obvious enough, and has probably struck any person who has bothered to think twice about these super-sellers and blockbusters of the 1970s. More speculatively, however, I would suggest that the extraordinary degree of graphically rendered violence and irrationalism in these films/novels and novelizations expresses a perverse resistance to the prevailing rationalism about child rearing, embodied in that bestseller of bestsellers, Dr Benjamin Spock's *Baby and Child Care*. With getting on for 25 m. sold this has outdone any novel ever published in the US, by 2 to 1. And — of course — Spock is bought mainly by the young (and therefore parentally inexperienced) marrieds. The same group, that is, as I have guessed make up the core of the film-going public for this kind of film.

Since the 1960s, and especially in the 1970s, parents in the English-speaking world have been instructed by Dr Spock that everything the child does has a 'normal' explanation. His manual is one of the great demystifying texts of our age. The name Spock has, in fact, become mythic shorthand for 'monstrous rationality'. This is not, of course, all the doctor's fault. In the tremendously popular and long-running *Star Trek* series, 'Mr' Spock (clearly inspired by the physician) is Captain Kirk's second in command; as a hybrid Vulcan and Earthman he is incapable of, and often comically perplexed by, human emotion. To every problem he brings the computer's icy, rational evaluation. Such, indeed, is his main role on board the USS *Enterprise*; he counterbalances the messily passionate and hasty assessments of his crewmates when confronted with the strange and terrifying worlds of outer space. He sees everything, and takes everything in without shock, emotion or prejudice; nothing human or inhuman is alien to this alien.

For Dr Spock, too, everything that customarily worries or surprises the parent has a rational explanation when seen in the whole light of the child's development. Be astonished by nothing, be angry at nothing, he tells us; it's normal. This, for example, is how the handbook explains 'contrariness' or 'balkiness' in your child:

It looks as though the child's nature between 2 and 3 is urging him to decide things for himself, and to resist pressure from other people. Trying to fight these two battles without much worldly experience seems to get him tightened up inside, especially if his parents are a little too bossy. It's similar to the 6-to-9-year-old period, when the child tries to throw off his dependence on his parents, takes over a lot of responsibility for his own behavior, becomes overfussy about how he does things, and shows his tenseness in various nervous habits.

It's often hard to get along with a child between 2 and 3. Parents have to be understanding. The job is to keep from interfering too much, from hurrying him. Let him help to dress and undress himself when he has the urge. Start his bath early enough so that he has time to dawdle and scrub the tub. At meals let him feed himself without urging. When he is stalled in his eating, let him leave the table. When it's time for bed, or going outdoors, or coming in, steer him while conversing about pleasant things. Get things done without raising issues. Don't be discouraged.

(Spock, 1974, p. 357).

In the heroic effort to be 'understanding' and not be 'discouraged', many Spock-enlightened parents must have desired, like Damon's mother, to knee the obscene little swine in the nose and batter him over the head with one of daddy's golf clubs. And in spite of Spock, parents surely from time to time have the instinctive feeling that contrariness and balkiness are altogether too tame words for what one gets at the tea-table or at bedtime. Naughtiness or wickedness must sometimes suggest themselves as proper descriptions, as must the possible benefits of giving 'the little devil' a quick spank.

It's all for the good, probably, that we have Spock and relatively new codes of patience and self-restraint in dealing with our children. But if one accepts the thesis that I have been putting forward it would follow that the authoritarian, arbitrary parent with his unspared rod and his intention to root out the devil in his offspring is not entirely purged from our society.

Chapter Six

Women's fiction I: *The Thorn Birds*

In the *New York Times Book Review*'s survey of the decade's top ten sellers there are only two works by women. One of the great realizations by the book trade in the 1970s, however, was that the woman reader accounted for much more than a fifth of the market for fiction. In fact, surveys — taken to heart by the book trade — revealed that women consumed around 60 per cent of all novels sold. It was a mark of this realization in 1979 when a work by Judith Krantz earned the highest ever advance sale for paperback rights to a novel ($3.2 m.). If the 1970s demonstrated anything to the publishing industry, it was that women's fiction was not restricted to genre products, but could have its 'blockbusters'. The following two chapters deal with the top-selling novel by a woman (*The Thorn Birds*), the top-selling woman novelist (Erica Jong), and the top-selling line of women's novel ('sweet and savages').

> *The Thorn Birds* has sold more copies than any other novel of the past ten years, and rights have been sold all over the world for more money than publishers have ever paid for a book before.
>
> (Futura blurb)

> The pokiest pig ever sold in the Australian sucker market.
> (Max Harris, in *The Australian*)

I

The Thorn Birds was indisputably 'the number one international bestseller' of 1977-9; according to its publishers it was also 'the publishing legend of the decade'. In fact, well before publication *The Thorn Birds* was legendary. Of the seven who started, Bantam and Avon 'slugged it out like gladiators' for two days at the paperback auction, to acquire rights from Harper & Row. The final price Avon paid, $1.9 m., topped Bantam's $1.85 m. for *Ragtime* in 1975 and stood as a record until the $2.2 m. given for Puzo's *Fools Die* in 1978. British hard and paperback rights were acquired by Futura for $266,000; German rights brought in $220,000; and together with the sale of Australasian rights *The Thorn Birds* drew in some $650,000 in overseas (meaning, here, outside-America) earnings. McCullough's agent held onto the film rights until a little after publication, turning down a *Rich Man, Poor Man* style TV mini-series, parting finally with the novel to Warner Brothers in September 1977 for an undisclosed sum, but one which added considerably to the overnight millionairess's investment fund.

The Thorn Birds was a presold winner. Harper & Row put $100,000 into their launch campaign in April 1977 achieving what they claimed (probably correctly) was 'the biggest publicity promotion blitz of the year' (*Publishers Weekly*, 11 April 1977). Among other things, 2,000 advance-reading copies were circulated through the American book trade. Three weeks before official publication day there were 225,000 hardback copies in print and some booksellers were already reporting it top of their list. Such was pre-publication excitement that it reached the #9 position in the official lists a week before anyone in America could legitimately buy the novel and it made the #1 spot on 6 June. By August, 362,500 copies had been printed. As a hardback it remained in the American charts for a year. As a paperback it was, by 1979, well on the way to becoming one of the very few 10 m. sellers of the decade.

As the *Guardian* observed, there was something of a 'publishing mystery' in this landslide success. Before *The Thorn Birds* McCullough was a virtually unknown writer — and an Australian at that — with only one obscure book to her credit. (*Tim*, 'a warm Australian romance', chronicles the love between a middle aged spinster and a mentally retarded — but physically magnificent — young man.) Why, then, did

Harper & Row, Avon and Futura go overboard, so early and so perceptively, for *The Thorn Birds*?

One reason was the new sense of global market which had developed in the American book trade following the abolition of the Traditional Market Agreement in 1976. This had opened the previously protected 'Empire' markets to America — and Australia, with its world's highest *per capita* book consumption — was now very much in the forefront of American publishers' minds. Significantly, on the publication of *The Thorn Birds* McCullough undertook three consecutive promotion tours — in the US, to the UK and to Australia.

For their part, Avon may have been induced to go over the odds by their proven ability to pick winners from the slush pile. They had done so with Rosemary Rogers and Kathleen Woodiwiss — probably the most valuable finds any paperback publisher made in the 1970s. And, by their 'open door policy', Avon, a paperback house, discovered them first; they did not inherit them from a hardback house. Although McCullough was not entirely unknown, and Harper & Row could claim to have recognized her potential first, Avon had by the mid-1970s a millions-strong, brand-loyal women's readership who trusted the firm to come up with steamy romances. And *The Thorn Birds* with its three heroines was clearly a book which would appeal to the women's market.

One may surmise that Harper & Row were less attracted by any one feature of *The Thorn Birds* manuscript than by its nice mix of selling points, in terms of what was currently dominating the charts. Two of the very biggest novels of the mid-1970s were *Centennial* and *Trinity*. Uris's novel made over seventy appearances on the *Publishers Weekly* list and gave him his first top-spot since *Exodus*. *Centennial* was such a surefire thing that it remained a bestseller even after the hardback publisher hiked the price nearly three dollars to an unprecedented $12.50. Like *Centennial* ('An epic American experience that captures the soul of a country') and *Roots* (an even bigger seller) *The Thorn Birds* is a panoramic saga of national emergence, narrated in terms of a series of representative individual lives. Like Uris's Ireland, McCullough's Australia is interestingly foreign — yet has a shared language and, in large part, a shared cultural tradition with America. And just as Ireland had the historical advantage (for the novelist) of a more recent revolution than America's, so Australia had the advantage of a more recent pioneer era. Both Australia and Ireland had freed themselves from the status of colonial possession, and the bicentennial had made a mild xenophobia a good selling point. There is, incidentally, an understated but quite audible anti-English sentiment in *The Thorn Birds*, whose main protagonists are all Irish Catholic: 'It is not causeless, you know, the Irish hatred of the English,' one of them observes.

The Thorn Birds has elements of the Michener/Uris/Haley 'birth of a nation' theme as well as these authors' massive spread of narrative. But in other ways it is closer to the family saga or 'dynasty' style of epic. These were also doing excellent business in the period that American publishers were making their expensive decisions about *The Thorn Birds*. John Jakes's 'Kent Family Chronicles' (the American Bicentennial Series) had come from nowhere to sell over 10 m. in two years. And for the specifically female readership there were the English Diane Pearson's *Csardas* (1975, the saga of a Hungarian family from the glittering late nineteenth-century Austro-Hungarian Empire to 'today's totalitarian state') and Susan Howatch's *Cashelmara* (1974), both of which had done extremely well in America. *Cashelmara* is as it happened, particularly close to *The Thorn Birds* in organization and subject matter. Both works offer the saga of a representative Irish family; Howatch's covers the period 1859-90 and is segmented into six narratives, each given to a narrator with a different point of view. McCullough offers seven segments, covering the period 1915-69 and taking as its focus a different member of the Cleary family (or, in two cases, associates by intimate sexual relationship). *Cashelmara*, *Csardas* and *Thorn Birds* were all insistently promoted as the 'new' *Gone With the Wind*, a label which seems to have irritated McCullough intensely, as well it might since her own authorial professionalism is in stark contrast to Mitchell's small-town amateurism.

II

The title of McCullough's novel is explained by the italicized 'legend' which prefaces it. Thorn birds spend their lives searching for a thorn tree. Having found one, they impale themselves 'on the longest sharpest spine' and dying sing 'one superlative song, existence the price . . . For the best is only bought at the cost of great pain'.

This prefatory legend (which I assume McCullough has invented) recalls the life-giving mother pelican tearing its breast to feed its selfish young. McCullough's symbolism is — however — more directly genital; and the suggestion of feminine surrender to the victimizing phallus is transparent. Also recalled is the swan-song — conventionally figurative of the artist's tragic sacrifice of life for art.

The opening sections of the novel descend a long way from the poetic prelude. One of the strengths of *The Thorn Birds* for overseas readers (less so for Australians, judging by Max Harris's home-town hatchet job) is the gritty evocation of rural life in a pioneer era which extended up to the Second World War. McCullough is very convincing in her descriptions of the filthy business of shearing and tending Merinos in the semi-desert of back-country Australia, or the rigours of cane-cutting in semi-tropical North Queensland. The scene painting of Australian landscape and of the sheep station/country town settings are (with a few gushy lapses for sunsets and so on) well done. And some of the set-piece scenes come off brilliantly (the lightning-exploded gum tree which immolates the Cleary patriarch, Paddy, stands out as a descriptive *tour de force*).

But the virtue of *The Thorn Birds* is not that it has a single strength or selling quality; rather it has a specific strength for everybody, man, woman, young, old, emancipated, reactionary, American, English, Australian. Its wide-ranging appeal can be conveniently gathered under four main heads, or component parts, each appropriate to a different market sector.

(1) *The Thorn Birds* offers the sweeping panorama of an 'epic moment' in the formation of a nation (historically

The Thorn Birds covers Australia's progress from minor colony, through dominion to national independence). The organization of the novel intimates that many small lives go to make up a family history and many small family achievements make up a national identity. This aspect of the novel depends on the assumption, legitimate enough in the early sections, that the Clearys are 'ordinary' immigrants. At the beginning of the narrative Paddy Cleary is an itinerant New Zealand sheep shearer who emigrates to the Australian outback to work as head stockman on a sheep station. In the subsequent drama of adaptation, McCullough evokes an anti-pastoral world where hardship is inseparable from the immigrant struggle with the continental spaces of an uncolonized country. The relationship between suffering and creativity, the thorn and the song, is clearest cut in this section of the novel.

(2) Grafted onto this stock is a novel of high life and gracious living, in the *Gone With the Wind* manner. By a most improbable chance, the indigent Clearys are the sole relatives, and eventually heirs (together with the Catholic Church, another odds-against likelihood) to the richest woman in Australia. Thus the vagrant family become masters of Drogheda's 250,000 acres. As the belle of Drogheda (sheep station and plantation interchange easily enough) Meg's life story is dominated by her fifty-years-long love affair with a grandee of the Catholic Church, Ralph de Bricassart ('a magnificent man'). De Bricassart's elevation in the novel is as precipitate as the Clearys'. He rises from priest, to bishop, archbishop and finally cardinal. (While just a bishop he fathers a son on the 26-year-old Meg.) Meg herself is revealed as a Perdita figure, the princess in peasant disguise. Through her mother's family we understand she has inherited aristocratic blood, 'titian' hair, natural breeding. This finer being is set off by her being the only Cleary girl (the numerous boys all take after the bog-trotting Paddy except, of course, the madcap Frank who is the by-blow of his mother's premarital fling with the brilliant Pakeha).

(3) 'At the heart of the tale', as the blurb tells us, are the forbidden loves of Fiona and Meg, the first two generations of Cleary women. Both have husbands who are worthy

'working men' and 'cultured, sophisticated, very charming' lovers whom society prohibits their openly acknowledging: Fiona's 'Pakeha' because he is half Maori; Meg's de Bricassart because he is a priest. The 'thorn' in this central situation is the woman's self denial of sexual gratification, denial which is given a final poignancy when the consolatory children of these love affairs are taken prematurely from them (Frank into life imprisonment, Meg's Dane by drowning). This masochistic aspect of *The Thorn Birds* would seem designed to appeal to the mature, married woman reader.

(4) Subordinate to the above is a preoccupation with female emancipation, designed apparently to appeal to a younger group of women. The chronicle of the three generations from Fiona through Meg to Justine Cleary follows, in social terms, an advance from the slavery of frontier womanhood to the liberation of modern woman on near-equal terms in the man's world. Justine (a rather Jacqueline Susannish conception) is a freebooting modern young woman. Her grandmother had half a dozen sons (girls didn't count); her mother two children; Jussy repudiates the whole breeding business with a breezy feminist scorn ('Not bloody likely! Spend *my* life wiping snotty noses and cacky bums?'). In her young womanhood Fee was a bondslave to the domestic economy. Meg has a less drudging time of it, though she is still indentured to the house and, in a larger sense, to Drogheda. Justine, by contrast, has a profession; she is an actress, and this removes her from home into the cosmopolitan world. In the last, climactic scene of the novel Justine is shown (at her mother's prompting) rejecting Drogheda's good earth and the bondage it represents. The thorn is now less sharp, and the modern, emancipated woman less likely to drive it into her bosom.

The Thorn Birds is a highly efficient, broad-appeal product. Few categories of reader can have been disappointed in their purchase. Nonetheless the novel does have weaknesses. The descriptions of Justine's jet-set life do not seem to me to come off. And the extended descriptions of the ecstatic physical consummation that produces Meg and de Bricassart's love-child is an embarrassing failure:

Did he carry her to the bed, or did they walk? He thought

he must have carried her, but he could not be sure: only that she was on it, he was there upon it her skin under his hands, his skin under hers. Oh, God! My Meggie, my Meggie! How could they rear me from infancy to think you profanation? Time ceased to tick and began to flow, washed over him until it had no meaning, only a depth of dimension more real than time (*The Thorn Birds*, 1978, p. 354).

As it happens, McCullough is not entirely to blame for this scene. As she explained to the *Guardian*'s reporter, she produced it only under duress:

My editor told me that the second half of the book needed a damn good love scene, and there is nothing I dislike writing more. Love-making is such a non-verbal thing, I hate that explicit 'he stuck it in her' kind of thing because it is boring. You can only say 'he stuck it in her' so many ways (*Guardian*, 15 April, 1977).

Chapter Seven

Women's fiction II: liberation and female masochism-Erica Jong and the 'bodice rippers'

> You can only say 'he stuck it in her' so many ways.
> (Colleen McCullough)

The sweep of *The Thorn Birds'* narrative gives an equivalent subplot status to both Meg's long-suffering domestic passivity in its historical setting and Jussy's liberated activity in the present. McCullough's superseller thus succeeds in combining profitably what elsewhere crystallized out into a distinct bipolarity in 'women's fiction' and its blockbusters of the 1970s. This bipolarity and its formal characteristics may be represented in a simple diagram:

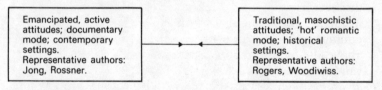

Emancipated, active attitudes; documentary mode; contemporary settings. Representative authors: Jong, Rossner.

Traditional, masochistic attitudes; 'hot' romantic mode; historical settings. Representative authors: Rogers, Woodiwiss.

Emancipated, active attitudes; documentary mode; contemporary settings

Although pioneers like Betty Friedan were writing in the early 1960s, it was not until 1968 that the women's movement was installed in the public consciousness and took off as a widespread campaign. A usual starting point is the much publicized burning of brassieres in Atlantic City, 7 September 1968. As regards the mores of fiction this particular event was significant as being both rebellious and as ostentatiously flouting a taboo, one of the sex's 'dirty little secrets'. In male fiction, the parallel, of course, was Philip Roth's *Portnoy's Complaint*, 1969 — a work which, as the current witticism had it, took the novel all the way from the bedroom to the bathroom. The women's movement thus took its stand on emancipation and gross, calculatedly pugnacious affronts to *The Feminine Mystique* (Germaine Greer's observation, for instance, that unless a woman could taste her menstrual blood with the same indifference with which she might lick a cut finger, she was not liberated). Out of the new enlightenment and rebelliousness came a number of bestselling novels in the early 1970s catering for an enlightened and rebellious reading public; Lois Gould's *Such Good Friends* (1970), Alix Kates Shulman's *Memoirs of an Ex-prom Queen* (1972), Marge Piercy's *Small Changes* (1973). And it was the sexual-political climate of the turn of the decade, together with the new market for women's fiction, that converted Erica Jong from being an experimental writer (disciple of Nabokov) and minor poet to a multi-million selling novelist:

I owe my decision to throw away my Nabokovian madman novel and begin writing *Fear of Flying* in 1971 partly due to this new women's consciousness and partly to the intercession of a good editor, who urged me to attempt a novel born out of the same authenticity I was beginning to discover in my poems. I must also credit the liberating influence of the outrageous Alexander Portnoy, and the courage-kindling fires of the Women's Movement, which, above all, decreed that women's emotions had as much validity as men's (*Bookviews*, August 1978).

Fear of Flying had a huge success, and the zipless fuck joined the burned bra as a notorious icon of what was universally sneered at as 'women's lib'. But in general the movement's relationship with fiction was uneasy. 'Authenticity' required either poetry (with its minimal readership and consequent freedom from commercialism) or the straight talk of non-fiction. In terms of sexual politics *The Female Eunuch* was generically sounder than *Fear of Flying*. The superselling novel with emancipated themes (*Fear of Flying*, *Perdido*, *The Woman's Room*) was inevitably suspect as being indirectly exploitative of women (making money for male publishers, fuelling male masturbation fantasies) or indicative of a repressive tolerance which insidiously sapped revolutionary energy and confused protest with entertainment.

Jong's second novel, *How to Save Your Own Life* (1977) demonstrated in a number of ways the dead end which enlightened women's fiction of the 1970s eventually encountered. First, it was a critical flop. (Jong put this down to 'backlash' and 'deliberate distortion' by reviewers.) Second, even those who admired the novel could not but see that fiction had melted into barely veiled autobiography, with a good selection of Jong's poems as epilogue. Briefly, Isadora Wing goes on to write a bestselling autobiographical novel and become a media celebrity. Her marriage has broken up. Jong introduces into the plotless narrative real life characters such as Anne Sexton, the poet, under transparent disguise. *Time* called *How to Save Your Own Life* 'up-to-date confessional bulletins', the *New York Times* critic said he felt as if he were reading 'gossip rather than fiction'. Jong retorted that the objection that her novel was mere autobiography revealed a 'literary double standard . . . what is it that men write about?' (*Observer*, 24 April 1977.) Third – and probably most painful for the author – the hard core of the women's movement discerned in *How to Save Your Own Life* a damaging 'romanticism', the implication being that fiction *qua* fiction cannot be otherwise than 'soft' on the issues. (See the interview between Jong and Roszika Parker and Eleanor Stephens in the feminist magazine *Spare Rib*, July 1977. Although the interview is good-natured superficially, the allegation of 'romanticism' comes up several times and Jong is driven to deny what she affirms elsewhere, when she finally declares: 'I never got a lot of nourishment from the movement'.)

What happened to polemical or enlightened 'women's fiction' in the 1970s is what one perceives happening to the 'Tendenz Roman' or 'social-problem novel' in other periods. In a few years the aspirations of the protest movement are too articulate, too urgent and too self-important to be contained within the limitations of mere fiction. Even the documentary novel is insufficiently documentary for the movement's needs, and is repudiated as false consciousness.

Traditional, masochistic attitudes; 'hot' romantic mode; historical settings

A less articulate consequence of heightened women's con-sciousness in the 1970s was the spectacular increase in the appetite for romance. This had always been a solid sector of the popular fiction market, but suddenly it boomed. The veteran Barbara Cartland was suddenly required to up her output from five to twenty titles a year; despite her advanced age she responded manfully, one might say. Firms like Avon in America, Mills & Boon in Britain and the multinational Harlequin expanded their operation dramatically. Avon, from virtually nothing, built up a stable of youngish new romance writers, whose paperback originals consistently made the bestseller lists selling millions of copies per title. Harlequin's sales rose from around 30 m. in 1974 to around 80 m. in 1976. Harlequin's affiliate, Mills & Boon, claimed a 33 per cent increase in sales between 1972 and 1974 (*Guardian*, 26 November 1975; *Author*, winter 1974). The Mills & Boon expansion was accompanied by a logical switch to paperback: in 1969 the firm was putting out twelve hardbacks and six paperbacks a month; by 1974 it was fourteen hardbacks and ten paperbacks.

The romance boom was not just a matter of bigger sales of the same kind of title. The most dramatic innovation in the field of popular women's fiction was the success of 'hot ones', 'bodice rippers', or 'sweet and savages' as they were called (this last after Rosemary Rogers's trendsetting *Sweet Savage Love*). These were works which, like *Fear of Flying*, exploited the new permissiveness of the post-Portnoy 1970s. The firms associated with this new wave were primarily Avon in America and Troubadour in Britain, though many others quickly got in on the act. And the fictional formula, pioneered by Rosemary Rogers and Kathleen Woodiwiss, involved erotically fantasized woman's bondage in an historical context. The unliberated condition of woman — incarcerated, flagellated, degraded, violated — was celebrated time and again, with a great deal of accurate sexual and inaccurate historical detail. The energy, which in Jong's fiction was directed to the activity of woman's emancipation was, in the sweet and savages, converted to a morbidly intensified masochistic passivity. In these novels the heroine does not quest, like the indomitable Isadora Wing; instead she is a chattel, a vessel and a powerless victim under the thrusts and lashes of the men who use her body. The summary of *Savage Eden* ('The power of *Sweet Savage Love* ... the passion of *Dark Fires* ... the intensity of *Love's Tender Fury*') is typical:

> It's the story of beautiful Caroline Fane, unjustly accused of adultery and murder, flogged naked in public ... and Justin Lawrence, the daring, flamboyant highwayman whose lust for Caroline was irresistible. Together they escape to the New World, only to be recaptured and sold into slavery. In the untamed, violent world of the notorious plantation known as Montrose, they fight for survival against a brutal master and a sadistic mistress with monstrous erotic appetites and, in spite of every obstacle, fulfil their fierce and tender love for each other (*Publishers Weekly*, 2 August 1976).

Love's Wild Desire, by 'Jennifer Blake' uses the same mythical American South setting, and makes the same woman=slave equation. The attractions of the novel, as proclaimed in Sphere's cover, are the standard ones: rape, flagellation and protracted humiliation:

> LOVE'S WILD ASSAULT!
> In a locked room in a notorious mansion, Catherine Mayfield first learned to fight against the power of a man's aroused desires — and her own awakened hungers. She learned what it meant to lose all pride, all pretence. And all control. . . . In a great plantation house, Catherine was placed to be mistress of all she surveyed. And to be a slave to one man's iron will and fierce possessiveness. . . . On a riverboat on the raging Mississippi, Catherine faced a captor whose hulking brutality and animal lust mocked her claims to respect as an aristocrat and virtue as a lady. . . . In a world where force and violence ruled supreme, Catherine was a woman whose passions were too strong and defences too frail to shield her from LOVE'S WILD DESIRE. . . .

These bodice rippers were clearly exploitative and commercially cynical. Some of the authors with extravagantly feminine names were later disclosed to be men. 'Jennifer Wilde', authoress of *Love's Tender Fury* and *Dare to Love* was unmasked as a former Texan schoolteacher, Tom Huff. 'Leonie Hargrave', authoress of *Clara Reeve* — 'a nightmare vision of Victorian sensuality' — turned out to be the two sf writers, Tom Disch and Charles Naylor. But a jollier cynicism about the corniness of traditional women's fiction (together with a respect for its newly evident lucrative possibilities) also produced the charmingly camped-up sex romps of journalists Jilly Cooper ('Barbara Cartland without the iron knickers') and Molly Parkin. The *TLS* catalogued the 'plot' of Parkin's *Love All* thus:

in seven days she fellates her father, takes on board her
two regular lovers, sleeps with her ex-husband, is half-
raped by a homosexual, has her anus enlarged by an adroit
French restaurateur, sleeps chastely with a Lesbian ex-
lover, picks up a buffet-car attendant, and is back for
more.

Her paperback publishers, Star, gleefully reproduced the *TLS*'s denunciation as an inducement to the prospective purchaser. Parkin, it would seem, knew lots of ways of saying 'he stuck it in her'.

By the end of the 1970s, the sweet and savages had lost their shocking novelty and, as is usual with breakthroughs in genre, the field was hopelessly saturated by 'me too' imitations. It was significant when, after four supersellers (*Sweet Savage Love*, *Dark Fires*, *Wicked Loving Lies* and *The Wildest Heart*) the category's hottest property, Rosemary Rogers, was deprogrammed and relaunched as 'the new Jacqueline Susann' with *The Crowd Pleasers* (*roman à clef* about the immoralities of the 1970s jet set).

Chapter Eight

Star Wars

A real gee-whiz book.

I

Like the hamburger, *Star Wars* can be consumed by all the
family, from the youngest to the oldest of both sexes. It is
less a novel than a market strategy designed to scoop up as
much cash and pocket money as possible. It was helped in
this aim by the commercial fact that in modern America
there is virtually no product which cannot be copyrighted,
patented, registered under a trademark, sponsored or franchised. The consumer could watch, read, listen to, drink, or
play with *Star Wars* products. It came as a Twentieth Century
Fox film, and a range of book, pictorial and print items,
from the Ballantine and Random House division of the RCA
conglomerate. LP records and myriad wall posters, comics,
drinks, drink vessels, toy laser guns, models, board games etc.
were everywhere to be had. In 1978 one could even buy
Darth Vader ice-lollies, a fraction of whose price — like all
the rest of the brand-named commodities — found their way
back to the 'Star Wars Corporation'. A whole thematic
industry was set up on the *Star Wars* logo (t.m. TCF. Twentieth
Century Fox went so far as to protect by trademark characters'
names, like 'Chewbacca'). Its turnover was incalculable; but
by 1979 the film alone was estimated to have made getting
on for $200 m. on its modest $6½ m. production costs.
   George Lucas had the idea for an sf film in 1971 and began
working on it full time in 1973. Production was finished in
1975, but it was strategically held back for a massive launch

programme. As part of the pre-launch mania-generation the novelization 'authored' by the film's director (Lucas) first came out in December 1976. This was six months before the film's release in June 1977, an epoch-making event in show-business history: 'it's madness,' one TCF official was quoted as saying, 'the queues at the cinemas are unbelievable.' As soon as the film hit the screen the paperback shot to the head of the bestseller lists. (In Britain the novelization was put out by Sphere, who reportedly gave $225,000 for rights.) 'Activity on the book has been incredible,' Ballantine reported in June. 3.5 m. copies were sold in three months. And the first novelization was only a part of the *Star Wars* trade. Billed as 'from the adventures of Luke Skywalker', the paperback opened the way for many follow-up adventures. The connoisseur could also purchase, in 1978, a 'portfolio' of paintings by Ralph McQuarrie; the film buff could invest in a chronicle, 'The making of *Star Wars*', and the screenplay. For the technical minded there was a volume of 'blueprints' with the specifications of the spaceware and weaponry. For the cultish there was an 'iron-on transfer book' with which to emblazon T-shirts, jeans and self. For the astrological, a '*Star Wars* calendar' ('a must for every fan'). A whole range· of low-priced comic books and fan-club products catered for the younger reader. And there were, of course, the usual rip-offs and cover jobs, from space epics called 'War Star' to a tract from Bible Voice entitled 'The ·Force of Star Wars' (this purported to tell the Bible story in terms of the film's icon-ography).

This *Star Wars* mania was methodically whipped up not once, but twice. The *Star Wars* film/book multi-media smash-hit circus was 're-released' in early 1979 in America and in summer in the UK. Supposedly it drew almost as many filmgoers the second time round. And it set off a new bom-bardment from the publishers. In Britain, for the re-release, Fontana published four new 'activity books' and two story books. These were mainly aimed at the junior market; the Sphere novelization and various other *Star Wars* items were still around, notably sequel and prequel narratives 'from the adventures of Luke Skywalker'.

By the time this second wave was played out there would

be *Star Wars*'s sequel, *The Empire Strikes Back* — and back and back and back, presumably, until the last note was extracted from the last pocket. Then television could have Lucas's 'intergalactic dream of heroism'. Meanwhile sf, which trade wisdom has always thought to be box-office poison, suddenly attracted all the smart money in Hollywood. Multi-million dollar investments were made (and handsomely returned) in *Alien, CE3K, Star Trek: The Motion Picture* and *The Black Hole*, which coined fortunes for their owners, not just as films and books of films, but in a whole range of ingeniously spun-off products on the *Star Wars* model.

II

'Escapist' was the tag universally applied to *Star Wars*, 'Escapist and proud of it' was the theme of its publicity. As in the concurrently successful MGM nostalgia binge, *That's Entertainment*, the come-on message put across was: 'We know it's not very heavy, but you deserve it — give yourself a treat.' Lucas originally had some trouble marketing the idea of *Star Wars*, but this matinée quality was the selling point that producer Alan Ladd Jr saw in the sketch, paste mock-ups and fourteen pages of story which were peddled around Hollywood in the early 1970s:

> When I heard about *Star Wars* I thought that it sounded like the kind of thing I used to love when I was a kid at the movies on Saturday afternoon — People still want to see films about human relationships and films with good escapist values that will make them laugh and cry (*Sunday Telegraph*, 1 April, 1979).

Lucas himself stresses the same artless appeal in his plug for *Star Wars*:

> I think that anyone who goes to the movies loves to have an emotional experience. It's basic whether you're seven, seventeen or seventy. The more intense the experience the more successful the film.
>
> I've always loved adventure films. After I finished *American Graffiti*, I came to realize that since the demise of the western there hasn't been much in the mythological

fantasy genre available to the film audience. So instead of making 'isn't it terrible what's happening to mankind' movies, which is how I began, I decided that I'd try to fill that gap. I'd make a film so rooted in imagination that the grimness of everyday life would not follow the audience into the theater. In other words for two hours, they could forget.

I'm trying to reconstruct a genre that's been lost and bring it to a new dimension so that the elements of space, fantasy, adventure, suspense and fun all work and feed off each other. So, in a way, *Star Wars* is a movie for the kid in all of us (*Star Wars*, 1977, p. 108).

Lucas is rather more candid than Ladd. *Star Wars* is not exclusively for kids (not, that is to say, like the Flash Gordon serials — an original model). Seven-year-olds are, of course freely admitted without parental guidance if they have the money. But *Star Wars* is principally for those in the seventeen-to-seventy bracket who can afford (without saving up) $3 for a ticket, $1.95 for a paperback and have something left over for a $2 'souvenir programme'.

It is probable that the creators and backers of *Star Wars* were inspired to put their millions of dollars and years of effort behind the project by the 1970s cult success of *Star Trek* (originally a 1960s TV serial). This recruited millions of self-styled 'Trekkies' — zombie (but adult) fiction addicts willing to buy anything connected with the serial. Trekkies were that advertiser's dream, consumers with the child's fanatic brand-loyalty and inexhaustible appetite for narrative pap together with the spending power of grown-ups. Children are wonderfully seducible by advertising; but one of the great problems in merchandising products for them is that they have so little cash. The greatest achievement of the American persuasion industry has been to induce in wealthy adults the appetites, enthusiasms and loyalties of their kids. Hence the extraordinary fact that American children, teenagers and adults all swill coke (though the weight problems of the older generations necessitate a 'low calorie' version). It is true to say that *Star Trek* and later *Star Wars* similarly achieved the all-generation appeal of coke.

Like all broad-spectrum family entertainment, *Star Wars*

makes a primary appeal at the kid's level. The borrowings from *The Wizard of Oz* (C-3PO = Tin Man, etc.) are blatant. None the less the publicity was careful to reassure the adult that it was OK — even smart — to pay to see (read) a kid's film (book). But more was packed in for the sophisticated than just the camp pleasures of old Flash Gordon or Buck Rogers replays. *Star Wars* makes a calculated bid for the 'intellectual' Tolkien cult-public, with its heavily laid-on mysticism about 'the force'. 'The force surroundes each and every one of us. Some men believe it directs our actions, and not the other way around' (*ibid.* p. 80). In some quarters the myth-mash of *Star Wars* was indeed taken very seriously. The *Journal of Popular Culture*, for instance, brought out an article in 1977 ('*Star Wars*: the yearning for a past future') which applauded the intricate symbolism of the work. Luke, it was solemnly pointed out, etymologically signified 'Light'; Darth Vader was, of course, 'the Dark Lord'; Ben Kenobi was a Merlin figure; the lightsabre Skywalker's (e.g. Arthur's) Excalibur; Moff Tarkin connoted Tarquin and so on.

In fact there are, I think, deeper meanings in *Star Wars*. But they are not to be found in its mythopoeia and mythical allusiveness. *Star Wars*'s seriousness is that it dealt with *war* in a historical period which made the subject unusually sensitive. 1976-7 was a time when, if for no other than bicentennial reasons, Americans craved fictions about the kind of justified recourse to arms that their republic was founded on. And yet, by a cruel historical coincidence, this was the aftermath of the first war which the country had ever lost. My Lai, returned POWs and the disgraced President who had promised peace with honour were recent and painful recollections.

One of the things which *Star Wars* would seem to have achieved is the reconstitution of the sustaining mythology of the good war for an America whose faith in it had been shattered. Any realistic reference to war was — of course — as tricky as it would have been in Germany or Japan in 1947. Hence the displacing *mise en scène* whose insistent message is NOT HERE, NOT NOW — above all *not* SE Asia:

Another galaxy, another time.

The Old Republic was the Republic of legend, greater than distance or time. No need to note where it was or whence

it came, only to know that . . . it was *the* Republic (*ibid.*,
p. 1).

This dislocation allows an extraordinarily daring metathesis,
in terms of the war recently waged between the United States
and North Vietnam. As the synopsis puts it: 'Luke Skywalker,
a twenty-year-old farmboy on the remote planet of Tatooine
is compelled to break from his dull chores on his uncle's
moisture farm . . . and challenge the Galactic Empire's
ultimate weapon, the Death Star.' One can make a fairly
obvious exchange of terms here: 'Luke Skywalker, a twenty-
year-old peasant in the paddy fields of a northern province, is
compelled to break from his dull chores . . . and challenge the
gunships and B52s of the Yankee imperialist.' Not to put too
fine a point on it, *Star Wars* permits the luxury of fictional
identification with a heroic *American* guerrilla force, who
defeat an alien, technologically formidable, superpower. In
their use of hit-and-run tactics, their consistent ability to hide
from Vader's 'stormtroopers', Solo and Skywalker (they have
American names, by the way, in contrast to the outlandish
Moff Tarkin and Darth Vader) are what the novelization calls
'Underground Freedom Fighters' – an American Viet Cong.

Given the bruised state of American morale, it was not
permitted to *Star Wars* to press its points too hard or too
directly. The narrative is detextured of any physical or 'felt'
quality. Distancing is achieved by encoding everything in the
extravagantly conventional modes of 'sword and sorcery'
(i.e. transposed medieval romance) and 'space opera' (i.e. transposed western). From the one comes the apparatus of regality
and aristocracy, from the other the numerous shoot-outs.
Luke, the first hero, is associated with S & S; he discovers
himself a Jedi Knight and sets out to rescue the 'Princess'
Leia from the 'Dark Lord' who holds her in thrall. The other
male hero, Han Solo, brings with him a large chunk of
western convention. As his name implies, he is a version of
the Lone Ranger, the unattached gunfighter or freebooter
with the survival skills which make him a broker between the
savage (here represented by the simian Wookie, Chewbacca)
and the civilized, robotic world of the Princess. And Solo's
final sacrifice of his independence when, after internal
struggle, he joins in the suicidal fighter raid on Vader's

battle star is in the best Shane traditions. Of course, at the end, he must carry through the tradition and 'travel adventurously on' literally into the sunset of another solar system) leaving Luke and the Princess united.

The violence of *Star Wars* is sublimation of the already sublimated physical violence of conventional western gunplay. In his *Six Gun Mystique* John Cawelti notes of the six-gun that it permits 'the largest measure of objectivity and detachment' while yet engaging in individual combat' (Cawelti, 1970, p. 60). Laser guns and light swords carry this detachment a step further. Combat is simply a matter of erasure. In a film where literally hundreds of people (at one point a whole world) are destroyed, not a corpuscle of blood is seen. In the climactic duel with light swords, when Vader slashes the body of Kenobi apart, the old man's corpse simply evacuates — there is only a robe left. This disincarnated quality is the case with all the mayhem in *Star Wars*; it leaves no physical residue.

III

Where they were not condescending, or desperately anxious not to be wrong-footed, film critics were scathing about *Star Wars*. Book critics ignored it. Yet the *Star Wars* 'phenomenon' was far from negligible; in the final reckoning the film alone will probably turn over half a billion dollars.

It may well be that *Star Wars* is inferior sf: a lightweight exploitative film. But it was clearly just what was wanted in 1976-9. No one could have coerced millions to pay for it, and its thematic derivatives, had *Star Wars* not been the right product at the right time with the right marketing techniques behind it. And its rightness seems to be explained by what Bernard Shaw, observing the intellectual flimsiness of the London theatre in 1919, termed the 'traumatic' escapism into romance which war induces in an exhausted population.

Battlestar Galactica

It is worth noting that *Star Wars*'s follow-up, Richard Colla's
Battlestar Galactica (1979), was no longer escaping from the
last war, but thinking aggressively about the next. *Battlestar
Galactica* is set up in the twelfth millennium (far past, or
far future — we don't know) 'in another Galaxy'. A weak
President is seduced by flabby and corrupt 'counsellors' into
signing an interplanetary SALT agreement with the subhuman
Cylons. His gallant and entirely admirable generals warn him
against this rash course, but he persists. Once the military
shield is lowered, the Cylons launch a sneak attack and destroy
all twelve human colonies ('Where are our defences?' a forlorn
voice is heard to cry from the burning city). The military
take over in the last remaining stronghold, Battlestar Galactica.
The effete counsellors continue to advise treaty and negotiation ('Throw down our arms,' urges the chief appeaser,
unctuously played by Ray Milland) — right up to the moment
that the treacherous Cylons launch their second sneak attack.
Only the vigilance of the warrior-caste saves the remnant of
the human race. (They also exterminate practically the entire
Cylon race — but that counts as 'victory' in total galactic
war.) Between *Star Wars* and *Battlestar Galactica*, which have
so much special effects hardware and plot in common, the
concern seems to have shifted from Vietnam and war- weari-
ness to SALT 3 and war-readiness. (The Egyptian sneak
attack in the Yom Kippur war seems also to be evoked in the
later work.)

Chapter Nine

Alistair MacLean and James Clavell

It is as if Edgar Wallace had collaborated with Conrad.
(*Daily Express*)

I

MacLean's outstanding popularity is hard to account for. He writes clumsily; his characters are wooden; his morality banal; his plots are virtually sexless; he is derivative and behind the latest thing where ideas for his highly contrived fiction are concerned. Yet sales of 100 m. or more are claimed for his twenty-odd novels. He is — in Fontana's old-fashioned description — the 'master story teller'; 'the leading adventure story writer in the world', according to his immodest hardback publisher, Collins, who also claim him as their *protégé*. (A Collins editor, Ian Chapman, spotted a prize-winning short story of MacLean's in the *Glasgow Herald*. He persuaded the young teacher to write a novel; the result was *HMS Ulysses*. A record-breaking 250,000 hardback copies of this work were sold in the first six months of publication.) 'Everything that MacLean writes', the *Sunday Mirror* correctly observes, 'is an immediate bestseller.' And often, too, a long-term bestseller. Fontana estimated in 1978 that MacLean had outdone the previous record-holder Ian Fleming's thirteen 1 m. sellers. According to Fontana's reckoning MacLean had no less than seventeen — which would make him, title for title, the bestselling English novelist ever.

A general impression of MacLean's loyal public can be gained from the rave reviews he gets in the sub-quality and provincial press. The terminology is that traditionally reserved for male action: his novels 'explode with action', they are 'utterly compelling', 'spine chilling' and 'throat clutching'; 'relentless express trains' in their 'pace', they feature 'breathless action', 'finger biting' and 'cliff hanging' suspense; 'unbearable', 'nail biting' and 'high wire' tension are MacLean hallmarks. The ideal reader goes through a lot and needs himself, it would seem, some of the square-jawed toughness of the MacLean hero if he is to make it to the last page.

Although it has broadened and internationalized over the decades (especially with the 1960s success of his films), the constituency of MacLean's regular readership is evidently masculine, low to middle-brow, middle-class or slightly higher and middle-aged or older. This profile is suggested by the chastity of his plots (as I recall, not a single bedroom scene or rape in over a million words of fiction), the decency of his language (MacLean's sole concession to twenty years of increasing literary permissiveness is a very occasional 'bastard' or 'Christ') and the tameness of his violence (in what is, by MacLean's standard, one of the more violent of his novels, *Puppet on a Chain* (1969), a drug-crazed, psychopathic dollybird exhibits her subhumanity by threatening to shoot the bound hero 'in the leg. High up'; *Puppet on a Chain*, 1971, p. 209). Rarely in MacLean's novels is it directly indicated that men and women have genitals, or that one sex's set is different from the others.

II

MacLean's bestselling career starts with what is often claimed to be his best novel and is his personal favourite, *HMS Ulysses* (1955). This chronicle of a 'mutiny ship' which redeems itself with a final heroic performance on the Russian convoy route in 1943 was inspired by MacLean's own wartime experience. To quote Fontana's blurb:

Alistair MacLean, the son of a Scots minister, was brought up in the Scottish Highlands. In 1941 at the age of eighteen, he joined the Royal Navy; two and a half years spent aboard a cruiser was later to give him the background for *HMS Ulysses*, his first novel, the outstanding documentary novel on the war at sea.

The hardback blurb — conscious perhaps of the higher tone of public library readers — adds that MacLean took a postwar honours degree in arts at Glasgow University and taught for a while. Something of the Scottish dominie as well as the torpedo-man remains in MacLean's frequently didactic narrative manner. For all its veracious first-hand documentation, *HMS Ulysses* prefigures the artifices of MacLean's later, formulaic fiction. We have, for example, the single-sex society, or crew, in an enclosed situation; their behaviour governed by 'manly' codes of action under crushing stress. Archetypally in MacLean's novels the closed society is that of the ship, the values naval and the stress that of war. In his later, largely peacetime, marine scenarios the MacLean fleet diversifies; we have the refugee boat (*South by Java Head*, 1958), the nuclear submarine (*Ice Station Zebra*, 1963), the Caribbean luxury liner (*The Golden Rendezvous*, 1962), the charter craft (*Bear Island*, 1971), the oil rig (*Fear is the Key*, 1977; *Sea Witch*, 1977). Other closed situations which MacLean has experimented with — usually less successfully — are the train (*Breakheart Pass*, 1974), the motorcade (*The Golden Gate*, 1976), the gypsy encampment (*Caravan to Vaccarès*, 1970), the sealed-off experimental weapons establishment (*The Satan Bug*, 1962), the circus (*Circus*, 1975) and, famously, the commando squad on a mission in enemy held territory (*The Guns of Navarone*, 1957; *Where Eagles Dare*, 1967; *Force 10 From Navarone*, 1968). The common features in all these situations is close confinement; the claustral tensions, frictions and camaraderie which result seem to fascinate MacLean. In most of his novels he also introduces an intramural traitor — a complication which seems not yet to have occurred to him in the writing of *HMS Ulysses*.

Typically, for MacLean, *HMS Ulysses* centres on the ordeal of men under extreme duress. Men who are, in the words of the Tennysonian epigraph 'strong in will to strive and not to yield'. The fortitude MacLean particularly values is unblushingly invoked in the address which the 'skipper' (otherwise the 'old man' — such patriarchs carry great authority in MacLean's world) makes to the crew of *Ulysses* over the

tannoy as they prepare for the Arctic rigours of the winter
Russian convoy:

No one has any right to ask you to do it, I least of all . . .
least of all. I know you *will* do it. I know you will not let
me down. I know you will take the *Ulysses* through. Good
luck, good luck and God bless you (*HMS Ulysses*, London,
Fontana, 1977, p. 55).

The 'impossible' mission, undertaken in full consciousness
and voluntary obedience to the authority that requires it, is
to reappear regularly in MacLean's later work (usually in a
tense briefing session rather than a broadcast appeal). What
makes *HMS Ulysses* different, and potentially a better novel
than its successors, is that MacLean has not yet localized the
extraordinary qualities of courage and daring in a single hero,
or pair of heroes. The whole crew become 'men above
themselves'. Later MacLean has an unfortunate penchant for
the superman who — like Mallory in *Force 10* — can take out
a whole German armoured corps single-handed.

III

HMS Ulysses flatteringly commemorated British wartime
endurance, within memory of its being actually required in
the home population. The novel was clearly aimed, if not by
MacLean then by Collins, at the same nationally narcissistic
readership who had made *The Cruel Sea* the British bestseller
of the 1950s. Like Monsarrat's book, *HMS Ulysses* is rather
lugubrious but clearly suited a reading public emerging from
austerity. MacLean, having struck it rich with his first novel,
followed it up with the similarly conceived *South by Java
Head*, a novel which chronicles the ordeal and adventures of
escape by sea from the Japanese invasion of Singapore. As in
Ulysses, the sterling quality of British (more particularly
Scottish) doggedness and British resourcefulness is celebrated,
although MacLean now allows a freer rein to his ingenuity.
There emerge the twists of plot and factitious 'suspense'
which is to be his later stock in trade (one passenger on the
escape vessel is a secret agent, another has the enemy's plans
for the invasion of Australia which the Japanese have to

recover 'at any cost').

MacLean has always shown himself an unusually restless novelist, unwilling to stay with any style of fiction. Presumably he could have remained a more or less repetitive spinner of sea yarns and — like Douglas Reeman, or Dudley Pope, for example — have sustained a healthy minor-league bestseller status. But he decided that 'war novels were not my metier'. This nationalist-narcissist phase of his career finishes with *The Guns of Navarone* and *South by Java Head* in the late 1950s. (The two later war novels, *Where Eagles Dare* and *Force 10 From Navarone* were foisted on MacLean in 1967-8 by film producers who originally commissioned them as screenplays.) In the novels of the early 1960s, however, one sees a lingering attachment to the military/naval adventure despite the resolutely up-to-the-minute settings. In *Ice Station Zebra* (1963), a homage to Natopolis, a British scientist is posted to an American nuclear submarine embarked on a dangerous, probably impossible mission to the north polar ice-cap. For all his civilian status and their military super-power, Dr Carpenter shows the Yanks a thing or two; after listening to a particularly insightful analysis of his men's behaviour under stress the American skipper grudgingly observes, 'I think . . . that I'd sooner have you — what do the English say, batting on a sticky wicket — than almost any man I know' (*Ice Station Zebra*, 1969, p. 131). He's quite right to think so, since it is the sharp-witted Carpenter who finally unmasks the saboteur responsible for the destruction of the vital weather station.

There is a certain geopolitical realism in *Ice Station Zebra*'s tacit acknowledgment that it is the superpower America which now has the ships that matter. But there is also a nostalgia for past power in the evident intellectual superiority of the sophisticated Briton over this technologically advanced, well-meaning but essentially naive ally. (The British hero's OSS buddy in *Where Eagles Dare* is similarly slow off the mark.) One suspects the decline of British power may have been painful to MacLean in this period. In *The Satan Bug* (1962) he resorts to that favourite compensatory fantasy of chauvinist thriller writers — the British secret weapon. The scientists of the world are represented as racing to produce 'a new toxin of frightening virulence' and 'Britain has succeeded — which is why the eyes of the world are on Mordon [i.e. Porton Down].' This bacteriological 'ultimate weapon' is 'our [the free world's] last but most powerful line of defence' (*The Satan Bug*, 1968, p. 211). Britain, modestly and clandestinely, guards the west. It is the kind of nostalgic dream of potency which one associates less with adult fiction than the *Boy's Own Paper* romance. By the mid-1960s the juvenile little Great Britain note has died out of MacLean's fiction. A last nationalist cheep is heard in *Sea Witch* (1977) where the Scottish tycoon Lord Worth controls the oil supply essential to the economic well-being of the US. But in many of Mac-Lean's 1970s novels there is not so much as a British character in the dramatis personae, let alone any hurrahs for empire.

Although he has recently tended to depreciate them, it seems to me that MacLean's best work remains the five Second World War stories, together with *Ice Station Zebra* which is set on a warship. War 'naturally' sets up the highly artificial and stringent conditions of the classic MacLean adventure. Women are conveniently excluded by the rules of the game. And combatant men are routinely thrown together in tightly knit and often uncomfortably isolated groups. They can plausibly be shown voluntarily enduring the kind of elemental inclemency (storm, sheer cliff face, ice cap blizzard etc.) that only lunatics would submit themselves to in peacetime. Under such pressure the MacLean military/naval hero, who is also typically a leader of men, displays not so much Hemingway's grace as what the author, in his arch way, calls 'intestinal fortitude'. The following scene from *Ice Station Zebra*, in which the *Dolphin* submerges to suicidal depths, indicates the 'guts' and the sang-froid which are the badge of MacLeanian manhood:

Seven hundred feet. Seven hundred and fifty. Eight hundred. I'd never heard of a submarine that had reached that depth and lived. Neither, apparently, had Commander Swanson.

'We have just set up a new mark, men,' he said. His voice was calm and relaxed. . . . The pressure gauge fell farther and still farther. I knew now that nothing could save the *Dolphin.* . . .'I'm afraid we're moving into the realms of the unknown,' Swanson admitted calmly. 'One thousand feet plus. If that dial is right, we passed the theoretical implosion point — where the hull should have collapsed — fifty feet ago. At the present moment she's being subjected to well over a million tons of pressure.' Swanson's repose, his glacial calm, was staggering. They must have scoured the whole of America to find a man like that (*Ice Station Zebra*, 1969, pp. 120-2).

For the MacLean man, war itself is often a perfunctory matter. Mere hostility pales beside the task of scaling Navarone's 'vast, impossible precipice', for example. Thus the mountaineers Captain Mallory and Oberleutnant Turzig forge an instant manly bond in *Navarone*: 'How easily one could respect, form a friendship with a man like Turzig if it weren't for this damned, crazy war' (*The Guns of Navarone*, 1976, p. 166) thinks Mallory. As they part (Mallory has meanwhile killed Turzig's superior officer and overpowered the German guards holding him) he chivalrously invites his disarmed opponent to come climbing with him when the damned, crazy war is over. At another moment Mallory muses on the slaughterous exploits of his comrade-in-arms Andrea, and bluffly cuts short any unhealthy speculation:

Andrea killed neither for revenge [his family was massacred by the pro-Nazi Bulgarians] nor from hate, nor nationalism, nor for the sake of any of the other 'isms' which self-seekers and fools and knaves employ as beguilement to the battlefield and justification for the slaughter of millions too young and too unknowing to comprehend the dreadful futility of it all. Andrea simply killed that better men might live (*ibid.*, p. 52).

MacLean often throws in phrases like 'the damned war' or 'the dreadful futility of it all'. In fact war is a supremely ennobling experience in his early realistic works (notably *HMS Ulysses*) and a downright romp in his later and best-known novel/film, *Where Eagles Dare*. This tale starts with the standard scene of a group of commandos ('all volunteers of course') having a mission born of the sheerest desperation outlined to them. They are to parachute in and rescue an American general, who knows about Overlord, from the German stronghold in the Bavarian Alps where he is being interrogated. If they fail, the invasion of Europe cannot go ahead, millions more will die etc. etc. (Later, in one of the many plot reverses the novel contains, we learn that the General is a plant — and that the whole elaborate exercise has been set up to root out double agents in the allied HQ.) As the raiders approach their objective, two are murdered and three are captured, leaving only the leader Smith and his OSS sidekick Schaffer. This pair perambulate the Bavarian village in Savile Row-made German uniforms; naturally they speak 'flawless' German. Equally polyglot is Birmingham-born 'Heidi', the 'top British agent' who displays her 'voluptuous charms' as a barmaid at the local Wein Stube. The means by which Smith and Schaffer penetrate Schloss Adel is pure MacLean; they ride the ice-covered roof of a cable car, using a penknife as a piton for both their weights (literal cliff-hanging is common in the novels). Once in the castle, the heroes secrete themselves in a minstrels' gallery, and witness that there were no less than three traitors in their original band (the supposed 'captives'). With a typical *coup de théâtre* Smith now reveals himself to the Germans (and a perplexed Schaffer) as 'Johann Schmidt', their double agent. He denounces the three turncoats as *British* double agents and tricks them into disclosing their espionage contacts (this, of course, is the 'real' purpose of the mission). But in fact, the wily Smith is a *treble* agent. Having secured the necessary information he and Schaffer fight their way out, burn down Schloss Adler, effect a precarious descent down the cable-car wires and make good their escape in a stolen post bus, hotly pursued to their pick-up rendezvous by the enraged Alpen-korps and a Tiger tank lobbing 88mm shells at them. On the plane home Mallory springs his final surprise by denouncing the 'most dangerous spy in Europe, the most successful double agent of all time' — namely the officer in charge of their rescue, Colonel Wyatt-Turner. (MacLean, incidentally, has a marked dislike of the English aristocracy.) This confounded villain throws himself out of the plane in pure frustration at being found out.

MacLean excels in this kind of escapade fiction, with its theatrical heroics and its thrill a page. But the basic recipe lacked certain ingredients for the mass, Anglo-American market of the late 1960s and 70s. Sex, notably, is lacking. Particularly for film adaptation, the ward-room, men-only aspect of MacLean's 'classic' fiction is bad box office. Hence in the film of *The Guns of Navarone* the Greek partisans who help the commando squad are transformed by Carl Foreman from gnarled, male peasants to beautiful sloe-eyed women. As preposterously, MacLean himself supplies the sexual omission by introducing a girl stowaway and the buxom barmaid into the raid on Schloss Adler. 'Sex', as MacLean's great rival Desmond Bagley puts it, 'gets in the way of the plot.' MacLean himself observed, to *The Book Programme*'s Robert Robinson, in one of his rare interviews, 'Sex? No time for it. Gets in the way of the action.' MacLean has made concessions on this matter, but not so many as ever to obstruct his action. Celibacy remains one of the cardinal MacLean virtues and while his recent heroes may have passing amours, they are very seldom married. In *Force 10 From Navarone* Andrea actually leaves his bride at the altar when the call to action comes from Mallory. This is a fair measure of the domestic imperative in MacLean's fiction.

A more intractable problem arises with the rather stuffy virtues of the quintessential MacLean hero. He singularly lacks the freebooting amorality of the late 1960s ideal — embodied famously in Bond's sex, sadism and snobbery. The MacLean hero-cum-leader typically understates, endures impassively, is moderate in his appetites (especially his sexual appetites, which are apparently entirely sublimated) and prefers the hard life to the good life.

Disastrously, it seems to me, MacLean was induced to modify his instinctive manner and imitate the fashionable Bond stories in the early- and mid-1960s. The secret agent narratives of this period are among his very weakest offerings. In *When Eight Bells Toll* (1966) a band of international thieves hijack £8 m. worth of bullion at sea (echoes of *Goldfinger*); in *The Satan Bug* (1962) an ex-mafioso steals the super-toxin in order to evacuate London and rob all the banks (Goldfinger again); in *Puppet on a Chain* (1969) another ex-mafioso is a 'narcotics king' in Amsterdam. Foiling these arch-villains and busting their crime rings sets up something like the 'impossible mission' of the war stories.

But MacLean's attempt to graft his para-naval code, and its ultimately patriotic values, on to a laconic secret agent fails comically. As Jacques Barzun has pointed out, the spy or secret agent is (unlike the detective) obliged by the terms of his dirty trade to be a sneak and criminal. He has, as Hamlet says of Elsinore's double agents, 'to make love to his profession', and thus forfeits any claim to unqualified approval. MacLean apparently has difficulty in accepting that a 'hero' of his can be motivated by anything other than the highest, most selfless motives. Thus in *When Eight Bells Toll* Philip Calvert, after killing three crooks, overhears his control, 'Uncle Arthur', singing his praises:

Philip Calvert is not what any reasonable man would call a killer. . . . He doesn't do this job for money. He's miserably paid for a man of his unique talents. . . . He doesn't do it for excitement, for — what is the modern expression? — kicks: a man who devotes his spare time to music, astronomy and philosophy [we never see this cultured side of Calvert in the novel, by the way] does not live for kicks. But he cares. He cares for the difference between right and wrong, between good and evil, and when that difference is great enough and the evil threatens to destroy the good then he does not hesitate to take steps to redress the balance (*When Eight Bells Toll*, 1970, pp. 141-2).

At moments like this MacLean flounders horribly, unable as he is to reconcile the simple affirmative codes of his wartime fiction with the perplexities of le Carré's 'looking-glass war' where values are reversed and substanceless. Nor can MacLean whip up the paranoia necessary to create an overpowering villain. The 'big time czars of American crime' who mastermind his international coups, like the Gestapo officers with their 'cold, dark, empty eyes' or the psychopath thugs who 'take an unholy joy in sadism' are hand-me-downs from B-movies. MacLean seems incapable of the fascinated attention which Fleming brings to his majestically depraved Auric Goldfinger, Dr No or Ernst Stavro Blofeld.

MacLean's career in the 1970s reflects his present international superseller status, and the fact that he now lives in, draws inspiration from and largely writes for America and its film industry. (MacLean made the really big time in films with the $12 m. budget 1979 production of *Bear Island*, starring Vanessa Redgrave and Donald Sutherland.) He increasingly relies on gimmicky plots and indulges his penchant for sudden surprises and ingeniously worked-up suspense to the full. In this last phase he has gone from bestselling strength to bestselling strength. But, at the same time, the ideas and settings for his recent novels have become increasingly and at times absurdly exotic. Novelty is something which he clearly regards as a prime selling point. In *The Golden Gate* (1976) a presidential motorcade is hijacked on the Golden Gate Bridge. *Breakheart Pass* (1974) is set in America of the frontier period and involves gunrunning and Indian fighting. In *Circus* (1975) a trapeze artist with 'near supernatural powers' is charged by the CIA to attempt the usual 'impossible' break-in on the 'impregnable' Lubylan Fortress (his task is made harder by there being an unknown Communist agent in the troupe — MacLean still makes regular use of the Judas figure). In *Caravan to Vaccarès* (1970) it is the annual gathering of European gypsies in Provence which provides the setting for secret service capers. In *Bear Island* (1971) a film crew are marooned in the Arctic — one of their number is a killer (echoes here of *Ten Little Niggers* — MacLean, oddly, has never tried his hand at a straight detective story; though he borrows many of its devices). In *Sea Witch* (1977) a cartel sets up a raid to sabotage the $100 m. oil rig of a rival 'wildcat' oil baron (the assault involves tactical nuclear weapons, the possibility of sparking off the Third World War and at the very least the 'largest oil slick in history'). In *Goodbye California* (1977) an earthquake threatens to slice off a section of the western state (where, incidentally, MacLean now lives and which, via Hollywood, provides him with the bulk of his income). One feels if Britain sank into the North Sea it would no longer qualify with him as a disaster, such is his current international perspective.

MacLean is that publisher's prize — the bestselling novelist who pulls it off, without fail, once a year. He is not, even by the relatively dim lights of the adventure story, a *good* writer nor even, at times, a very competent one. One explanation for his pre-eminent sales success is his canny eclecticism. He judges which are the fashionable coat-tails to catch hold of and skilfully traffics in 'nearly-new' fictional styles (thus his first novel tags along behind *The Cruel Sea*; his last, *Goodbye California* jumps on the disaster bandwagon).

Many mediocre novelists are derivative, however, and the vast majority are unrewarded for it. MacLean's talent is not that he imitates but that he knows which imitations his readers will go for. 'I write for my public,' declares MacLean. He appreciates that 'his' public do not want genuine shock or disturbance but 'thrills'. They do not want literary skill or innovation. 'His' public do not even want the 'research' which Hailey offers (MacLean makes a show at technical informativeness — as in the technical prologue to *Sea Witch* which explains the distinctions between the three main kinds of oil rig; but since Hailey may spend as long researching one novel as MacLean does in writing three, there is a necessary flimsiness in the facts department). What the brand-loyal MacLean customer wants is the untaxing excitements of a 'good read'. MacLean supplies it annually, and sometimes even twice a year.

MacLean and James Clavell

A survey of MacLean's soggy achievement is a depressing business. But that the adventure genre has literary life in it is witnessed by the work of a writer whose career runs parallel to MacLean's on a higher plane. James Clavell has three novels to his credit, two of them vast (they would, apparently, have been still vaster but for the economizing influence of Clavell's American editors). *King Rat* (1962) is a prisoner-of-war story set in Changi, where the very young Clavell was himself for three years a prisoner of the Japanese. *Tai-pan* (1966) is an historical epic set in Hong Kong; and *Shōgun* (1975) another set in sixteenth-century Japan.

Clavell's fiction and the films with which he is creatively concerned revolve around certain obsessive themes — notably the pressures of wartime defeat and a connected obsession with the victor's chivalrous yet brutal martial codes. *King Rat* chronicles an unlikely friendship between an eccentric young RAF officer and an opportunist American enlisted man, who not only survives in the death camp but actually prospers and grows fat by ruthless capitalist exploitation of the prison black market. (The title comes from his enterprisingly marketing battery-raised rats as 'small deer'. The 'king rat' is the stud beast who survives, finally by cannibalistically eating his weaker fellows when the camp is evacuated.) Clavell does not simplify matters. The Japanese are beastly to prisoners because they are a worthier military caste. The equivalent caste of British officers are wholly unworthy (it is only the unwitting officers, incidentally, who buy and eat the rat meat). In *King Rat* British and American officers steal their men's rations and unfairly assume privileged work roles. They survive by contemptible parasitism. The 'King' survives by virtue of his capitalist cunning, as extreme in its way as the code of the Japanese samurai. *King Rat* ends with the 'tormented' question in the hero's mind — is it right to adapt, to submit absolutely, without compromise, to the arbitrary conditions of war?

Shōgun transposes and develops the *King Rat* situation. An Elizabethan English buccaneer, Captain James Blackburn, is marooned on mainland Japan. At first he is merely a captive, in which condition he and his crew are subjected to the vilest abuse. (One, for example, is slowly boiled alive to provide a 'poetic' poignancy to the evening musings of the warlord who has taken him.) Blackburn does not merely survive. He becomes himself a Japanese samurai warrior, giving himself entirely to the society which took him prisoner. A barbarian, Blackburn comes to understand and accept the highly stylized brutalities of the Japanese military caste. He embraces a militarism which exists without ideology, theology or material interest, and which justifies itself purely in terms of personal honour. He never returns, or wants to return, to England. (Clavell, incidentally, though born British is now listed in writers' directories as American.) The progression from fierce resentment (the Japanese are animals) to admiration (the Japanese are civilized) is a crucial one in the novel, and, one suspects, crucial as well for Clavell, the ex-prisoner of war. It is interesting that in *Publishers Weekly*, 5 May 1975, it was reported that a film of *Shōgun* was to be made with Japanese finance. Few survivors of Changi can have devised fictions suitable for the Japanese mass market.

Clavell is what his publishers term 'a bestselling author' and a 'master storyteller'. In terms of category he belongs centrally in that adventure, male-action area which MacLean dominates. Yet his work has a dimension lacking in MacLean or — say — Wilbur Smith. Its probings of the complex nature of what can be achieved in defeat (personal survival) and what in victory (personal grace) are subtle, provocative and inconclusive.

Yet Clavell is only a part-time novelist. More profitably he is a successful writer, director and producer of films. *The Great Escape* (1963) which he scripted (and won a prize for) is a pallid, toned-down version of *King Rat*, which was itself made into a poor film in 1965, though Clavell had no part in it. *633 Squadron* (1964), *Where's Jack* (1968) and *To Sir With Love* (1969) are best not mentioned. *The Last Valley* (1969), which Clavell wrote and directed, is set during the Thirty Years War and deals with an as-yet unravaged village, taken prisoner by a troop of mercenaries. The film's situation and its central characters 'the Captain' and 'the Scholar' carry on Clavell's personal debate as to whether military honour can coexist with liberal, civilized values. As always, those who merely choose to 'survive' at the lowest level are contemptible. This is the only film which Clavell has been solely responsible for, and it can stand with the best of his fiction.

Chapter Ten

Jaws

I

The term is often used loosely, but *Jaws* is a true superseller of the 1970s. In just six months as a Bantam paperback it sold over 6 m. copies, and within a couple of years had come up to the maximal 10 m. mark. In Britain, Pan's paperback sold a million in its first year and almost twice as many in its second, boosted by the film. The film itself, whose costs reportedly escalated during production from $4 m. to $8½ m. (largely due to shooting problems at sea) eventually rewarded the budget overrun with gross returns of $400 m. in box-office and $200 m. in film rental receipts by mid 1978 (Loynd, 1978, p. 16). '*Jaws* mania' received America's highest popular acknowledgment: front cover commemoration on the *Time*-style magazines. For one week (and this during the Vietnam war's critical aftermath) a film centred on 'Bruce', the plastic shark, was certified as the single most important news-story in the world.

Corresponding as its paperback publication did with the beach season in the US (when most cheap-format bestsellers are consumed) and the press silly season, reports of shark attacks appeared in the newspapers every few days, often competing for space with interviews with oceanographers, most of whom asserted that sharks weren't so bad, 'that they really didn't bite people much' (true enough, it seems). When the film was launched in Britain, the BBC was sufficiently carried away on the *PM* magazine programme to broadcast an item from some crackpot arguing that the Loch Ness monster was, in fact, a giant white shark. There's money in mania, however, and the usual spin-off industry sprang up, extending from the chic (and franchised) use of the *Jaws* motif and logo on pricey Magnin swimwear, through T-shirt transfers down to such 'novelties' as strap-on shark fins. Shark's-tooth necklaces and pendants became *de rigueur* decoration at European and American resorts — though at $400 a fang few were genuine.

As with *The Godfather* and *The Exorcist*, the film *Jaws*, directed by Steven Spielberg, was felt by most critics to have surpassed the original novel by Peter Benchley. Although they shared the same general narrative and employed the same, highly effective sales symbolism (naked swimmer, threatening 'penis with teeth' rising through the depth towards her) *Jaws* film and *Jaws* novel are significantly different. Thinking cinematically, Spielberg stripped away layers of redundant Benchley subplot; notably the motel adulteries of Hooper and Ellen Brody. (Spielberg had his artistic motives; but partly the removal of this 'adult' material was designed to get the valued 'PG' rating which would admit children into the cinema. This aim was cruder in *Jaws 2*, which made its appeal principally to the youth market and removed not only sex but the bloodiness of *Jaws 1*). Spielberg also achieved 'filmic thrust' by excising the parallel plot of the Mafia's secretly buying up Amity — the small New England town which is at risk from two kinds of shark in the novel. The film *Jaws* concentrates on the reciprocal victim-victimizer relationship: the shark hunting humans and humans hunting the shark.

When he took on *Jaws*, the 26-year-old Spielberg, like Coppola and Friedkin before him, was the *Wunderkind* of the film industry. He had just finished a successful 'chase' movie, *Sugarland Express*, and a similarly dominant pursuit structure was imposed on the *Jaws* screenplay. Spielberg also built into the film one of his favourite dramatic devices, that of the glimpsed but not clearly seen attacker. In *Duel*, the director's first and best feature work, an innocent car driver is terrorized by a predatory trucker whose face is never seen, nor his homicidal motives understood. In *Jaws*'s successor, *Close Encounters of the Third Kind*, the aliens' invading presence is sensed only; their actual irruption as something seen is delayed until the final scene. In the film *Jaws* the shark is not clearly seen until the last moment, two-thirds through the film, when he pops up beside an electrified Chief Brody. The novel, by contrast, began with a thorough anatomy of the White Shark in Haileyesque pedagogic manner: '. . . lacking the flotation bladder common to other fish, and the fluttering flaps to push oxygen-bearing water through its gills, it survived only by moving. Once stopped, it would sink to the bottom and die' (*Jaws*, 1975, p. 3). The film *Jaws* gives no lessons in zoology. Nor does it present the shark *qua* shark until the tactically effective moment, late in the action.

II

The 1970s have been notable for a number of bestselling animal narratives directed at an adult rather than the traditional young persons' market. Three of them have been supersellers: *Jonathan Livingston Seagull*, *Jaws* and *Watership Down*. Oddly enough, all three have been by authors previously unknown to the mass reading public.

Jonathan Livingston Seagull, *Jaws* and *Watership Down* share a stress or 'gravity' which can be clearly related to one of the great causes of the age, ecology. They draw their 'relevance' from a cluster of negative and positive emotions provoked by concern for vanishing or endangered wildlife and wilderness. At one pole is guilt about man's depredation of his and other species' environment, at the 'silent spring' which he has brought. Over the last twenty years this environmental guilt has discharged on such issues as the extinction of whales, myxomatosis, pollution, nuclear power generation, urban decay, indiscriminate use of pesticides and consequent disruption of food chains, overpopulation, defoliation programmes in Vietnam, deforestation in the Amazon basin, the clubbing of baby seals. In fact, given the myriad interrelationships which the pseudo-science of ecology proposes, anxiety diffuses to the point where it takes in everything and anything that has gone wrong in the natural world. A typically random formulation of eco-issues is offered by Benchley in one of his many ecologically concerned asides:

Nothing touched them [i.e. the Long Island beach crowds]
— not race riots in places like Trenton, New Jersey, or
Gary, Indiana; not the fact that parts of the Missouri River
were so foul that the water sometimes caught fire
spontaneously; not police corruption in New York or the
rising number of murders in San Francisco or revelations
that hot dogs contained insect filth and hexachlorophine
caused brain damage. They were inured even to the
economic spasms that wracked the rest of America.
Undulations in the stock markets were nuisances noticed,
if at all, as occasions for fathers to bemoan real or fancied
extravagances (*ibid.*, pp. 49-50).

The over-all effect of such ecological concern is to create a
vague but infinitely far-reaching sense of wrong-doing and
apprehension of nemesis — the so called 'doomwatching
syndrome'.

At the other, positive, pole is a churchy 'reverence' or
'wonder' at the achieved perfection of natural creation and at
the fullness of animal relationship with the universe — a
fullness which, by implication, man has lost in his search for
political utopia. As the icthyologist Hooper puts it, on first
seeing the shark which is eventually to kill him: 'that fish
is a beauty. It's a kind of thing that makes you believe in a
god' (*ibid.*, p. 253). Such transcendent or 'Aquarian' response
is authoritatively evoked in the ecological bestseller. *Jonathan
Livingston Seagull*, for example, is dedicated coyly to 'the
real seagull in all of us' — our soul. *Watership Down* ends
with the assumption of Hazel, conducted to a higher plane of
existence by the race father.

Of the three works Bach's is the simplest. Its narrative is
composed of a fictional reconstruction of a seagull's flight
from A to B. In prose-poetic fashion it celebrates airy free-
doms and adds faint chauvinistic and humanistic overtones.
Jonathan — archetypal American forename — reminds us that
America pioneered human flight. Livingston evokes man's
questing, exploring spirit. Such connections are hard to
validate, but it is likely the phenomenal appeal of this abysmal
'novel' (it sold 2 m. copies in hardback in 1972) has to do
with the late-1960s/early 1970s resurgence of *Wandervogel*
idealism, more realistically depicted in that other tract for

the times, *Easy Rider* (1969).

Watership Down is a more subtle and intricate re-creation of the fullness of animal experience. Like *Jaws*, it is unsentimental about the conflicts between species and the historical inevitability of the eco-crisis. Adams's novel begins with a rabbit cosmogony which establishes the rabbit as central to the universe. In this creation myth, Frith, maker of the world, punishes the Adamic rabbit, El-ahrairah, for his insolent progenitiveness, by making all other animals his enemy, and he their prey. In compensation Frith bestows on the chastened El-ahrairah speed and cunning wherewith to survive:

All the world will be your enemy, Prince with a Thousand Enemies, and whenever they catch you they will kill you. But first they must catch you, digger, listener, runner, prince with the swift warning. Be cunning and full of tricks and your people shall never be destroyed.

This mixed curse and blessing creates the terms of the 'natural' environment where the rabbits are discovered living in their first warren at Sandleford. But the environmental contract, drawn up by Frith, is breached by man. A new threat emerges from whom the rabbits cannot run or dig, and against whom their cunning is futile. The inexplicable notice-board is sensed by the precognitive Fiver as betokening blood: the developers with their poison gas and bulldozers are imminent. Migration, the all-or-nothing animal gamble for survival, is counselled. In the course of their migratory adventure the rabbits discover and escape new animal and human aggressors. More significantly, they discover 'political' opposition in the totalitarian regime of the Efrafan warren. The Efrafan system has replaced the benign tribal hierarchies of Sandleford and its wise 'chief rabbit' with a military apparatus under the fearsome General Woundwort. Woundwort substitutes for the traditional survival strategies of speed and cunning a 'revolutionary' reliance on ferocity and the rule of tooth and claw. He and his order are destroyed by the farm dog whom Frith, presumably, has more liberally endowed with teeth and claws. At the end of the narrative, with Woundwort dead and the resettlement achieved, the natural, Frith-decreed life of the rabbits is re-established in Watership Down. The eco-system is restored, old ways rule again and the narrative subsides into the timeless legend with which it began.

The main trick of *Watership Down*, like *Jonathan Livingston Seagull*, is to frame the narrative within the imagined limitations of animal consciousness. *Jaws* does this only intermittently and briefly, locating the main action in human responses to the mysterious shark menace. This witnesses to the source of the novel in Benchley's apparently life-long study of marine life and his enthusiastic horror for sharks. From childhood he claims to have been fascinated by their 'inherent menace' and their primitive, violent perfection: 'they are prehistoric eating machines', he notes, 'that have not evolved in thirty million years' (Morgan, 1978, p. 142). The author's fascination, his mingled wonder, contempt and fear, are elaborated in the opposition of *Jaws*'s two principal shark experts. For Hooper, the icthyologist, the giant white is 'perfect':

Sharks have everything a scientist dreams of. They're beautiful — God, how beautiful they are! They're like an impossibly perfect piece of machinery. They're as graceful as any bird. They're as mysterious as any animal on earth (*Jaws*, 1975, p. 117).

'Horseshit' responds Quint, the Hemingwayesque old fisherman. In his unlyrical view sharks are neither mysterious nor wonderful. They are 'dumb garbage buckets' and 'cock suckers'. The dualism is sustained up to the crisis of the novel in which both men die killing the shark. By this point Hooper has gained something of Quint's detestation of sharks, just before his horrific death in the underwater cage; Quint, on his part, learns something of Hooper's respect for the 'dumb' shark which finally outwits him. Benchley creates a further baffling ambiguity by associating the shark's atavistic lunge at its prey with Hooper's sexual aggressiveness towards Ellen Brody whose cuckolded husband, of course, is the third man on board the *Orca*. Ellen is haunted by a 'vision of Hooper, eyes wide and staring — but unseeing — at the wall as he approached climax. . . . Hooper's teeth were clenched, and he ground them' (*ibid.*, p. 172). The last thing that Hooper sees, before the shark's teeth crunch down on him, 'was the eye gazing at him through a cloud of his own blood' (*ibid.*, p. 288).

Benchley is astute enough to confect a crust of literariness
which the critic detects to be as thin as Jacques Cousteau did
Jaws's shark-lore. Cousteau's scorn, incidentally, wounded
Benchley more than all the unkind reviews by clever literary
people. Thus in the death of Quint, tied by a snarled line to
the dead shark, Benchley knowingly evokes Ahab's 'quenchless
feud' with Moby Dick and their final submersion together.
Quint is also made to recall Hemingway's Old Man. The plot —
in which mayor and aldermen hush up the disaster — is lifted,
apparently, from Ibsen's *Enemy of the People*. But such
allusive claims on seriousness are not creditworthy. Essentially
Jaws belongs not to the 'literary' tradition but to a bestselling
entertainment fashion, or gimmick, of the early 1970s — the
disaster story.

The inspiring 'disaster' idea and its primacy in Benchley's
mind is evident enough in the short synopsis the novelist first
delivered to his publisher:

> The purpose of the novel would be to explore the
> reactions of a community that is suddenly struck by a
> peculiar natural disaster — not an earthquake or a flood . . .
> but a continuing, mysterious devastation that, as time goes
> on, loses its natural neutrality and begins to smack of
> evil. . . . Suppose a Long Island resort community was
> suddenly visited by a great white shark? A young woman is
> killed. . . . How does the community cope with this
> inexplicable menace? (Morgan, 1978, p. 142).

Benchley's question points to the main emotional gratification
of the disaster genre, whose appeal he clearly understood.
The community 'copes' by the political equivalent of religious
revivalism. In disasters new faith is evoked in the 'old ways'
and more particularly in the governors of society. It is, for
example, the benign federal government which declares a
region to be a 'disaster area' and thus eligible for 'aid'. *Jaws*
has as its hero a small-town police-chief, a figure whose social
role in other than disaster fiction would automatically render
him villainous or at least demoralized and at odds with his
job. In fact, it *is* as a weak and self-doubting figure that we
encounter Brody in the early chapters of *Jaws*. But in the
mounting emergency created by the shark's invasion, Brody
achieves his proper authority and power as the guardian of

his small town. This regeneration is typical of the disaster genre, where pilots of planes, captains of ships, fire chiefs, city managers, all recover an unambiguous social dignity. Scientists, elsewhere sinister and politically untrustworthy, also do well in disaster fiction. In Herzog's execrable *The Swarm*, for example, killer bees sweep up from Brazil to devastate the US. The government mobilizes a team of top scientists to combat the menace: they are given the resources of Fort Detrick in Maryland which is, outside fiction, America's main research centre for chemical and bacteriological warfare. The novel thus converts leaders, their scientific servants and their factory of hideous mass destruction into imaginary saviours. Another example, even more transparent, is found in the 1980 disaster film (and novelization), *Meteor*. A meteor is heading towards earth, and will probably destroy it:

> NASA immediately calls upon the services of America's leading astrophysicist, Dr Paul Bradley (Sean Connery) and asks him if he can develop a plan to change the meteor's course and save the world from destruction. . . . When Bradley gets down to business he decides that the only chance he has — and it's a slim one at that — is to use intercontinental missiles to divert the meteor from its course. When Bradley has finished doing his sums, however, he realises that America's stockpile of missiles will be insufficient for the plan he has in mind. He therefore approaches the President of the US (Henry Fonda) with the revolutionary proposal that Russia be invited to join the enterprise. The combined missile power of the two super-powers might then be enough (*Film Review*, January, 1980).

A similar eventuality is conceived in *The Hab Theory*, where a capsize of the earth, due to the excessive weight of the ice-caps, is proposed to be averted by the detonation of the US's supply of thermonuclear devices. What these preposterous 'disaster scenarios' intimate to us is that America's 10,000 warheads are stockpiled for some unforeseen planetary emergency; that only scientists can save the world; and that we need *more* missiles (to save the world) and must trust the President to look after things.

Actual disasters cohere society and restore faith in government and military in proportion to their physical disruption. In fiction, the disaster scenario throws a heroic halo over figures the relaxed citizen usually suspects as likely tyrants or abusers of power. Apprehension of elemental disasters (flood, earthquake, meteor, fire, shark) which cannot be attributed to an enemy, criminal malice or maladministration thus serve to syphon off rebellious or cynical sentiments and render society docile to its masters and managers. Beneath its mantling of progressive ecological concern, *Jaws* is a profoundly conservative novel. Like other works in the disaster genre it asserts the need for constant vigilance in a society forever on guard against mysterious, unpredictable visitations ('sharks do so many uncharacteristic things that the erratic becomes the normal . . . we'll never understand'; *ibid.*, p. 92).

III

Following *Jaws*'s triumph there was the predictable goldrush by lesser writers. Fictional America, and its minor colony Britain, were ravaged by plagues and pests: dogs, rats, bats, crocs, worms, alligators, spiders, piranha, crabs, rattlers, frogs. One of the most successful tricks of *Jaws* had been to invest the cosy summer holiday on Long Island with hideous menace. Other writers' attempts to combine holiday and horror resulted in plots of such desperate ingenuity as to be almost worth reading for their unintended comedy — Berton Roueché's *The Cats*, for example:

> Too many city folk have been turning their cuddly kittens loose when they leave their holiday homes on Long Island. Out in the woods, the cat colony has been growing and changing. . . . They used to prey on rats and birds.
> Suddenly packs of blood-crazed mutant wildcats, with razor-claws and inch-long teeth are attacking homes and humans.

There was also a cheapie *The Cats* for the British market by Nick Sharman. The leader in British *Jaws* me-tooism was James Herbert, author of *The Rats* etc. For all his derivativeness Herbert had a nice line in East End settings.

Authors realized that *Jaws* was not just a novel but a film
scenario, and thought ahead in choosing their toothsome
predators. *Jaws* the film had been enormously difficult and
expensive to make. Roger Corman circumvented the huge
expense of Bruce the robot shark by using goldfish-sized
attackers in *Piranha* (the cover of the novelization and film
advertising made great play with them, but somehow the
little 'jaws' didn't seem as frightening). Benchley's most
successful imitator in commercial terms was Arthur Herzog,
whose novels about killer bees and killer whales were made
into big budget movies. *The Swarm* is warmed-over sf but
Orca (the name, incidentally, of Quint's boat) capitalizes
directly if perversely on trendy ecological concern about the
commercial exploitation and possible extinction of the
whale. Orca belongs to a species of whale which, untypically,
turns on man. A clear-cut if understated implication of
Herzog's unpleasant novel is that if whales choose to behave
like this, they deserve all they get. One of the odd features of
Jaws and sub-*Jaws* fiction is the way in which it often moves
from an initial eco-OK position to frank, Darwinian delight in
struggle to the death. In the film performance of *Jaws* which
I saw, the audience was moved to cheer when Brody shoots
the gas cylinder which detonates in the shark's jaws, blowing
it to fishpaste. Yet few, I imagine, would consciously applaud
the Japanese use of the explosive harpoon. This eco-sadism –
the justified slaughter of wild things – is clearly one of the
disguised gratifications of the genre. A 'straight' ecological
adventure, *Leviathan*, by John Gordon Davis, though it was
handled by the same editor as *Jaws* and given major publicity,
seems for this reason not to have caught the imagination of
the public. *Leviathan*'s plot, which involves the vengeful
hunting of factory ships to save the whale, is somehow too
'tame' and pious.

Following bestsellerism's familiar line of 'the same but
better', *Orca* takes as its premise that there are larger jaws
than the white shark's around. The poverty of imagination
in this novel/film is well indicated by the breathless synopsis:

Massive jaws and savage teeth combined with a powerful
intelligence make Orca, the killer whale, the most feared
monster in the deep. He is the only creature – apart from

man — who kills for vengeance. If his mate is harmed by a man, Orca will surely take his revenge in terror, mutilation and death.

Orca is just as dire a performance as the above summary suggests, and the film (starring Richard Harris) was a resounding, and absolutely deserved, flop with the critics (though it seems to have done good business). Little good fiction or film has, in fact, followed *Jaws*. One work which does, perhaps, deserve some attention is John Godey's *The Snake*. In this novel the *Jaws*-like plot device (an eleven-foot Mamba loose and killing in Central Park) is made secondary to grisly comedy about New York's free-floating, always-on-the-boil hysteria. In consequence, *The Snake* seems to be as much a satire on *Jaws* mania as an imitation of the other novel:

The snake in the park became a jewel in the crown of the city's obsession with its own eccentricity. The public reasserted its prideful conviction that it inhabited the most put-upon city in the whole world. When bigger and better and more unendurable disasters were contrived, they were visited justly upon the city that matched them in stature; which was to say, the city that was superlatively dirty, declining, expensive, crime-ridden, unmanageable, and glamorously unlivable beyond any other city in the world. By lunchtime, gallows humor jokes were already epidemic. And never mind that most of them were retreads of stale ethnic jokes; they worked surprisingly well with the mere substitution of the word 'snake' for 'Italian' or 'Polish'.

Manufacturers of novelties, famous for their opportunism and dazzling speed of production, succeeded by late afternoon in flooding the city with snake buttons, snake decals for auto bumpers, stuffed snakes of many lengths, designs, and colors. Not long afterward, strikingly realistic, battery-powered snakes of great technical sophistication were to appear. There was a run on canned rattlesnake fillets in gourmet specialty stores, and the brave people who ate them inevitably compared their taste to that of chicken, only better.

Four Hollywood film companies filed notice of intent to make a movie about a snake in Central Park; by nightfall, one of them had brought a lawsuit against another, charging infringement of its title, 'Black Mamba'. The news division of all three television networks patched together half-hour films about snakes for presentation following the eleven o'clock news, with full commercial sponsorship. A porno film, in which a young woman performed the sex act with a squirming and unhappy snake, was revived and did turn-away business at the box office. A nightclub introduced a snake-charming act: a man in a turban playing a flute for a cobra so lethargic from being refrigerated that it could barely spread its hood. Educational paperback books dealing with reptiles flooded the newsstands and bookstores. Herpetologists and zoo curators were at a premium for guest appearances on television talk shows. Snakeskin shoes, jackets handbags, ties and belts were snapped up in clothing and department stores. Sheets, pillowcases, and window drapes with a serpentine motif appeared almost overnight (*The Snake*, 1979, pp. 177-8).

Godey's narrative focuses on the same trio of hunters as *Jaws*: an eco-OK herpetologist (who wants to save the reptile), a hard-nosed cop with a mid-life crisis and a vicious Jesus-freak sect who want to destroy the snake as the incarnation of evil. (Godey, incidentally, is the author of another effective, off-beat New York-set novel, *The Taking of Pelham 123*).

Chapter Eleven

Harold Robbins: the *roman à clef* I

> Harold Robbins . . . is affecting the emotions of the world.
> That's obscenity.
>
> (Pauline Kael)

The *roman à clef* is a main form of the modern bestseller and a main strand in many bestselling novels. (The Fontane subplot in *The Godfather*, for example, is a *novelette à clef* set in a wider, more hard-boiled, gangster narrative.) Historically we can trace the contemporary *roman à clef* back to those 'silver fork' novels of the 1840s (like Disraeli's or Mrs Gore's) which fed the curiosity of the Victorian middle classes as to the sophisticated delinquencies of the power elite. Such novels would sometimes have unofficial 'keys' attached to them, the better to appreciate their piquancy. Since libel laws are now more rigidly enforced, today's keys are more likely to be found as hints on the cover, or intimated by the novelist's gossip-column aides. Harold Robbins is well served by a whole series of 'insider' articles in the popular press like this from the *Daily Mail* under the headline, 'What Harold Robbins left out':

> Harold Robbins certainly has a rich enough imagination to
> include the world's biggest divorce action in one of his
> bestsellers, but in *The Pirate*, based in part on the world of
> 'Mr Fixit', Adnan Khashoggi, it is the one bit of action he
> left out (*Daily Mail*, 1 September 1979).

The article goes on to 'report' Khashoggi's wife's billion-dollar divorce suit. In this way the worlds of romance and cheap journalism feed each other, mushing fact and fiction into a vicariously thrilling fantasy world for the consumption of the millions (Robbins's *The Pirate* had another lease of bestselling life, for instance, following the British popular press's interest in the 'scandal' of Mrs Khashoggi's affairs with British politicians.)

The aim of the *roman à clef* is to render itself into an open (but not actionably open) secret. Hence such transparent, but still not explicit, cueing as we find in one of the most successful of recent *romans à clef*, Jacqueline Susann's *Dolores*. The British and American cover illustrations display two of Jackie Kennedy's most recognizable features, the mane of downswept, raven-black hair and the dark glasses. (The plot of *Dolores* concerns the widow of an assassinated US president, etc.)

In social terms, the *roman à clef* is the tribute which the fantasizing middle and lower classes pay their aristocracy; or, in modern terms, what the tourist class pays the jet set. The cynosures of *romans à clef* are a homogeneous 'club' whose distinct life style exhibits immense wealth, conspicuous consumption, absolute power and seigneurial sexual potency. Harold Robbins, the bestselling of contemporary writers in the style, picks on appropriate heroes for his fiction with great skill (arguably it is his principal, and, critics might say, his only skill). In *The Pirate* we are made to recall Khashoggi, the arms entrepreneur, flying round the world in his private jet, a paradisal harem in the air. In *The Carpetbaggers* the allusion is to Howard Hughes, the Hollywood tycoon and flier who 'invented' Jane Russell and her special bra, and became one of the richest men in the world. Jackie Susann is the dedicatee, and unmistakably a part of the heroine of *The Lonely Lady*. This is Robbins's only novel with a heroine rather than a hero, and it stands as a queer testimonial to his own branch of the fiction industry. *The Adventurers* has a South American playboy-diplomat hero — evocative of the younger Trujillo and, more strongly, of Porfirio Rubirosa, who married or had an affair with every beautiful woman in Hollywood and every heiress in the continent. *Memories of Another Day* picks on the new class of robber barons in American society, the union leaders; men whose patronage, privilege and power is beyond the law.

Robbins's heroes (and heroines) constantly display their status as life's superstars by repetitious acts of sexual domination, the exertion of insatiable and gigantic libido. The big, powerful and beautiful people in Robbins's novels are marked by one common feature — super-potency. Thus we recognize that the young Daniele Huggins in *Memories of Another Day* has greatness in him, by virtue of his astounding cockmanship:

> . . . a born eroticist, strong, uninhibited once set free, he never seemed to tire. It seemed to take no effort for him to have four or five and sometimes more orgasms in the course of a night's lovemaking. More than once she had been surprised at his readiness. One time she had touched him by accident and found him hard. She laughed. 'My God, Daniel, do you walk around like that all the time?'
> (*Memories of Another Day*, 1979, p. 137).

In later life, 'Big Dan' at the age of fifty-six marries a seventeen-year-old girl, who is amazed, as are all women, by his prowess. This elision of all power with superior sexual potency (superior, that is, to the Kinsey-average potency of the presumed reader), and the wearisome stress on orgiastic satisfaction, is one of the manifestly juvenile satisfactions which the *roman à clef* offers. In Robbins's fiction we have the child's obsessed view of paternal sexual privilege and familial authority. As Orwell observes (in his essay on the trash novel *No Orchids for Miss Blandish*) people worship power in the form in which they understand it. The immature child understands power in terms of the father's monopoly of family wealth and family sexual pleasure. This immaturity pervades the world of Robbins's fantasy. The advertisements for *The Carpetbaggers* announce, aggressively, that 'this is a book for adults' but the preposition is wrong; it is a book *about* adults as the limited child's conception half observes, half distorts them.

Robbins's novels all recount life histories in which will triumphs. His characters make themselves, by a series of conquests. They are themselves alone — the notion of a 'happy marriage' or a life-long relationship is anathema; a potential dropping of the will's guard. Robbins's heroes characteristically have no family. (He himself was apparently an orphan, and there remains a traumatic trace in all his fiction.) In his most violent novel, *The Adventurers*, the hero loses his mother in childhood in circumstances of sickening sadistic brutality. Having witnessed the murder and gang-rape of the female members of his family it is Dax's duty, as a mere *nino*, to machine-gun the captured bandits in the 'cojones'. It is described as a sexual fulfilment:

I walked over to him. He rested the gun across his forearm and guided my hand so that my finger was on the trigger. He held the recoil barrel in the crook of his elbow. 'Now,' he said, 'look down the top of the barrel. When you see it is aimed at their *cojones* pull the trigger. I will do the rest.'

I squinted along the blue metal barrel. I pointed the gun at Garcia. I could see his white legs and hairy belly just below the end of the short metal barrel. I squeezed the trigger.

The noise exploded in my ears and the white body shattered into a thousand tiny bloody fragments. I felt the general sweep the gun down the line. And everywhere it pointed was white flesh dissolving into torn and bleeding flesh. I felt the trigger turn hot under my finger but there was an exultation and excitement in me and I wouldn't have let it go even if it had burned my fingers (*The Adventurers*, 1977, p. 28).

Thus released and initiated into 'manhood', Dax's life adventure can begin.

In *The Carpetbaggers* the young Nevada Smith (né Max Sand) returns to find his parents tortured with branding irons, the mother raped and skinned alive. In later life he discovers one of the torturers still using her tanned breast as a tobacco pouch. Smith's revenges are typically violent and genital. The first of the murderers he catches up with he leaves to have his 'pubis' (an oddly favourite Robbins term) eaten by ants, after slitting his eyelids and staking him in the sun. The second he judicially shoots twice 'in the belly' and once 'in the balls' — so he can watch him die at the proper leisurely rate. The other, Hughes-inspired, hero — Jonas — starts his adult life with the motto 'mi padre ha muerto' — my father is dead. In the most extravagant of Robbins's fantasies, *The Pirate*, the hero is ripped from the belly of his dying mother. *Memories of Another Day* starts with the young hero's father's death ('The last time I saw my father, he was lying quietly on his back in his coffin', Dan's mother had previously died giving him birth), and then flashes back to the father as a young hero himself. As a youth, he, in his turn, was obliged to revenge his brutally murdered parents by means even more brutal.

It is essential to the scheme of Robbins's novels that family should be obliterated, that there should be no dependence. Thus liberated from human connection, his heroes and heroine embark on a life's struggle of Darwinian intensity. And typically they achieve their 'dreams' in middle age. But they carry with them into middle age the adolescent's values and systems of survival: *sacro egoismo*, refusal to form lasting relationships, machismo. The dream world they create and inhabit is one in which there is no political or social dimension: only power expressed in the crude biological units of sexual domination (his 'first woman' is the principal milestone for the hero of *The Adventurers*), and the sexual accessories of wealth and power.

A characteristic climax in Robbins, is when 'the dreams fade'. Having achieved the fantasized goal, it is found to be empty, 'tinsel'. Pseudo-moralities intrude here: the rich aren't really happy, poor little rich girl etc. In *The Lonely Lady*, this goal, banally enough, is the winning of an Oscar. To express her disenchantment, the heroine indulges in a supremely infantile act of defiance. On the rostrum, she takes her clothes off, and displays her naked painted body:

Her voice came over the crowd. '. . . Last, but not least, I want to express my appreciation to my fellow members of the Academy for electing me their Token Woman Writer, in honour of which I want to unveil a painting I had done especially for them.'

She smiled gently as her hand reached behind her neck. Suddenly her dress fell from her body. She stood motionless on the stage, a huge inverted golden Oscar painted on her nude body. The gold paint covered her breasts and stomach, the flat head of the figure disappeared into her pubic hair.

Pandemonium broke out in the auditorium. The audience came to its feet, staring, cheering and booing as men rushed from the wings to surround JeriLee. Someone threw a coat around her. Contemptuously, she threw it off and marched from the stage in naked dignity (*The Lonely Lady*, 1977, p. 399).

In spite of Robbins's extraordinary use of the word 'dignity' here, and the invocation of the bra-burning stereotypes of women's liberation, we recognize the phallic defiance of the child, still selfishly obsessed with its own genitals. (There is something very similar in *Dreams Die First*, where the hero's main Hefner-style innovation in his magazine is a centrefold which features nothing but the model's pubis — 'Supercunt of the month', as it is called.)

Sex is the main element in the *roman à clef*, and in it sexual gratification is always achieved by domination or captivation. Thus in the *roman à clef* subplot to *The Godfather* we are told as part of his character build-up that Johnny Fontane (Italian, New York-born crooner, gangster connections, guess who?) has 'maybe a thousand pubic scalps dangling from his belt' (*The Godfather*, 1977, p. 158). The grotesquely large number, as well as the notion of sex as a predatory game of cowboys and indians, is typical of the genre.

The most appropriate and salesworthy authors of *romans à clef* are those who are themselves members of the written-about club. Thus, for example, a nineteenth-century novel of high life will recommend itself as being by 'Lady ****'. It was not unknown for works to be written under aristocratic *noms de plume*, by which common hacks were promoted to brevet marquesses, duchesses or ladies, so as to suggest spurious membership. In the 1970s two notable club members turned *roman à clef* novelist were Spiro T. Agnew and John Ehrlichman. Such big fish are not easy to catch, however, and once caught they may not, with all the editorial help in the world, be able to write. Harold Robbins, who *can* write, has been given the 'Lady ****' treatment. That is to say, we are led to take him not as some sordid key-hole peeper, but as someone actually on the inside, one of the set. Thus the *Daily Mail* confirms Robbins's credentials for writing about Khashoggi: 'Robbins, a millionaire many times himself, flits around in such a world.' The same assurance is given,

implicitly, by the NEL back cover for *Dreams Die First*:
Gareth Brendan, young, power-hungry and ambitious,
dreams of expressing his personal vision of liberated
sexuality in a magazine that will deal openly and honestly
with sex. So *Macho* is born, to shock and fascinate with its
outspoken views.
But for Gareth success also brings threats and obstruction
— from the underworld, from the law, from rivals. Violent
confrontations follow one after another as Gareth converts
his dream into a flamboyant private empire of total
pleasure and hedonism, in which money and sex go hand
in hand, in a world so rich it becomes almost too
enormous for Gareth to control.
Dreams Die First is a raw and passionate novel that
exposes the behind-the-scenes world of one man's sex
empire — a man who sacrifices his dreams to the reality of
success.

Figure 1 Harold Robbins on the back cover of *Dreams Die First*

Of course Brendan *is* (insofar as the *roman à clef* permits)
Hugh Hefner and *Macho* is *Playboy*. And there is the usual
wrapping everything around with infantile sexual fantasy.
But the illustration at the bottom is not Brendan/Hefner but
Harold Robbins, lounging on one of his many limousines
(see Fig. 1). He has twelve Rolls Royces — the playboy-

tycoon's *only* mode of land transportation, as the private yacht and personalized Lear Jet take him by air. Robbins is not, we understand, an onlooker like us, but an insider.

This sense of his being 'inside', 'one of them', validates all Robbins's fictional enterprises as we see from the publishers' blurbs:

The Lonely Lady: In this searing, poignant novel, Harold Robbins . . . rips the deceit and pretence from a society where money, appearance and fame seem to be the only values.

The Dream Merchants . . . dissects with intimate precision the glittering, amoral world of the movie moguls.

The Carpetbaggers is full of sharply drawn characters who search endlessly for power and love, and seek to dominate others even at the expense of self-destruction. Their sins are as great as their successes and Harold Robbins leaves nothing of their lives uncovered.

This ripping away, dissecting, uncovering, is best performed by someone on the inside, with an *entrée* and member's privileges. But, of course, Robbins finds himself playing a dangerous game. He celebrates the glamour of a life-style which is allegedly his own, while denouncing it, 'stripping it bare'. This ambivalence ('it's glamorous/it's ultimately empty') is a contradiction which Robbins is incapable of resolving; nor, incidentally, would his readers want him to.

Chapter Twelve

The *roman à clef* II

Pierre Rey's *The Greek*

This novel is something of a rarity, in that it is translated from the French and stands as 'Europe's greatest fiction bestseller of the year'. The year was 1973, although the book really took off in the Anglo-Saxon market with its translation in 1974 and the hype about the related film starring Anthony Quinn and Jacqueline Bisset. Since it is 'the Giant Inside Novel of Life among the Jet Set' in the Riviera, Paris, London, Washington, 'from superyachts to international palaces', a European origin is not entirely inappropriate.

Somewhat exotic in origin, *The Greek* offers the staple commodities of the slushier variety of modern *roman à clef*. The publishers are careful to align Rey with well-known Anglo-American practitioners: '*The Greek* moves with lightning pace and deft touches from one superb scene to another, a sure-fire mass of enjoyment to all those who wait avidly for the next novel from Arthur Hailey, Harold Robbins or Jacqueline Susann.' Rey prefaces his sure-fire mass of enjoyment with the ritual disclaimer: 'It is not a *roman à clef*.' How seriously we should take his protestation is suggested by a résumé of the plot, which centrally concerns the vendetta between two fabulously rich ship owners: Socrates Satrapoulos and Herman Kallenberg. These tycoons are rivals despite being related by having married sisters (heiresses to a former shipping tycoon's fortunes). The Greek of the title becomes enamoured of a famous, stunningly beautiful concert pianist, Menelas, a woman of icy beauty and tigress temper. Kallenberg has a propensity to sexual brutality. Alongside the main conflict is a subplot centring

on a young, beautiful American society belle, Peggy Nash-
Belmont; a reporter for a chic magazine, she falls in love
with a rising, brilliantly handsome young politician, Scott
Baltimore. He is the scion of the Baltimore dynasty (super-
rich, super-Catholic) and has been indoctrinated from childhood with the fact that his destiny is to be President of the
US (this destiny passed on to him with the death of his older
brother; he has two younger brothers). He has, we are told,
'that indefinable something which some call style' (*The
Greek*, 1975, p. 258. One of his aides is called, incredibly,
Herb Trendy — a measure of the complete absence of any
sense of the ridiculous in the *roman à clef*). Peggy marries
Scott, but intends to divorce him just before he comes up
for the Presidential nomination. She is persuaded out of this
course by the patriarch of the Baltimore clan with a $1 m.
douceur. Baltimore is eventually assassinated driving in an
open-air motorcade through New Orleans; the assassin is
himself promptly rubbed out, but he was only a front-man
anyway. Behind him were a conspiratorial consortium of
fifteen of the most powerful financiers in America, who
feared that Baltimore's liberal policies would deliver the
country to 'the beatniks and the blacks' (*ibid.*, p. 378).
The widowed Peggy becomes the Greek's new bride (he has
meanwhile dumped the temperamental Menelas). American
public opinion is infuriated ('Scott Baltimore's widow has
disgraced America'). But it is one in the eye for arch-rival
Kallenberg, who beats his wife to pulp, so driving her to
suicide. Satrapoulos's happiness and triumph are dashed,
however, when his son, Achilles, is killed in a mysterious
air crash.

Of course, Onassis, Niarchos, Callas, Bouvier, Kennedy
may have been names that never once occurred to Rey in
the writing of *The Greek*. And since those who hadn't been
beaten to death, assassinated or killed in suspicious aircrashes
were still around to sue, he had no option but to take refuge
in the 'any resemblance is purely coincidental' formula.

The *roman à clef* naturally gravitates, for its subject
matter, to the super-rich and omnipotent — people who,
like Satrapoulos, 'have the world by the balls' (*ibid.*, p. 275).
Yet it is not financial or commercial power that the novels

concern themselves with. 'Business', as these novels present
it, is no more than the occasional phone call, some boardroom manoeuvring and the spectacular coup from time to
time. What fictions like *The Greek* are centrally concerned
with is the sexual lives of the principal characters. (Less than
principal characters usually have no sex lives at all; they are
eunuchs in attendance.) For these tycoons the real business
of life is the continual orgy and battle of their personal
relationships.

In this world, dominated by the monotonously base values
of the gossip column, the most important information we
receive about *The Greek*'s principals, and the main explanation
of their antagonistic personalities, is that Satrapoulos has a
very large 'organ' (commensurate with his large nose) and
Kallenberg a 'laughably small' penis — a deficiency which, we
understand, explains everything about him:

Kallenberg was perfectly aware of the diminutive size of
his organ, and he compensated for it ferociously by an
unrelenting aggressiveness, an aggressiveness which
expressed itself in his Homeric delight in victory, his
sudden rages, his thirst for conquest and domination, his
desire to humiliate (*ibid.*, p. 59).

What a novel like *The Greek* suggests most vividly is the
child's curiosity about his parents' genitalia, and his taboo-
intensified fantasies about their sex lives. The super-rich, as
presented in this kind of *roman à clef*, are caricatured parent
figures: all-powerful, all-potent and mysteriously capricious
and cruel in their moods. 'What are their "organs" really
like?' — this is the question which the novelist assumes in a
reader consumed with an exciting mixture of penis envy (for
Satrapoulos's majestic organ), castration fear (at Kallenberg's
homicidal rages) and infantile voyeuristic wonder. Thus a
whole chapter is devoted to the sophisticate Peggy's shaving
her pubic hair into the shape of a heart to express her infatu-
ation for Scott. The 'relationship' isn't important — what she
does to her pudendum is.

One could multiply examples to show that the sexual
behaviour, obsessively depicted in this novel, is patently a
projection of regressive fantasy. The orgies, of which there
are many, culminate in one where a Scots lord (kilt and all)

has his penis sliced off (he wasn't wearing knickers — the playground joke is inescapable). In another scene Peggy discards a fiancé for the new-found Scott. When the rejected lover comes round to complain she holds a .38 pistol to his head, forces him to take off trousers and pants, and whips his 'bronze posterior'. An Arab potentate (in his native state an austere Islamic puritan) spends a chapter making tiny nicks with a razor blade on the rumps of six beautiful call-girls, rewarding them with diamonds for their pains. After this fetishistic ritual he turns with relish to a couple of twelve-year-old boys, supplied by the omnicompetent, jet-set ponce. All this is not, as it should be, horrifying or titillating; rather it strikes one as transparently infantile, a residue from the genital and anal phases with all their aggression and prurient obsessions.

The world in which these super-rich live is portrayed exclusively in terms of surfaces and style. Everything has a pedigree which guarantees it as out of the ordinary. A fabulously rich decor and ceremonial is the impression aimed at, even where the everyday transactions of life are concerned:

Dodino picked up the telephone and ordered breakfast without bothering to consult Raph. 'Some caviar,' he said, 'you know, the kind with the large white grains. The kind you serve my friend Reza Pahlevi — the Shah. And a bottle of Veuve Cliquot '51' (*ibid.*, p. 225).

This is a prime example of the style of fictional description the Victorians called 'silver fork'. In this plated style everyday objects and ordinary activities (here breakfast) are always specified as being *special*. To start the day these playboys need not just refreshment, but a breakfast fit for a Shah. The fact that for the orgy-exhausted subject a soft-boiled egg and Nescafé might be more welcome to the stomach is unimportant. *Richesse oblige.*

Behind Closed Doors

It was one of Norman Mailer's many observations about 'Jack' Kennedy that in him America for the first time had a President who, as the most powerful man in the world, was a sex object rather than a father figure. Mailer's own *Marilyn*, Judith Exner's *My Story* and such studies as Joan and Clay Blair's *The Search for Kennedy* ('uncovers . . . startling material') spun off a vogue for sensational *romans à clef* liberated from the pieties of, for example, Allen Drury's White House sagas.

In bestselling fiction of the 1970s, American Presidents are prone to act in the most unpresidential ways; they 'hump' and 'bang' their secretaries and female aides all over the White House (even in the sanctity of the Oval Office itself) as well as on Airforce One and in campaign trains. (See, for instance, William Safire's *Full Disclosure*, and Patrick Anderson's *White House*. As she fellates the President one of Safire's aides observes: 'I'm going down in history'.) They are embroiled in *crimes passionels* (see Anderson's *The President's Mistress*). They hang out in brothels (Jonathan Black's *The House on the Hill*).

The range of Presidential delinquency was further enlarged by Watergate, *The White House Transcripts* and the muckraking of the *Washington Post*. Arguably Watergate was the most massive conversion of private to public life in American history; certainly it was disclosure at the highest conceivable level. A President's private (or at least 'covered-up') affairs were subjected to the whole apparatus of modern electronic data capturing, combined with the publicity machineries of investigative reporters (less hampered by libel laws than in the UK) and trial by television.

Post-Watergate Presidents and candidates were paranoid, blackmailers or downright crooks. The President in *The Whole Truth* 'destabilizes' a South American country to preserve business interests. In Walter Stovall's *Presidential Emergency* the President actually defects to China. In *Side Effect* the President covers up for an illicit transplant operation his brother had by murdering the innocent and heroic couple who have revealed the scandal. *Side Effect* ends with the President about to go on television and mislead the American people; for in the Nixonian *romans à clef* Presidents lie as readily as they fornicate in Kennedy *romans à clef*. The Nixonian two-faced President is somewhat more metaphorically embodied in T. Allbeury's *The Man with the President's*

Mind which fantasizes a duplicate usurping the genuine
leader, and in Ben Bova's *The Multiple Man* where no less
than six clones secretly conspire to play all the various
Presidential parts.

The Vice President is, notoriously, an unglamorous post
in the US. But Spiro T. Agnew did his best to perform a
'full disclosure' job on the deputy leadership in *The Canfield
Decision* where Porter Canfield is portrayed as a selfish
schemer, a conspirator and a murderer.

John Ehrlichman's *The Company* is by far the best of the
mud-slinging presidential *romans à clef*. Written after the
reverse journey of the Assistant for Domestic Affairs from
White House to log cabin via prison, the novel came out in
May 1976. The TV mini-series, brilliantly retitled *Washington:
Behind Closed Doors*, put the novel back into the bestseller
lists in autumn 1977.

The Company is based distantly, but unmistakably, on the
alleged CIA murder of Diem, which (again allegedly) Kennedy
connived in. The other Kennedy Presidential misdemeanour,
the Bay of Pigs invasion, is fictionally combined with this
earlier assassination. In *The Company*, President William
Curry (JFK) arranges the murder of 'Father Julio Benitimes ...
chaplain and inspirational advisor' to the 'Free Dominican
Forces'. This murder, a few hours before the ostensibly US-
supported invasion of a pseudonymous Caribbean left wing
dictatorship, ensures failure — the 'Rio de Muerte fiasco'.
A secret CIA report looking into the matter after Curry's
premature death (in a plane accident) concludes 'that the
President had decided to insure the failure of the operation
while, at the same time, not calling it off' (*The Company*,
1976, p. 32). When Esker Anderson (LBJ) retires from
the Presidency with heart trouble, the facts about Liberal
Democrat Curry are available to his neurotically envious
Republican rival, Richard Monckton.

The TV series was a cult success in both Britain and
America, and newspapers were prompt in providing 'keys'.
No key was necessary, however, for the reader to jump to
the identification of Monckton with the novelist's former

boss Nixon (especially given Jason Robards's mimicry in the part). None the less, in the novel Ehrlichman prudently employed the *roman à clef*'s traditional legal disclaimer:

This is a story about people, events and the forces that impel them. The people are wholly fictional. But the forces — the stresses, pressures, fears and passions — that motivate the characters are real.

And in the course of the narrative there are a number of blocks to any automatic (and legally actionable) connections. Esker Anderson, for instance, is folksy Oregon rather than folksy Texan. Monckton is from a mid-West farming rather than Californian shopkeeping background. Ehrlichman catches supremely well and with uncanny accuracy, however, the flavour of Oval-office diatribes, as rendered in the semi-coherent gabble of *The White House Transcripts*. The following is a typically effective vignette of a paranoid President at bay, justifying a 'plumber's job' on the grounds of 'national security':

'The miserable fags at the State Department don't like the idea of a strong White House hand on foreign policy. They hate it; so they squirm and squeal and leak all over to try to ruin it. What only the sophisticates in the White House, and a few others, realize is that they are also ruining the Presidency — the ability of the President to carry out his constitutional duties — to conduct foreign policy. Well, by Christ, we aren't going to let them bring down the Presidency! We owe it to the country to prevent that. And that's where you fellows become so important.' Monckton paused and looked directly at each of them in turn. 'We've got to know what the enemy is doing. And we can't rely on the FBI and the others to tell us' (*ibid.*, pp. 222-3).

Chapter Thirteen

Full disclosure: research and insider novels

I tried a book about land once, but I found all the research materials were owned by a film producer. To hell with that. I can do my own primary research on the sea.

(Peter Benchley)

Nowadays the bestselling author must often be prepared to sacrifice some of his originating role, and the glory of sole ownership which goes with it. Hence one sees such title-pages as this, in which the author shares his credits as a screenwriter would:

330 Park

Stanley Cohen

Produced and Developed by R. Smith Kiliper

or advertisements like the following:

ANNOUNCING

THE HALL OF FAME

SERIES

the latest from

Lyle Kenyon Engel,

Creator of the bestselling

Kent Family Chronicles

The 'author' of the bestselling 'Kent Family Chronicles' is
John Jakes. Engel, the 'creator' provides the ideas for Jakes
to write up, and receives 50 per cent of the royalty from the
series — which by the late 1970s was advertised to have sold
over 10 m. of its various instalments.

An author thus denied the dignities and traditional free-
doms of the onlie begetter in the shift of real power upwards
can respond in a number of ways. He can demote himself to
the level of a hack or writing machine. Alternatively, he can
divert his main creative effort to a phase of the production
sequence other than origination. He (or more often she) can,
for example, support the selling of the book by starring in a
promotional media blitz. 'Most writers of fiction', observed
the *New York Times* in 1976, are 'electronic wallflowers'.
Increasingly, however, some aren't; and in the circus of
launch publicity they find the author's traditional ego
rewards.

A third response, and one favoured by many ambitious
novelists (especially male novelists), is to affect that they are
not primarily novelists at all, but journalists. There is enough
overlap in the two forms of writing to make this pseudo-
journalism of the novelist at least superficially plausible. The
bestseller, for example, has an intimate connection with
news. Frequently it presents itself as 'tomorrow's headlines'.
(This line is often pushed in promotion campaigns for bestsellers: e.g. 'Alfred Coppel: *34 East*. Read it today while it's
still fiction!') Often popular fiction assumes in this way a
privileged and almost mystical inwardness with the big stories
of the day, as if the novelist were in a position to 'scoop' the
journalist. When Mountbatten was murdered by the IRA it
was a main news item that the assassination had been pre-
figured in a bestseller of a year or so earlier. The implication
was that, in some magical way, life had imitated fiction. In
Britain in 1979-80 the whole Blunt affair melted miasmically
into the bestseller ethos of the televisation of le Carré's
immediately previous *Tinker, Tailor, Soldier, Spy*, so that
one could hardly tell where headlines about moles finished
and fiction started.

More materially, the journalist resembles the bestselling
novelist in that he has his job on an assignment, not an

inspiration basis. None the less, in performing his assigned task the journalist can achieve an honoured, and sometimes heroic status. (One thinks of Woodstein, Pencourt, or the *Sunday Times*'s Insight team in their crusade for thalidomide victims.) It is this glory — or at least professional self-respect — that the displaced and diminished novelist aspires to in his research fetishism.

The journalistic styles most conveniently borrowed by the bestselling author are those of the investigator ('muckraker') and the researcher ('expert'). The attraction of both is that they allow the novelist to simulate an activity (and sometimes actually perform it) recognized and rewarded outside the judicial area of literary criticism. In consequence, for example, Hailey can ignore the critics of his fiction (who have been very unkind) and console himself that *Hotel* — whatever the mandarins of the English department think — is on the hotel administration course at Cornell. Where research is concerned, Hailey — an otherwise unpretentious man — affects a Flaubertian conscientiousness:

> When he writes, everything must be impeccably accurate.
> He won't write off the top of his head, hoping the facts are
> correct, no matter how relatively unimportant these
> minute details are to the main story. If he were going to
> write a sentence about installing a U-bend pipe under a
> kitchen sink, he'd ask a plumber how it was done. He
> argues: if the sentence doesn't ring true to a plumber, then
> the plumber will doubt the information in the rest of the
> story (Sheila Hailey, 1978, p. 86).

Jaws author Peter Benchley was, apparently, less upset by the bad reviews of his novel-*qua*-novel than at the scorn of Jacques Cousteau about the novel's 'expertise' on sharks. That is to say, he was more vulnerable, because he had his *amour propre* invested in his 'research' rather than in his 'art'.

Readers are induced to fall into a corresponding double-think. *The Godfather* may be a clumsy, soggy novel — but it 'takes the lid off the Mafia'. Forsyth writes what may be thought wooden, amateurish prose (Hutchinson's first reader's report on *The Day of the Jackal* made this point strongly, advocating a rejection that would have cost the house dear) but his fiction is 'meticulously researched'. It is doublethink because there is, logically, nothing a novel can do in this department that a newspaper can't, and important things which novels can't do, since fiction is inherently untrustworthy and subject to libel laws (newspaper reports, if they keep to the facts, aren't).

Muckraking and Deep Throat fiction

The fearless, crusading journalist like Jack Anderson, Ralph Nader or Daniel Ellsberg occupies an honoured place in recent American history. Such men take the lid off society and reveal the corruptions beneath. They are the guardians of democracy, and the free press is the source of their power. The muckraking role is one which popular fiction eagerly mimics. The following is the blurb of a would-be muckraking novel, *Condominium*, by John D. MacDonald (the narrative concerns jerry-built sunset homes, sold to unsuspecting American senior citizens in the prosperous evenings of their lives):

> *Condominium* is a blockbuster in the grand tradition of
> Arthur Hailey and James Michener. . . . *Condominium* is
> the first book to spell it all out; the real estate chicanery,
> the political corruption, the sexual immorality, the endless
> exploitation of the retired. . . . It's the 'inside' novel of
> 1977 that packs the two-fisted wallop of one of America's
> master-story tellers.

Wheels was sold under the same claim as the 'inside' novel of 1971: 'the biggest name in blockbusting bestsellers takes the lid off Detroit'. That it 'takes the lid off', or is an 'inside' story is one of the main promises of modern bestsellerism. One even has it from authors whose attitude to muck is less that of raking than wallowing in it; thus Jackie Collins's steamy *roman à clef*, *Lovers and Gamblers*, will recommend itself as 'one helluva good big read . . . for anyone who wants to know what it is really like in the superstar belt'. What it is 'really like', of course, is 'A beauty queen and a rock superstar . . . riots, bomb scares, orgies and drug trips.' Familiar stuff to any insider, presumably.

For obvious reasons, Hollywood and show business have

their lid taken off more frequently in bestselling fiction than does Detroit. Thus William Goldman's 1979 novel *Tinsel* could retell the well-worn Marilyn Monroe story yet again and claim to be '*The* Hollywood Novel', spilling the industry's 'best kept secrets' and 'portraying today's Hollywood as only an insider can'. (Goldman has academy awards for *Butch Cassidy* and *All the President's Men*.) Three years earlier Delacorte Press (Goldman's publisher) put out *The Users*, with a big advertising campaign that declared:

Joyce Haber knows more than anyone about the X-rated lives of Hollywood's 'A-list' superstars. . . . Only the columnist *Time* calls 'Hollywood's #1 voyeur' could have written this novel of sex and social climbing in Sodom-on-the-Pacific. THE USERS includes anybody who is anybody in the New Hollywood's social hierarchy, among them: the most boisterous novelist in America; the most powerful agent in show business; the most unpredictable superstar in films; the most celebrated hostess on the West Coast; the most passionate lover in Los Angeles; the handsomest studio chief in the world; and many, many more. Already, THE USERS is causing more shock waves among Hollywood insiders than the San Andreas fault.

That the novel is making shock waves is a common claim. 'Hollywood', Delacorte claimed, 'will never be the same' after *Tinsel* (*Publishers Weekly*, 14 May, 1979). Authorities, supposedly, quake when they read such works as *Dress Gray*, set in West Point. '*Dress Gray* will not be read happily at either West Point or the Academy,' observed the *New York Times*, 'but it will, you may depend on it, be read.' This superior murder mystery, written by 'insider' Lucian K. Truscott IV, a West Pointer, presents the academy as a kind of Sodom on the Hudson, and follows on newspaper disclosures of violations of the 'honour code' in the mid-1970s.

Following Watergate and the spate of Washington exposés in the 1970s, the capital has rivalled Hollywood as the centre with the most sensational muck to rake. Thus Les Whitten's *Conflict of Interest* tags along behind the hilarious Wilbur Mills and 'Fanne Foxe, the Argentine bombshell' revelations, carried by the *Washington Post*, then by the national press. It packed extra punch since Whitten has some claim to be a

muckraker proper:
THE WASHINGTON INSIDER'S NOVEL THAT HAS
OTHER INSIDERS SAYING 'IT'S DYNAMITE'. . . . Les
Whitten, the veteran investigative reporter who shares Jack
Anderson's byline, has written a novel about sex, payoffs,
and power in Washington that exposes the real world
behind the recent, shocking headlines.

In CONFLICT OF INTEREST, an investigative reporter
named Aubrey Warder digs into the life of an alcoholic
Speaker of the House and comes up with more
incriminating evidence than he bargained for.

Veteran investigative reporters of the Anderson/Whitten
kind have been somewhat eclipsed in the 1970s by the young
journalist superheroes, Woodward and Bernstein, the *Washington Post* reporters who took the lid off Watergate ('opened
the can of worms', as the then current metaphor was), and
who, with the help of their mysterious informant 'Deep
Throat', brought down a President. In 1976, the largest-ever
advance for paperback rights for a first novel went to Safire's
Full Disclosure. Safire was touted as a fiction equivalent to
'Woodstein', probing and disclosing all. The publishers'
advertising material stresses their author's credentials as a top
journalist and inside informer whom they have, in the language of spy fiction, contrived to turn':

New York Times columnist and former Presidential
speechwriter William Safire offers a privileged insider's
view of the moulding of opinion and the play of power.
He has written the hottest political novel of our time — a
savage, witty spellbinding exposure of the inner workings
of the world's most powerful office . . . and the men who
run it.

The key word 'novel' appears only once in this blurb, and is
there overshadowed by the neighbouring epithets 'hottest
political . . .' which contrive to suggest that fiction is merely
a protective membrane, which will not in any way impede
any moderately perceptive reader from appreciating the
'privileged insider's' complete 'exposure'.

Even Safire's throat is shallow compared to Spiro T.
Agnew's (*The Canfield Decision*) or John Ehrlichman's
(*The Company*). Ex-convict Ehrlichman mischievously

entitled his second *roman à clef The Whole Truth*. According to its publisher's advertisements, *In the National Interest* (by CBS and ABC reporters Kalb and Koppel) was a Washington novel that 'could only have been written from the inside'. And the crowning achievement of the American book trade in the late 1970s was to recruit not just insiders such as network investigative reporters, but *top* insiders. Thus some of the 'plumbers' employed by Nixon took on a new career after conviction; Gordon Liddy, for instance, produced *Out of Control*:

> With the precision and accuracy only an insider could bring to the job, G. Gordon Liddy has written a gripping novel of espionage and corporate intrigue that immediately establishes him as a novelist of the first rank. His story takes us behind the scenes at the Central Intelligence Agency into an investigation led by a 'rogue' CIA agent, aided by his beautiful Chinese mistress, and backed by millions of Mafia dollars, culminating in an incredible duel in the New York skies.

How far this kind of recruitment will eventually go under the pressure of bestsellerdom remains to be seen. But it is not inconceivable that some day we shall have an American Disraeli, ambidextrously premier politician and superselling novelist.

Research

Gordon Williams tells us an amusing story on the subject of research and the modern novel. Once in a public lavatory in Holborn he observed some fine overhead glass cisterns. Wouldn't it be quaint, he thought, if someone put goldfish in them. Williams stored the idea away for future use in his fiction. A week or so later he read in a novel by bestselling American author Richard Condon a description of the same lavatory, the same glass cisterns and the imaginary goldfish. Williams wrote to Condon, remarking on the coincidence and asked how the other author came by the idea. He received a courteous reply saying that Condon did not bother with such narrative details himself; he had a research assistant to turn up 'local colour' (*The South Bank Show*, 4 March, 1979).

Bestselling novels of the 1970s are packed hard with factual detail, authentication and solidity of specification, all acquired by 'research' (usually, however, novelists do the legwork themselves — Condon's Tayloristic approach would seem to be logical but extraordinary). According to Hailey, as mentioned above, it takes him a year to 'research' his novels — as long, that is, as it takes actually to write them (he regards the writing as much the more mechanical task of the two). Sheila Hailey describes how her husband goes about this all-important research phase of his work:

Once the subject is chosen, Arthur reads everything he can about it. This is not to crib from other writers, but to have an intelligent reservoir of knowledge before he goes out to gather information from experts.

His first introduction to the new project is a meeting he either sets up himself, or asks Doubleday, his US publisher, to arrange. If the approach is to a big organization, this may involve a lunch with the vice-president of public relations. From then on, other interviews are set up.

Beyond these, Arthur fans out in all directions — to talk with chairmen in board rooms, office workers at a lunch counter, disgruntled employees eager to dig up skeletons, retired executives spinning out empty days at home and longing to relive their careers before an attentive audience (Sheila Hailey, 1978, pp. 79-80).

Having accomplished his fieldwork, Hailey marshalls his material into notes, all catalogued, cross-referenced and filed. In this he is, as Sheila Hailey puts it, 'ultra methodical', 'infinitely patient'. He has, it would seem, displaced a large part of his writer's conscience from 'creation' to this area of research activity. Indeed, the conscientiousness of some bestselling novelists in the matter of research often seems far beyond the call of duty. Jack Higgins, who claims to be able to throw off a novel in three months or less, spent three weeks in a funeral home to get factual details just right for one of his thrillers.

Desmond Bagley (twelve novels in fifteen years, estimated 10 m. plus sales by the late-1970s) follows the same, painstaking research programme as Hailey in the construction of his thrillers:

His work is famous for its highly technical content. He has had to learn geology, ship-building and Mayan history; he knows about hurricances and avalanches, genetic engineering and computers. He reads a book every day of his life (*Evening Standard*, 29 September 1976).

Publicity handouts foreground such information as Bagley's taking out a three months subscription to the *Vancouver Sun* before getting down to work on *Landslide*, a novel which is set in British Columbia. Bagley himself has divulged what preparatory work went into his 1975 bestseller, *The Snow Tiger*. The *idea* was formed in 1963 when he wrote to his editor, proposing a book about an avalanche. 'Avalanches', Bagley observes, 'are highly technical'. Presumably many of his daily books were on the subject. 'In 1968', he recalls,

'I had the great good fortune to go to Antarctica with the US Navy where I could talk to the physicists who specialised in snow and ice. They gave me lots of specialised stuff, six mathematical equations to the page. Oh of course I understood them, though I had to simplify them for the reader' (*ibid.*)

The next problem was the setting, which also entailed field-work in hunting down a location – research of a more practical kind. 'There's no point in setting your avalanche in Antarctica', Bagley deduced, 'there are thousands of avalanches but nobody underneath.' Looking around Bagley discovered some 'ice fields' by the Cook Mountain in New Zealand with the required number of people underneath them. A trip there supplied the necessary local colour. It was now 1974. The research was done and all that remained was the mechanical business of writing it up around a simple melodramatic situation. The novel was executed to formula (Bagley uses a small computer for writing purposes – it enables him to insert, calculate wordage and play back at will), and *The Snow Tiger* emerged to take its place at the top of the British lists in 1976.

The most respected researching novelist in Britain is probably Len Deighton. So saturated is his work in period and technical construction that it is a fine decision whether he writes a novel (*Bomber*) or contemporary history (*Fighter*).

Deighton does his own legwork (though he has some well publicized aids — as everyone knows a computer was used to work out the intricate time sequence of the raid in *Bomber*). Deighton's approach is, however, fiendishly hard work, and his rate of production is slow. One obvious short cut for the researching novelist is to take specialist guidance. Thus Herbert Lieberman's densely factual chronicle of the every-day life of a New York Chief Medical Examiner ('strangled whores, battered babies, dismembered corpses') carries a dedication to 'Dr Yong Myun Rho, Deputy Chief Medical Examiner, City of New York, who served so graciously as technical adviser on this book'. Dr Rho provided the un-pleasantly detailed and specific postmortem material which made *City of the Dead* into 'the shocker of the summer'. Such assistance is not always a shortcut, however. The acknowledgments to learned individuals and institutions for Michener's *Centennial* run to three pages and read like a degree ceremony procession, as every academic title is religiously cited. Any impudent doubts as to Michener's ability to recount a few billion years of earth's history is flattened by the academic avoirdupois he drops on the reader at the beginning of his massive saga.

Privileged information

Hailey, Deighton, and Bagley are grafters; they work at their research. They start as outsiders and get into a subject by diligence. Other writers claim or discover a more direct access. Thus many bestsellers claim to be informed by leaks or confidential inside dope from 'connections'. Classified information, mysteriously come by, is what the cover des-cription of Robin Moore's *The Set Up* promises us. The novel deals with the subsequent police theft of *The French Connec-tion*'s $90 m. worth of heroin:

> Brilliantly told by the author of the original *French Connection* from information that comes directly via the confidential files of the New York narcotics squad, this thrilling story emerges as a whirling typhoon of corruption and greed, which is impossible to put down.

Robin Moore is famous, as well, for his 'legwork'. He trained with the Special Services as a civilian and went into battle with them in Vietnam in order to write *The Green Berets*.

'Privileged information' is the guarantee of many sensational plots. In Jack Higgins's *The Eagle Has Landed*, for instance, a prelude to the main narrative follows an investigative reporter called 'Patterson' (Harry Patterson is Higgins's real name; he has also written as Martin Tallon, Hugh Marlowe and James Graham). This reporter is on the track of an astonishing story. During the war, it would seem, a band of German paratroopers attempted a Skorzeny-style raid to capture or assassinate Churchill. Much research by 'Patterson' among ledgers, army records and tight-lipped survivors winkles the truth out. As the prologue puts it:

> This book is an attempt to re-create the events surrounding that astonishing exploit. At least fifty per cent of it is documented historical fact. The reader must decide for himself how much of the rest is a matter of speculation, or fiction.

A good percentage of the part of Higgins's novel which is not documented historical fact would seem to be indebted to the master of this kind of meticulously researched thriller, Frederick Forsyth. Forsyth was a journalist before he was a bestselling novelist, and the convention underlying his fiction is that he has a bombshell story to reveal (de Gaulle came within an inch of being assassinated, the Nazis all but took over the Bundesrepublik). Covers always make much of Forsyth's research. Thus *The Odessa File* carries the endorsement of the *Chicago Tribune* that the novel is 'a carefully thought out, meticulously researched, documented, instructive and eventually highly suspenseful work of fiction'. The work is dedicated 'To all Press reporters' and the extra-literary, journalistic thoroughness of *The Odessa File* is certified by the 'Author's note' which carries an FF byline. In this preface, 'FF' modestly intimates the vast amount of legwork which went into the novel, while striking the journalist's pose of scrupulously protecting the anonymity of his sources of information:

> It is customary for authors to thank those who have helped them to compile a book, particularly on a difficult

subject, and in doing so to name them. All those who helped me, in however small a way, by assisting me to get the information I needed to write *The Odessa File* are entitled to my heartfelt thanks, and if I do not name them it is for three reasons.

Some, being former members of the SS, were not aware at the time either who they were talking to or that what they said would end up in a book. Others have specifically asked that their names never be mentioned as sources of information about the SS. In the case of others still, the decision not to mention their names is mine alone, and taken I hope for their sakes rather than for mine.

We are in a grey area here between journalistic veracity and fictional authentication games; games which go back at least as far as the 'found manuscript' of gothic fiction. But what is important here are the roles assumed and the poses struck which insist that the writer is primarily something other than a mere novelist.

Institutional fiction

As the investigative novel has its passive counterpart in the 'informant's' novel, so the 'researched' novel partners the 'institutional' novel — that is to say the work whose author is already a knowledgeable insider, professionally possessed of the specialized information which writers like Hailey have to soak up by research.

In the 1970s there has been a vogue for authors whose primary expertise is blatantly non-novelistic: doctors (Crichton, Cook), politicians and politicians' aides (Agnew, Safire, Ehrlichman, Anderson), jockeys (Dick Francis, whose racing background is so authentic that, as one critic put it, 'You can smell and taste it'), above all policemen and policewomen. Police novels parade the novelists's curriculum vitae in such a way as to make novel-writing a mere accessory to the first profession of the cop-turned-author. Thus in the come-on for Robert Daley's *To Kill a Cop* we are much more likely to be impressed with the novelist's professional background than anything else:

'Authentic and breathlessly fast' . . . As exciting as *The
Day of the Jackal'* . . . 'The explosive new thriller' . . .
Never has the brutal world of the big-city cop been
portrayed with such vivid accuracy. Robert Daley, former
New York City Deputy Police Commissioner, has drawn
on real-life headlines of Black Liberation Army cop
murders for his devastating novel about a small band of
revolutionaries and their plot to machine-gun high police
officials at a patrolman's funeral. Standing between the
guerillas and their deadly objective is one man — Earl
Eischied, Chief of Detectives — tough, relentless,
determined [etc. etc.] . Combining a novelist's gift for
breathless tension with absolutely authentic details of
police procedure, Robert Daley has written his finest work
to date — a thriller that echoes the terrifying reality of
recent history.

One suspects, incidentally, an invisible division of labour
here — namely that Daley provides the 'authentic' element;
his editor at Crown the 'breathless tension'. This was, for
instance, the main teamwork at Doubleday on *Jaws*; Benchley
brought his shark expertise and Congdon eliminated the
'limpness' and 'uncertainty' of the narrative, making everything 'tight'. Sometimes there is even a dual byline, as in the
successful team of T.N. Scortia and F. Robinson. Scortia is a
scientist, Robinson a former *Playboy* editor. In their technical
disaster scenarios, like *The Prometheus Project*, or *Towering
Inferno*, one imagines that the first partner is responsible for
the hard science, the other for the 'excitement'. An opportunistic 1979 novel, *Phoenix*, which fantasizes an Arab
assassination plot on Dayan to delay the peace treaty, similarly
has as its authorial team Amos Aicha, former head of the
Israeli police force, and the professional author Eli Landau.
Such partnerships are logical crystallizations of the writing
function, and come to resemble the Hollywood star-director
team.

Daley is fairly small in this field (though his novel did
inspire a short-lived, abysmally boring television series,
starring Joe Don Baker). Supersellers in the police genre are
the East Coast ex-cop Dorothy Uhnak and, above all, her
West Coast counterpart 'Sergeant' Joseph Wambaugh, with

his new order of police chivalry (*The Blue Knight, The New Centurions*). Wambaugh initially insisted on keeping his job with the LAPD even after his first novel had made him rich. 'He doesn't plan to give up work', *Publishers Weekly* (23 August 1971) reported, 'because he still thinks of himself as a cop who writes in his spare time, rather than a writing cop.' (Judging by *The Choirboys*, writing is a more decent employment of spare time than Los Angeles cops usually go in for.) All the covers of Wambaugh's paperbacks have a police motif — handcuffs, cap, truncheon, badge, service .38, usually set against a blue background. This iconography serves to remind us that the author is a policeman who writes novels, rather than a novelist who writes about policemen. The whole Wambaugh package is de-emphatic where 'novel' is concerned, stridently emphatic where 'police' is concerned.

The same stress is found in the publicity for Dorothy Uhnak's novels. Thus in the blurb to *The Investigation* we are told:

Dorothy Uhnak is also the author of *Law and Order*, *The Bait*, *The Witness* and *The Ledger*. She was herself a Detective in the New York Transit Police Department, promoted three times and decorated twice for performance.

Critics agreed; according to *Newsweek* 'Uhnak's strength lies in her firm, unsentimental knowledge of the harsh world of crime, policework and city politics.'

Uhnak and Wambaugh write novels which are largely clichéd and conventional in their narratives. (*The Investigation* resolves itself into an old-fashioned whodunnit in which the detective-hero falls in love with the prime suspect. All Wambaugh's novels are in the 'thin blue line' mode.) But their fiction is crusted over with a solid layer of privileged, inside information. Such things as police procedure and city topography are given with a detailed precision which only 'research' could otherwise supply, and yet research could not produce it as casually. Writers like Uhnak, Daley and Wambaugh are also careful to cue the reader that they are not as other crime novelists are. Typically they indulge in the logically contradictory game of 'This is a true fiction unlike those other false fictions which you're used to.' The following sarcastic put-down of 'Hollywood cops' comes from *The Investigation*:

> Any cop worth his shield knows that unless a homicide is
> committed by someone close to the victim the odds are
> that the perpetrator will remain at large. Unless you get
> lucky and an informant comes through for you.
> Informants — what the Hollywood cops call 'snitches' —
> are the backbone of any successful police department. The
> informant is generally the scum of the earth, and when his
> usefulness is over, any cop would throw him to the wolves
> without a blink. Which is not exactly the cute relationship
> of the television-series Homicide Squad hero, who sleuths
> out solutions week after week, using ten bucks' worth of
> information and a head full of clever ideas (*The
> Investigation*, 1977, p. 53).

Needless to say, Uhnak, Daley and Wambaugh's work has
been acquired by Hollywood, and has inspired TV series. But
their superior insiders' authority is sustained by constant
publicity reminders of their career records, and by works of
reportage like *The Onion Field* or *Prince of the City* — 'true
stories' of urban police life.

The special-plea novel

Typically the insider's novel by an institutionally knowledgeable novelist has set itself the task of 'taking the lid off' (as in
Hollywood and Washington fiction by former Hollywood and
Washington people) or 'telling it how it is' (as, for example,
in Robin Moore's *The Green Berets*). In the 1970s, however,
bestselling success has been achieved by a variety of insider's
fiction which sets out to make a special plea for sympathetic
understanding. Such a plea is found at the core of Wambaugh's
police novels. His cop-heroes customarily have stomach ulcers,
nervous complaints, are stressed alcoholics and frequently
their marriages break down as a consequence of doing their
job well. *The Onion Field* (a 'true story') chronicles the
crucifixion of a 'good cop' by a legal system skewed towards
the criminal. This is a favourite theme of Wambaugh's,
epigrammatically summed in the advertising tag for the film
of *The Onion Field*: 'the real crime comes after the arrest'.

The titles of Wambaugh's early fiction (*The Blue Knight*, *The New Centurions*) indicate his sub-Hemingwayesque endorsement of grace under the intolerable pressure of modern American police work. In *The Black Marble*, one of his later and better novels, the hero is an LAPD police sergeant (as was Wambaugh in his pre-literary career) in the terminal stages of a nervous breakdown. Sergeant Valnikov is tormented by a recurrent and mysterious nightmare in which a rabbit is skinned in horrific detail. The narrative records Valnikov working through his crisis, with the therapeutic assistance of a suitably attractive woman police partner. Finally the cause of his nightmare is revealed. The last straw in a traumatic working life had been a harrowing postmortem of a young murder victim:

'The picture changes but I still see it. I . . . I had to keep looking at the little arms and hands to remember it's still a rabbit. Because the face was all swollen and deformed from the beatings. . . .'
'Yes? Yes?'
'He starts skinning it then. He tears the face right back over the skull. The face is pulled inside out, the little swollen deformed face. The hair is fine because it's so young. The hair goes inside out too!' Valnikov sobbed.
'Yes,' Natalie said. 'What then?'
'I have to keep looking at the arms and hands to . . . to remember it's a rabbit! I think it's a fish he treats it so brutally.'
'The hunter?'
'Yes. He says the anus is still open. After death!' Valnikov was crying now.
'Yes. Go on.'
'I know what that means. I've investigated hundreds, hundreds. I just had four others. This is too many!'
'What does it mean? The anus being open?'
'Sodomy after death,' Valnikov cried. 'I thought it was only the mother! I believed the father because he seemed so pathetic. He said he'd been away. He cried so much I believed him. But there was semen in the anus. The neighbors didn't want to get involved. He screamed in the night. Five in a row. That's too many!' (*The Black Marble*,

1978, pp. 305-6).

Less a superseller than anything of Wambaugh's, though still a bestseller in 1972, was Peter Gent's *North Dallas Forty*, subsequently made into a film starring Nick Nolte. This novel and its tie-in film lets the public into the agony of being an American professional football player. Off the field the hero is a virtual cripple, sustained by beer, amphetamines and pain killers. He is not a sportsman; he is a victim of sport. Like Wambaugh, Gent knows what he is writing about – he was himself a footballer with the Dallas Cowboys for five years. According to Gent:

My book was about people who are in pain. Outsiders tend to think of athletes as stereotypes. 'They're just a bunch of dumb animals.' 'They enjoy hurting each other.' None of this is true. Just because they're big doesn't mean ballplayers like to run at each other (*Observer*, 23 March 1980).

What is striking about both Wambaugh's and Gent's novels is their tendency to contradict common 'outsider' stereotypes. Cops and pro football players are conventionally regarded as the toughest of all law abiding American citizens. American policemen carry guns and clubs legitimately, nor are they reluctant to use them. American footballers approximate physically to the exaggeration of comic book supermen; they too wear armour at work. Yet both Wambaugh and Gent set out to convince the reader of the 'soft' nature of these hard men, avatars of the most violent society in the world. Cop and footballer are human and vulnerable within the hard, protective casing of their uniforms. It is the kind of apology which could only be persuasively urged by a fellow sufferer turned novelist.

Chapter Fourteen

Death Wish: from stetson to hard hat

All over the Western world a hideous unknown disease is striking teenagers, turning them into raving maniacs.
(1977 publisher's synopsis of *The Minotaur Factor*)

I

The romance of vigilantism has a long tradition in popular fiction, and goes back as a main stem at least as far as Edgar Wallace's *Four Just Men*. At almost any time in the postwar period one could have found a top-selling novel featuring a lone avenger or death squad on the bookstands. (As I write, *Death List* is the current candidate.) The emotional gratifications this formula offers are those of drastic surgery or (favourite politician's phrase in 1979) the 'sharp shock'. And this fantasized short way with social problems appeals particularly to the irritable, conservative temperament. A typical, successful and very British example of the vindictive novel is *The Chilian Club*. In it a quartet of St James's veterans get together to liquidate the trade union officials, student leaders and Trotskyist scum who are ruining 'their' Britain. ('Four heroes . . . and I mean *heroes*', noted the *Sunday Express*, approvingly.)

In the late 1940s and early 1950s in America the lone vigilante par excellence was Spillane's Mike Hammer, who, with massive egotism, assumes in his own revenging instincts the prerogatives of constituted authority (*I the Jury*). 'God's hit man' as one critic called Hammer, purges society by the same judicial short cuts as his contemporary, Senator Joe McCarthy — a figure with whom he has plausibly been linked.

Until the great 10 m. blockbusters of the 1970s, Spillane was the all-time fiction bestseller — holding the first half dozen places in Hackett's 1960s surveys. His publishers still proclaim his sales power over the years as their defiant answer to the distaste which Spillane's 'pornography of violence' provokes among liberal intellectuals: 'Mickey Spillane is read in fourteen languages every minute of the day. Since *I the Jury* was published in 1947, his books have sold more than 55m copies throughout the world. People like them.' In spite of this ya-boo, people liked them less in the late 1960s and hardly at all in the 1970s. For modern readers the private eye (a survivor of the 1930s pulps) had lost credibility. The great lone avenger of our decade has been the Garfield/Winner/Bronson creation, Paul Benjamin (Kersey, in the film), the milque-toast commuter with a .32 in his pocket and thirty-odd notches on it for as many justly slaughtered 'punks'. As in another superior tale of 1970s vigilantism, David Morrell's *Testament*, the one revenger is a decent family man, striking back after a grievous assault on his domestic normality.

II

Although Garfield's book (1972) preceded the movie, *Death Wish* really took off with Michael Winner's highly controversial film (1974: it went on general release and was re-released in 1979). The film caused a sensation by its frank appeal to the blood lust of 'law abiding' citizens. In New York audiences were reported as bursting into spontaneous applause when the middle-aged, middle-class commuter-vigilante at last strikes back and slays would-be muggers in Central Park and on the New York subway. (These scenes are not in the novel, incidentally, where Benjamin's hits are all furtive, back-street affairs.)

The story of *Death Wish*, to which Winner is only moderately faithful, owes much to the westerns with which Garfield served his literary apprenticeship. The novel opens in a downbeat way as Paul Benjamin, a 47-year-old, out-of-condition accountant, drives through New York after too heavy a liquid lunch. How did the city become this hooker-, addict- and porno-merchant-infested 'combat zone', he wonders? On his return to the office a colleague jocularly invites him to join a new 'guerrilla war' as one of the 'computer haters'. Joshing over, Benjamin gets down to his tedious afternoon's business, helping a millionaire evade taxes. Then comes the bombshell. 'Animals' have broken into his apartment and assaulted his wife and daughter. The older woman's neck had been 'twisted like a rag doll's', and she dies shortly after arrival in hospital. The younger woman has been brutalized into what eventually becomes irreversible catatonic withdrawal. The 'animals' are identified as young addicts ('kids', 'probably teenagers', 'filthy little monsters'). Benjamin discovers that even if they are apprehended (which they never are) the law is biased towards leniency for young 'disadvantaged' offenders. The scene is thus set for *lex talionis:* not against the now undetectable assailants, but against the whole juvenile criminal classes of New York.

Winner, whose approach is more sensational than Garfield's original novel, aggravates the assault by making it grossly sexual as well as homicidal. More significantly the film transforms Benjamin physically, professionally and morally. As Garfield conceived him he is forty-seven, and an overweight 180 lbs. He is, as we first meet him, a Jewish professional man of modest appearance and knee-jerk liberal sentiments. Winner chose to cast Charles Bronson as this character; Woody Allen would have been more appropriate. (Reading the novel, Bronson's own nomination was Dustin Hoffman.) Bronson had made his mark as a ruthless 'technician' (contract murderer) and 'stone killer' in a series of films where he played hard machismo parts (so successfully that by the early 1970s he was the highest paid film actor in the world). It is hard to see Bronson, with his impassive slavonic face and superb physique, as fitting the original conception. Nor, by any stretch of a somewhat limited technique could Bronson play a mild, urban Jewish intellectual. Consequently Winner reconstructed him. Paul Benjamin becomes the non-semitic architect Paul Kersey (his wife Esther becomes 'Joanna Kersey'). Kersey's background is crudely different from Benjamin's; Winner/Bronson's character is the son of a backwoods 'gunman' (or 'hunter') converted by his pacifist mother from the gun-toting manly paternal code. In Korea, Kersey was — following his mother's Quakerish anxiety — a conscientious objector. Now, his wife and daughter's death bring him back to his father's 'realistic' way of handling life. He rediscovers his 'American' origins with the gun. Garfield is reported to have disliked what Winner did to Benjamin and declared the whole film 'a fairly half-assed job' (Whitney, 1978, p. 185). None the less in *Death Sentence* he gratefully took over the ending of the film, in which Paul moves to Chicago; he also took over — incongruous as it is — the gun-loving paternal heritage.

In adding muscles and masculine style to Benjamin, Winner also subtracted conscience. In the film, revenge is an immediate response, a lashing-out. The greater part of the novel (120 of its 190 pages) is taken up not with violence suffered or violence administered but with the paralysed reaction time between the attack on Benjamin's family and his first vigilante murder. In this long interlude Garfield portrays, with some subtlety, Benjamin's conversion from 'bleeding-heart' values to a 'police mentality'. And it is conversion, not just emotional backlash. Garfield is careful to discriminate Benjamin's thoughtful vigilantism from the automatic conservatism of his older colleagues ('these young scum . . . these radicals . . . honest hardworking citizens like you and me'; *Death Wish*, 1974, p. 74) or the blue-collar, roughneck violence he over-hears in bars: 'I see any black son of a bitch prowling round my place he's gonna get killed first and asked questions later' (*ibid.*, p. 95). It is implied, though not definitely made clear, that the original 'animals' were black. Benjamin's victims are about half and half.

In the novel Benjamin's conversion goes through three stages. First is blind anger: 'they ought to be hunted down like mad dogs and shot on sight' he tells his 'smart-ass' son-in-law who works in legal aid and makes half-hearted attempts to put the 'reasonable' point of view. 'Think of it as a tragic accident' (*ibid.*, p. 43). The second stage of the conversion occurs during a business trip to Tucson, Arizona. In this Goldwater stronghold, which is also cowboy country, (and where Garfield lives), Benjamin is reborn. He loses weight, has a successful encounter with a woman and becomes 'younger' (he and his wife had grown 'strangely old before their time' he notices, *ibid*, p. 53). On his return to New York he begins to plan his campaign with accountant's thoroughness. His *modus operandi* is simple. He goes into danger areas, looks vulnerable, and when the punks accost him, he blasts them with his concealed .32. Sometimes he leaves his car, hides and mows down hub-cap hustlers and auto-strippers. Always he makes sure that he is absolutely secure from witnesses. His precaution fails him only once. In the last scene of the novel Benjamin discovers that a cop has watched him shooting down some youngsters bombing a subway train with lumps of concrete. But the cop ostentatiously turns his back — he has chosen not to see the vigilante, his unofficial partner.

It requires no great insight to see Wild West codes and conventions in *Death Wish*. (Garfield, incidentally, under various pseudonyms wrote some thirty westerns in the ten years before his bestselling vigilante novel — works as unmemorable as *Lynch Law Canyon*, by 'Brian Wynne', or *A Badge for a Badman* by 'Jonas Ward'). New York, with its overworked police and its 'soft' courts easily transposes to the frontier town with the weak sheriff, dependent on the strong citizen who takes things (more particularly, firearms) into his own hands and, by technically breaking the law, establishes justice. But there are also a number of features in *Death Wish* which distinguish it from the stereotype of either the western or the more recent Spillane formula. The first is the curiously joyless, back-street nature of Benjamin's vigilantism. There is, for example, a moment in Spillane's *Kiss Me, Deadly* (1952) when Hammer imagines his prospective criminal victims and observers, with typical lip-smacking relish: 'they'd find out the hunters were being hunted. Just for the fun of it' (*Kiss Me, Deadly*, 1967, p. 62). Benjamin has no fun at all in his hunting; he retains throughout the accountant's punctiliousness as well as his daytime camouflage of mild professional man (when not hunting, Hammer is a drinking and womanizing man of the world). Again, Hammer is usually set up against 'the mob' ('gangs' in westerns). Garfield's world — in *Death Wish* and other novels — is one of atomistic individualism. Crime is not organized. It is random. At most the animals form loose 'packs'. But there is no sense of an alternative society with strict hierarchies such as one finds, for example, in *The Godfather*, that other violent classic of the 1970s. In *Death Wish* there is no mob, no syndicate, no 'Family', no outfit. Nor is there a 'Mr Big' or Godfather for Benjamin to root out, as there always is for Hammer. There are only petty individuals, as independent and solitary in their criminality as Benjamin is in his execution of justice.

But the most striking feature of *Death Wish* and its sequel *Death Sentence* (1976) is the age difference between Benjamin and his victims. Hammer hammers down 'hoods' or 'gorillas' his own age and often bigger in size. In Benjamin's case the target is always a 'kid', or a 'punk'; teenage addicts and hoodlums are his game. In the most unpleasant of his executions Benjamin shoots and lames for life two schoolboys who are molesting a schoolgirl. The nature of the enemy is spelled out most clearly in *Death Sentence*, where Benjamin (now pursuing his vengeful way in Chicago) muses:

The ones who'd attacked Esther and Carol had been young; no one knew exactly how young but they'd been boys, not men. The young ones were the worst: they hadn't learned inhibitions. He'd read somewhere that the chief reformer was age. You rarely found a forty-year-old mugger; as they matured they learned fear (*Death Sentence*, 1977, p. 107).

(The last phrase is significant — not 'ethics' but 'fear'.)

This monotonous paedophobia in *Death Wish* serves to remind us that in the narratives of popular culture there is a constant war between the generations being fought. It is important to note that the animals in *Death Wish* strike Benjamin at that point where every middle-aged man feels weakest — the family whom he has vowed to protect. Can he — in crude zoological terms — protect his herd and his territory against the young bulls constantly prowling around its edges? This fear is articulated more sharply in a novel exactly contemporary with *Death Wish*, *The Shrewsdale Exit*, by John Buell. This novel opens with a middle-aged, middle-class man stopping with his family for a coke in a wayside cafe; a banal, quotidian *mise en scène*, as in *Death Wish*. But the wife and young daughter (the same family dependents as in the other novel) catch the fancy of a trio of motor-cycle crazies, who later ambush the family saloon on a lonely road (the Shrewsdale Exit). The crazies rape and disembowel the women, leaving the man for dead. In fact he recovers, and dedicates the rest of his life to revenge after the young thugs have been acquitted for insufficient evidence. ('They were sweet tail, man,' one taunts the husband, as they leave the court free.) The paperback cover for the Pan *Shrewsdale Exit* conveys the novel's fascination with the violent young: the anarchic lout, with his long greasy hair and aggressive stare, drinking *milk* − enriched milk at that − which dribbles down his chin in a parody of the nursing baby at suck.

The Shrewsdale Exit did not do all that well in Britain, where motor cyclists have always had a rather flabby image. But both Britain and America combined to make Kubrick's *A Clockwork Orange* a box-office smash in 1971 (Burgess's novel was originally published in 1962). In the film, the director stressed teenage Alex's violence against the old and the middle-aged. The first attack is on an ancient tramp; the most violent is the rape and beatings which the droogs inflict on the occupants of 'Home' (the name, emblazoned in neon on the forecourt, is a neat Kubrick invention); and finally Alex kills the cat woman, whom Kubrick converts from Burgess's aged crone to a middle-aged, trendy health fanatic. (In the film Alex batters her to death with a gigantic phallic *objet d'art*.)

Burgess's work is so complex as to defy brief analysis. And Burgess's motivation is, one suspects, deeper felt than Garfield's or Buell's. One of the 'inspirations' for *A Clockwork Orange*, for example, was, apparently, the assault of Burgess's own wife by three GI thugs during the war. Yet, for all this, Burgess does not draw the us/them line as distinctly as the other two; indeed he goes out of his way to blur it. In *A Clockwork Orange*, film and book, the owner of Home is a novelist writing a book called 'Clockwork Orange': the attacker is Alex de Large, whom the newspapers (in Kubrick's version) called 'Alexander Burgess'. In the first version of the novel (changed in later editions) Alex himself is seen as becoming middle aged, in an epilogue to the narrative — entering into the class and age group he earlier persecuted. Victim and victimizer, attacker and prey, novelist and hero are thus all run together provocatively in Burgess's fictional game.

Anthony Burgess/Stanley Kubrick remind us that the death wish of Garfield's novel is literally that. For if society can find no way of living with the young, it is doomed. And yet the conflict is fought over and again in mass-market narratives. And the printed novel (unlike the prime-time TV serial where heroes are young and villains old) is a main channel for transmitting the universal fear of the middle aged that the young are inevitably going to take over the world by violence.

The image of the teenage crazy is a variable thing and has changed over the years — especially during the great youth resurgence of the 1960s. (In *Bomb Culture*, Jeff Nuttall dates 1968 quite precisely as the year when open war was declared between the young and the old.) For the Pan blurb writers of 1962, Alex and his gang were 'juvenile delinquents', 'cosh kids', 'teddy boys' and returned National Service thugs (the cover illustration shows them as mid-twentyish). By the time Kubrick turned the novel into what Burgess called 'Clockwork Marmalade' the droogs were properly young, freaked out on hallucinogens and stereo music, outrageously psychedelic in their fashions. (There is nothing in the novel to suggest McDowell's sinisterly made-up eyes.) In *Death Wish* the punks are drawn from the local street crime and ghetto world of New York City. Garfield's vision, incidentally, is drabber and more fiftyish than that of a film success of the late 1970s, *The Warriors*, which shows New York juvenile criminals as a rich, exotic subculture among the ruins of Coney Island. This is a distortion of what Sol Yurick had presented in his novel, which, like *A Clockwork Orange*, was first issued in the 1960s. Yurick's novel presents a more conventional picture of street-gang culture, with none of the Woodstock exoticism.

More recent novels have drawn on the folk demonology of the Baader Meinhof terrorist (e.g. Herbert Kastle's *The*

Gang) and the specifically British teenage football-fan armies
(e.g. *Albion, Albion* by Dick Morland; 'makes *Clockwork
Orange* seem a gentle fantasy,' observed *Time Out*).

The appeal of *Death Wish* is not merely its retributive
fantasy of counterattack in the grim war of the generations.
Garfield's novels (*Death Wish* and *Death Sentence*) and
Winner's film celebrate the release of the individual from the
complex tensions of modern city life and 'responsible'
adulthood. Benjamin has an emancipated area of his life,
a free-fire zone unknown to his office colleagues, where his
will is absolute; where he can do what he feels to be right
without interference from authority, or the dictatorship of
'civilized values'. The liberal's well-meaning paralysis is
periodically relaxed by the satisfactions of the cold-blooded
executioner. It is, as Garfield presents it, highly therapeutic.
Benjamin develops a 'positive' attitude to his daytime work
and his new zest for accountancy earns him a long-desired
partnership in the firm. His is a Jekyll and Hyde split personality that works, a functional schizophrenia. Paradoxically,
by meeting the young on their own terms ('the only match
for a gun was a gun of your own') Benjamin himself is
rejuvenated. There is clearly some symbolism in the name,
with its connotation of 'the youngest'. The most potent
appeal of *Death Wish* does not lie in its superficially crude
code of vengeful violence, but in the suggestion (which was
also being made by the 'Playboy philosophy' of the period)
that one could profitably absorb into one's middle-aged
existence elements of youth's 'swinging' irresponsibility.

Chapter Fifteen

The 'new western' and the middle-aged reader

The 1970s saw a boom in many genres: women's romance, sf and the western particularly. The new western which emerged in this period was more violent and sexually explicit ('adult') than the old J.T. Edson or Louis l'Amour norm. It was, for example, portentous when *Playboy* moved into the field with a series of team-written new westerns. In these novels the sado-sexuality, previously latent in the genre, is rendered grossly manifest. And typically these westerns were spawned out as a series around a cowboy who could be labelled 'a new kind of western hero'. Among the more successful of these low-grade 'savage' sagas was John G. McLaglen's 'Herne the Hunter' — 'A violent man in a violent land.'

The series begins with Herne, a gunfighter in the big league (he has ridden with Quantrill, hung out with Earp, walked tall with Doc Holliday etc.) retiring into domesticity and hanging up his guns, never to pull leather again. After only a couple of years of marriage, however, he returns home to find that a gang of seven assorted drunks (they include a senator's son, a pair of psychopathic twins, a gambler and various riff-raff) have raped his wife Louise: 'every orifice of her body was running over with their lust' (*Shadow of the Vulture*, 1977, p. 7). She hangs herself, and Herne sets out on his vengeance trail.

To make such a comeback from domestic life is — clearly — the dream of the middle-aged married man. This compensatory aspect of Herne is emphasized by the fact that he is 'old — old for a gunslinger' (*ibid.*, p. 22).

The early narratives, especially, are punctuated by ritualistic encounters with 'kids', 'punk kids with their diapers still wet' who taunt Herne as 'old man' or 'white-haired'. Thus in Herne 2 a rash youth faces up to the veteran gunslinger with ritual insults as to his senility:

I reckon you only wear that Colt of yours to keep you balanced aright. Take it off and you'd fall to your knees like the dribbling old fool you are! You couldn't outdraw nobody any more (*River of Blood*, 1976, p. 61).

Like all the other kids who tangle with Herne he learns his mistake. As they expire these upstarts typically improve their manners: 'Help me, Mister,' they will plead, suddenly and properly deferential at the point of death. (Herne is always laconic at such moments, though sometimes he has a wistful little think about what he would have been like at their age.)

The white-haired Herne takes what few partners he has from his own age group; the only exception as regards the younger generation is his ward, Becky. She has survived the same gang of rapists as violated Herne's wife; now she is orphaned, and Herne takes charge of her education. First he sends her to a local western boarding school; this doesn't work out since the headmistress is a rabid flagellant. Herne drops by unexpectedly to find Becky tied to the bed with weals over her buttocks. The headmistress is reaching her climax by biting her pupil (her false teeth have usefully 'sharpened edges') when buckskin nemesis breaks down her dormitory door:

The full force of his fist landed on her nose with a crunch that sounded like a man stamping on the shell of a crab.
The fist moved back, returned: this time it was a man walking on egg shells' (*ibid.*, p. 28).

Becky is eventually sent off to the safety of an English boarding school, but not before she has a number of adventures in which her fifteen-year-old virtue is put at risk. Sometimes she falls in love with the punks who cross Herne's path. They are always killed. As he stands over them, bleeding in the dust, Herne is not immune to a touch of impersonal pity as he delivers the *coup de grâce*:

'Mister. I'm only twenty one.' [Like all punks he dies polite.]
He looked younger, vulnerable, and in pain.
Jed carefully took aim with the Colt and shot him

between the eyes, watching the blood-rose flower in the centre of the boy's forehead. The body twitched once and then lay quite still in the snow (*The Black Widow*, 1977, p. 65).

This forty-year-old, grey-haired revenger, utterly punitive to young men who dispute his masculine prerogatives, utterly protective to pubescent girls (Herne is rarely sexually aroused by Becky, though the whole of the rest of red-blooded Western male and pervert female society seems to froth at the sight of her), is clearly a projected image of the father. Similarly, in his return from marriage to the pursuits of his youth (gunslinging) Herne is a projection of parental frustration.

In the early novels Herne has little to do with women. Those that do appear are whores, saloon proprietoresses or monsters. The voluptuous mother in *The Black Widow* ('Herne 3'), for instance, raises her twin sons to be one a sadist, the other a masochist, both bisexual and heroin addicts (this addiction is arranged by mother so she can have her incestuous pleasure of them). Herne shoots all three together, economically taking the mother and the masochistic son with one carefully placed .45 slug that penetrates the 'soft part' of the maternal abdomen through to the 'belly' of the boy hiding behind his mother's skirts. (This kind of virtuosic 'gut wound' – often in the genitals – is something Herne specializes in).

Women do figure centrally in 'Herne 4', *Shadow of the Vulture*. By this time Herne has run out of victims from the original gang of seven. To support Becky's new style of life he turns bounty hunter. One of his first commissions is to rescue a rancher's wife from the Apaches who have abducted her ('Herne 5', *Apache Squaw*). In this novel the psychic revenge visited on the wife figure is pathologically intense and protracted. The rancher husband is, in the first instance, fiercely possessive of his young wife, and only lets her out on a supervised ride, once a week. In the Apache camp, however, she is raped by the whole warparty:

after seven of them had spent their lust in her, the woman had begun to roll and kick and cry out. At first in anger. But she had cried out and the Mescalero men had laughed for they knew that it was no longer anger, but a need to be taken and taken brutally and often (*Apache Squaw*, 1977, pp. 67-8).

Herne rescues her from the stronghold, single-handedly killing five squaws, one baby and innumerable braves in the process. In gratitude she gives herself to him. On the way home, they are captured, yet again, by an outlaw Mexican band. They follow the Indian example with Emmie Lou (she is, the narrative observes, looking ten years older and somewhat bruised around the thighs by this stage). One of her ears is casually removed, for ransom purposes. After a while Herne contrives to massacre the Mexicans as thoroughly as the Apaches. At last Emmie Lou is returned home to her pathologically jealous husband. As he rides off, Herne hears 'the rattling of chains and a scream'.

In the Herne series (and many like it), a clear set of middle-aged, married male fantasies are played out. Women are evil; they exist either as predators (*The Black Widow*) or as receptacles to be punitively raped when they are not properly locked up. Young men are rivals; they have to be exterminated after having had a salutary lesson in manners. In his mature masculine power Herne is lonely, a wanderer who is fated never to settle down to family domesticity but who must go through life, a boy eternal. In 'Herne 7' the hero is in some danger of succumbing to the now nubile Becky, 'just at that age that Louise had been when she had married the infamous Herne the Hunter' (*Death Rites*, 1978, p. 10). But to prevent this Becky is carried off by tuberculosis. The novel ends at the series' starting point: 'Jed Herne rode on. Alone.'

Chapter Sixteen

Images of war I: secret histories

The secret history of the Second World War

War is subjected to innumerable falsifications in popular fiction. Arguably the truest reflection comes in that depressed, post-bellum trough a few years after victory: the period that in America produced such bestsellers of the late 1940s and early 1950s as *The Naked and the Dead*, *The Young Lions*, *The Caine Mutiny* and in Britain *The Cruel Sea*. Naturalistic treatments of war (which is essentially what the foregoing are) represent an interlude, or hangover phase, between the headlines of wartime propaganda and peacetime's mythic, reductive, romantic, wish-fulfilling and fantastic treatments. At all periods, however, war is a popular subject. Any decent-sized W.H. Smith's will have a whole section devoted to 'war' and various kinds of war novel in it. (The largest European invasion of British bestseller racks has taken place in this genre, with the works of H.H. Kirst and Sven Hassell.) From the currently fashionable formulas of 1970s war fiction I have taken two. The first is 'the secret history of the Second World War', the second 'fantasies of Nazism resurgent'. Both formulas are heavily imbued with a paranoid suspicion that the *real* course of events and state of things are very different from what the authorities and their 'official' histories would have us believe.

A multitude of bestsellers and would-be bestsellers of the 1970s have alleged to give us a rewritten and absolutely authentic history of the 1939-45 hostilities. They disclose hitherto 'best-kept secrets of the war'. Beneath the frustratingly slow mass-movements of 'open' history there is opened up an 'action-packed' narrative. In the secret history,

alarmingly close calls for the forces of international order
and decency are revealed — near disasters which were only
just averted by acts of undercover individual heroism and
desperate remedies. The style of this kind of secret history
and the claims it makes are evident from the back blurb to
the American paperback of the superseller in the genre,
Jack Higgins's *The Eagle Has Landed*. (Higgins, of course, is
a British writer: one of the interesting features of the secret
history is that it is an area where British writers — often
originally little thought of in their home market — have made
it very big in America and become international bestsellers.
Higgins, Frederick Nolan and Ken Follett are the most
famous examples.)

> At precisely one o'clock on the morning of Saturday,
> November 6, 1943, Heinrich Himmler, Reichsführer of the
> SS and Chief of State Police, received a simple message:
> 'The Eagle has landed.' It meant that a small force of
> German paratroopers were at that moment safely in
> England and poised to snatch the British Prime Minister,
> Winston Churchill, from the Norfolk country house where
> he was spending a quiet weekend near the sea. This book is
> an attempt to re-create the events surrounding that
> astonishing exploit. At least fifty percent of it is
> documented historical fact. The reader must decide for
> himself how much of the rest is a matter of speculation, or
> fiction.

Some other representatives of this bestselling genre can also
usefully be described from their advertising copy and display
material. Owen Sela's *An Exchange of Eagles* (clearly echoing
Higgins's *Eagle* and his follow-up *The Valhalla Exchange*),
gives us a double assassination plot, directed towards Roosevelt
and Hitler:

> The time is 1940, just before America's entry into World
> War II. Two secret intelligence agents — one Nazi, one
> American — join in an underground plot to prevent their
> governments from forging the ultimate weapon. Their plan
> involves incredible risks — and a terrifying exchange that
> holds the fate of the Western world in precarious balance.

The notion of 'the precarious balance' of world history is of
course crucial to this kind of chronicle. One assassination can

wholly alter its direction.

In James Barwick's *Shadow of the Wolf*, it is Roosevelt and Churchill who commit the act of clandestine assassination (such turnabouts, all based on 'known facts', are routine in secret histories):

On the evening of May 10, 1941, just seven months before the fatal attack on Pearl Harbor, the second most powerful man in Hitler's Germany, Deputy Führer Rudolph Hess, parachuted from a two-seater Messerschmitt 110 over Scotland. When captured, his ankle broken, his identity unknown, he first gave his name as Alfred Horn.

History has it that Hess came to arrange a separate peace with Britain. Locked away since that day and later sentenced to life imprisonment at Nuremberg, Hess, now considered insane, remains the lone occupant of Spandau Castle Prison.

What awful secret was locked away with Hess? Why will neither Britain nor the USSR nor the United States implement his release after almost 40 years?

And was there a second man with Hess in the two-seater Messerschmitt? Was he the real Captain Alfred Horn and did he escape Hess's captors and reach the United States to carry on the true purpose of the Hess mission?

Did in fact, Horn secretly bring to a famous former U.S. ambassador to Great Britain — and through him to the President of the United States — not only a 'perfect peace plan' but the foreknowledge that the Japanese would strike at Pearl Harbor — if the U.S. did not heed the Hess warnings?

Did both Horn and Hess then become, ironically, the victims — of Churchill and FDR as well as Hitler?

Another and more vigorous Hess is given us in J.S. Thayer's *The Hess Cross*. In this novel Hess is not the pathetic lunatic of history but a 'plant', no less than 'the deadliest double-agent of the war', whose mission is to set up the kidnap of Enrico Fermi by German commandos. The 'father of the Atom Bomb', once abducted from America, 'will deliver the whole world to Nazi domination'.

Duncan Kyle's *Black Camelot* offers yet another secret drama of world-shattering consequence (the 'raid' idea clearly

derives from Alastair MacLean's *Where Eagles Dare* and the
ubiquitously influential *The Eagle Has Landed*):
> A secret raid on Himmler's Arthurian fortress in the heart
> of Nazi Germany is the climax to a fast action packed
> story which moves from Berlin to Stockholm and Dublin.
> Duncan Kyle's tense and exciting thriller is fiction — but
> its settings are meticulously researched and authentic. How
> much, then, is true? Says the author, 'All of the
> background. And much more of the foreground than you
> may think.'

In Clive Egleton's *The October Plot* an attempt to murder
Bormann (Operation Leopard) is the history-changing exploit.
If successful it will bring the war to an end a year early. In
The Valkyrie Encounter (*Eagles* again), Stephen Marlowe
gives us the secret history of the 1944 bomb plot on Hitler.
As is always the case with this kind of novel, the 'truth' is
supposed to be infinitely more complicated than the given
historical account. It would seem that in 1944 the von
Stauffenberg assassination plans were well known to all
interested parties. The Gestapo wanted them to go ahead,
Goebbels wanted them foiled. The allies and Russians,
independently, wanted the plot *nearly* to succeed (to flush
out the subversives): to this end they sent in secret agents
to nurse the coup to the point of failing. 'Hanging in the
balance', as the cover puts it, 'is the death of Hitler, the end
of World War II.'

Garfield's *The Romanov Succession* has much the same
plot, but with a different target:
> 1941 — Stalin's pact with Hitler has crumbled. Soviet
> Russia reels under the shock of the mighty war machine
> that has already crushed Europe. In a Barcelona villa, a
> small group of Russian exiles conceive a plan to save
> Mother Russia from the German invader and the Bolshevik
> tyrant . . . the assassination of Joseph Stalin and a daring
> coup to restore the Romanovs to the Kremlin.

In Frederick Nolan's *Brass Target*, the victim is different
again. Eisenhower, it is suggested, had Patten liquidated
because of old Iron Guts's anti-Soviet intransigence. There is
also a fortune in Nazi gold (a common motif) involved in this
'most audacious conspiracy of World War II'. A full house of

assassinations is posited in William Copeland's *Five Hours From Isfahan*. At the 1943 Teheran conference Churchill, Stalin and Roosevelt are all three to be killed by German commandoes on a raid 'that could change the course of history'.

One assumes that it was the superseller success of *The Day of The Jackal* and *The Eagle Has Landed* which inspired the large number of assassination scenarios one discovers in this kind of novel. Necessarily they are usually just foiled (Patten's death is an exception — Nolan goes to extraordinary lengths to devise a plausible murder out of what was, ostensibly, a road accident). In *The Rommel Plot* by John Tarrant, the English intelligence invent 'Foxhound' — a plan to assassinate Rommel. Then they discover the existence of 'Valkyrie' — the German plan to assassinate Hitler. In this circumstance it becomes necessary to abort the Rommel plot, so as to leave him as a 'reasonable' leader after the Führer's death. They are thus obliged to hunt down and assassinate their own killer. In Robert Vacha's *The Black Orchestra*, the English intelligence service again infiltrate the generals' conspiracy ('Craig an agent fluent in German . . .' they always are). Assassination figures in a rather more diffused way in Craig Thomas's *Wolfsbane*, in which Allied death-squads are directed to eliminate communist Free French, just before the liberation, so as to forestall a Red putsch.

A somewhat more straightforward 'best-kept secret of the war' is J.D. Gilman and John Clive's *KG 200*:

They flew Flying Fortresses. They wore American
uniforms . . . but they were Germans! KG 200 — the
phantom arm of Hitler's Luftwaffe. From a secret base in
occupied Norway, these crack pilots plan their ultimate
mission, the raid that would bring allied defeat crashing
down from the exploding skies. Inspired by the best-kept
secret of World War II, this is one of the most enthralling
novels of air warfare, espionage and manhunt ever written.

Patterson (a.k.a. Higgins) employs a similar element of masquerade in *The Valhalla Exchange*. The 'desperate last throw' gimmick also figures. To prepare his escape from the Berlin bunker, Bormann has a perfect replica made of himself called 'Strasser'. One of these lookalikes is then murdered.

Strasser/Bormann moves to the next stage of the escape plan, which is to hijack a group of VIP allied prisoners with which to negotiate terms. He is frustrated and bolts to South America. But which one — Strasser or Bormann — survived?

Patterson, following on the Churchill kidnap or assassination plot of *Eagle*, brought out *To Catch a King* in 1979. As the American advertisements put it (like Follett, incidentally, Patterson is routinely published first in the US): '*To Catch a King* by Harry Patterson is one of the most exciting unknown histories of the Second World War, based on documented historical fact.' Essentially, the novel deals with Hitler's plan to kidnap the Duke of Windsor, and persuade him to figurehead a Nazi takeover of the British Empire.

In the late 1970s Patterson/Higgins was obliged to cede his place in this genre to Ken Follett, a young English writer of no previous great distinction, who did very well in America with his *Eye of the Needle* (*Storm Island* in the UK). This tells of a top German spy ('the Needle' — so named after his penchant for the stiletto as a killing weapon). As the blurb puts it: 'His code name was The Needle. He was a tall, handsome German aristocrat of extraordinary intelligence — England's most dangerous enemy. He knew the secret that could win the war for Hitler.' The secret, of course, is Overlord. In the *de rigueur* 'Is it fact or fiction?' preface, Follett candidly admits that there were, in historical fact, very few German spies in Britain in 1944:

But it only needs one. . . . It is known that the Germans saw the signs they were meant to see in East Anglia. It is also known that they suspected a trick, and that they tried very hard to discover the truth. That much is history. What follows is fiction. Still and all, one suspects something like this must have happened.

II

According to J.M.S. Tompkins, in her *The Popular Novel in England, 1770-1800*, the 'secret history' style of fiction was stale even in the eighteenth century. Its revival in the 1970s and its association with the Second World War has two main sources of inspiration. The first is ineradicable popular belief that the *real* facts of history are never given. The public is always duped by a cover-up. 'They' have not told you the truth — 'they' dare not. Thus the publishers of *Brass Target* present it as 'A shocking thriller that goes beyond what you've been told . . . 250 million dollars says it [i.e. Patten's death] was no accident.'

The other source — and one which explains the mid-1970s timing of the fashion — is the historical threshold of thirty years. It is after this period that government papers normally become declassified. In the mid-1970s official historical graves began to give up their secrets. *The Eagle Has Landed* begins with a prologue emblematic of this, as the narrator physically turns up a gravestone to discover the hidden resting place of the German commando squad. 'Secret histories' like *The Eagle Has Landed* are the fictional shadow of the relaxation on official records which produced such factual bestsellers as *The Secret War*, *The Most Secret War*, *Ultra Goes to War*, *The Murder of Rudolf Hess* and *Victims of Yalta*. (It should be noted that the factual accounts often sadly deflate the fictional. Simultaneous with Follett's *Eye of the Needle* in 1978 came David Kahn's *Hitler's Spies: German Military Intelligence in World War II*: based on newly released papers, Kahn's study concluded that 'German intelligence was a colossal flop'.) Perhaps because they have tumbled out so quickly after each other, secret histories of the Second World War are a highly formulaic and stylized form of fiction, which can often be reduced to a set of fixed elements of historical world view, narrative device and technique. Most, for example, conform to the following four categories:

1 The critical moment
The first and most important historical tenet of this kind of novel is that there are supremely critical moments in world history. At such moments one decisive act (usually assassination, but also an air-raid, or the introduction of a new weapon, a double cross or a crucial piece of intelligence) can change everything. The security of the western world and its future hang in the balance at such junctures. Typically, the way in which things will turn out depends on the weak link

of a single life (Hitler's, Churchill's, Stalin's, the Needle's etc.). Often too, a single act of heroism is critical; or, as the blurb of *The Strasbourg Legacy* puts it, 'only one man can stop them' ('them' are 'the Brotherhood' — a resurgent Nazi secret society). In *Eye of the Needle* everything depends on the girl who is harbouring the Needle: 'She was Lucy Rose, a beautiful young Englishwoman torn between her burning desire and her binding duty. She was the only one who could stop him.' And he of course, is the only one who can win the war for Hitler.

History, as those novels conceive it, is a thing of drastic possibilities, and hairbreadth chances. There is no 'inexorability', no 'forces', no 'weight of history'. Everything, in the final analysis, is a matter of risky, personal interventions at the right moment. One man with one bullet can rewrite history. Another man with a gun can prevent him doing so. A woman using her body as a weapon can rewrite history a third way. In line with this conviction, the real, secret course of history is represented as devious and intricate — a matter of plots, ruses, intrigue and doublecross. A typical doublecross plus the 'single crucial life' and 'single critical moment' scenario is John Kerrigan's *The Phoenix Assault*:

Trapped in the bunker a Nazi leader is in touch with the Russians. For the Allies the unthinkable was about to happen; a plot that would create a new and infinitely evil regime to rise from the ashes of Hitler's Germany. Three men — two Britains and an American — set off on a desperate mission behind enemy lines. Their task: the assassination of one of the most closely guarded men in Germany.

2 Human motives

It is part of the folkloric wisdom of the bestseller, part of its 'revelation', that the *real* reason for fighting wars is spoils. At the centre of the conflict is not ideology or morality, but loot, gold, booty. In *Brass Target*, for instance, it is not merely the averting of the Third World War and the holding back of communism which precipitates Patton's assassination, but $250 m. in gold. The Nazis are commonly seen not just as absolutely evil and fascistic — but immensely rich. The plundered Nazi war treasure is the main object of desire in Nolan's other (and far superior) novel, *The Mittenwald Syndicate*, and in William Goldman's *Marathon Man*. In Madelaine Duke's *The Bormann Receipt*, the disappeared Nazi mastercriminal is connected with the confiscated and still unrecovered art treasure of European Jewry. The same idea is picked up in Jack H. Crisp's *Dragon Spoor*:

A seemingly inconsequential murder in Marseilles reveals a secret arrangement reaching back to war-ravaged Berlin and leading to only one conclusion; priceless Nazi art treasures were not destroyed in a desperate Allied recovery attempt and somewhere some organization waits with this staggering wealth.

Robert Ludlum's sequence of bestsellers insist that the underlying *casi belli* of the Second World War were economic. Big business and private fortunes were what the fighting was *really* about.

This concern with financial motives seems to arise from a simplifying aspect of the secret histories' world view. Human behaviour is comprehensible only in appetitive, non-ideological terms. That men fight wars because they are greedy is easier to take on than that they should fight them in furtherance of political aims.

Not everyone in these secret histories is driven by gold fever. There are psychopaths (Himmler is a favourite), and the heroes are, typically, motivated by personal, supra-national codes of honour and ascetic manliness. But the general tendency with these types, as with the gold hunters, is to reduce the motives of the actors in the secret history to comprehensible, apolitical, human forms.

3 Pseudo authenticity

The main narrative device of these novels is that of pseudo authenticity. Secret histories go to extraordinary lengths to tantalize the reader on the matter of their factuality. The advertising men strain every resource to ensure that we shall be left in two minds. 'The reader,' we are told of *Exchange of Eagles*, 'is left with a lurking suspicion that this incredible story might have a grain of truth after all.' Higgins puts it more riddlingly in his preface to *The Valhalla Exchange*:

'only the more astonishing parts are true'. Of course, no sane man would write history in the form of a popular novel, nor would any sane man expect to find sound history there. So the 'historical hypothesis' line (it may well have happened) is frequently put forward; thus *The Valkyrie Encounter* rehearses the main events of the July 1944 assassination plot and concludes:

> The attempt to assassinate Hitler was the culmination of a carefully planned conspiracy. . . . Whatever responses these efforts drew from Washington, London and Moscow remain to this day shrouded in secrecy. The relevant archives remain sealed. The narrative that follows, although a work of fiction, attempts to reconstruct these events.

The most laborious attempt to authenticate a secret history was Frederick Nolan's bringing Patten's jeep driver with him on the promotional tour for *Brass Target*. (The ex-GI resolutely disbelieved the novel's assassination hypothesis, by the way.) Brian Garfield's attempt to create a similar 'real' revelation on the same lines in 1980 was a notable flop:

> Just once in a lifetime, a novelist finds a story so incredible and so explosive that it can only be told as fiction. . . . *The Paladin* is the incredible story of a fifteen-year-old schoolboy, employed directly by Winston Churchill, who before he was twenty became one of the most valuable — and ruthless — British agents of World War II. It began in the Spring of 1940 as an adventure and it ended on D-Day with the most extraordinary and agonising double-twist which was to save thousands of Allied lives. 'The hero of this story is a real person. He is now in his fifties and his name is not Christopher Creighton,' writes Brian Garfield in the foreword to his remarkable novel.

4   Technicality

Stylistically, these novels affect a technically encrusted manner of narration, with a surplus of authenticating technical detail, especially on such things as guns, aircraft and intelligence apparatus. A plane is never simply a plane, but 'a tri-motor JU 52, powered by three understrength 1,250 hp Jumo engines, known affectionately to the "Schutz" on the ground as the three-nippled-sow . . .' etc. Towards the same effect of inwardness with things military, there are glossaries of technical terms, weaponry, German acronyms etc. The layout of these novels is frequently segmental, abrupt; the aim, apparently, is to create a superficial resemblance to documentary or military-report layout.

The secret history of the peace

The fictions of secret world-war history transpose quite easily to the postwar period. Novelists like Frederick Forsyth have a strong line in contemporary secret histories. In their world view the balance is just as precarious, and only a vast and continuous cover-up blinds us to the near-misses, flash points and hairbreadth escapes of the last decade. *The Day of the Jackal* is a famous and typical example. If the bullet had hit de Gaulle, it would not have meant quicker promotion for Pompidou, but fascist takeover in France and the end of western civilization as we know it.

A representative and rather good example of the postwar secret history is Harold King's *Four Days*. Set in March 1953, this novel plausibly chronicles near world war, brought about by Stalin's death, a bombing exercise gone wrong and a series of 'human errors' (the recurrent nightmare of 'fail-safe' narratives, very popular in the 1950s and early 1960s). Forsyth takes King's approach a logical step further in his latest novel, *The Devil's Alternative*. In this 'future history' a combination of the hijack of a super-supertanker, grain harvest failure in the USSR and political assassination bring the world to the brink of the unthinkable thermonuclear war.

The revelation of the CIA's covert operations in the 1970s Senate hearings inspired a spate of novels dealing with the agency's secret manipulation of world events — works such as Lawrence Sanders's *The Tangent Factor* and its 'Tangent' sequels (Sanders is a great sequelizer) in which African politics are shown to be masterminded from Washington. And there continue to be works like Gerald Browne's *Green Ice* in which the *real* power in the postwar world is conceived as 'the Concern' (i.e. an emerald and precious gem consortium) which can dictate to any government anywhere.

Arguably its most wide-awake practitioners discerned that the 'secret history of the Second World War' gimmick had exhausted its bestselling potential by the end of the decade. In his 1979 work *Triple*, Follett followed Forsyth into what the publicists call 'new history in the making':

> The smash bestseller, *Eye of the Needle*, was hailed as 'the World War II thriller that makes history'. TRIPLE, the new novel by its author, exposes history — specifically, the most audacious and mystifying intelligence coup of modern times, acknowledged to have a basis in fact, involving a lone Israeli agent, up against the Russian KGB and its extremist PLO 'allies', all gambling on one world-threatening power play that could literally determine the survival or death of the state of Israel — and probably did. TRIPLE is loaded with the same high-caliber suspense and excitement of new history in the making.

Triple duly made the #1 spot in the US (as did *The Devil's Alternative* in the UK).

Chapter Seventeen

Images of war II: the nightmare that wouldn't die

'They say I'm dead — Shot in a cafe in Asuncion. Lured into Brazil and mown down by an Israeli assassination team. . . . Let them come, I say. Let them come if they've stomach enough. I'll bury them all.'
(The 'Dark Angel of Auschwitz' — i.e. someone like Mengele, whom the author can't name — Herbert Lieberman, *The Climate of Hell*)

I

According to Hannah Arendt, contemplating the trial of Eichmann, Nazi evil is essentially banal, 'uninteresting'. According to the bestselling novel of the 1970s it is immensely glamorous, inexhaustibly interesting. Fiction, usually packaged in shiny SS black with prominent Nazi insignia, expresses a romantic fascination with the evil of the Third Reich. It also expresses a belief that Nazism, despite the victory of 1945, is ineradicable — a serpent's egg. Time and again these novels assert that the Nazi bacillus can never be exterminated, that it will return victorious and erect a Fourth Reich. The belief is evidently paranoid. Robert Ludlum, whose bestselling string of novels constantly deal with the installation of the next Reich and the evils of the last, declares himself frankly pathological on the subject of Nazis:

I believe the world is going infinitely beyond conservatism and communism to fascism — it's the child of the Nazi. In my own modest way I'd like to proclaim it to the whole goddam world. . . . I'm paranoid. I hope it doesn't interfere with my stories (*Publishers Weekly*, 21 February, 1977).

Far from it. Ludlum's fiction like that of William Goldman (*Marathon Man*), Ira Levin (*The Boys From Brazil*) and Forsyth (*The Odessa File*), revels in the paranoid's capacity for wild inventiveness, the discovery of plots and conspiracies in the face of all the historical evidence. *The Boys From Brazil*, for example, has a wonderfully extravagant conspiracy plot. Conspiracy is the mainspring of all Levin's fiction. In the best known of his works the devil, through a diabolist sect, fathers a child on the world via unsuspecting Rosemary. In *The Stepford Wives* husbands conspire to convert their wives into robots. In *The Boys From Brazil* the Angel of Death (Mengele – a favourite villain) conspires to resurrect not one, but close on 100 cloned Hitlers. Cuckoo-egg Führers are adopted out on to unsuspecting parents and childhood circumstances just like little Adolf's are arranged. (This, for instance, involves the assassination of ninety-four drunken fathers at the appropriate idiogenetic moment.) The plot is uncovered single-handedly by a Simon Wiesenthal figure (Wiesenthal, with his 'Vienna Documentation Centre' appears directly, or in thin disguise, in many of these fantasies). The novel ends with the list of the Hitler clones and their hosts discovered. But rather than give the names to the Israeli secret service, Liebermann destroys the record. The Manichaean game must be played out. The Hitler seed must again be scattered through the world. *The Boys From Brazil* finishes with a shot of one of the embryonic Hitlers drawing a stadium (he has inherited his genetic father's love of banal neo-classical architecture with the dictatorial megalomania):

> Who would he be, this man on the platform? Someone great, that's for sure, with all these people coming to see him. Not just a singer or comedian; someone fantastic, a *really good person* that they loved and respected. They paid fortunes to get in, and if they couldn't pay, he let them in free. Someone that nice. . . .
>
> He put a little television camera up at the top of the dome; aimed a few more spotlights at the man.
>
> He thinned the brush to a real fine point and gave little dot-mouths to the nearer bigger people, so they were cheering, telling him – the man, that is – how good he was, how much they loved him.

He bent his sharp nose closer to the paper and gave dot-mouths to the smaller people. His forelock fell. He bit his lip, squinted his pale-blue eyes. Dot, dot, dot.

He could hear the people cheering, roaring; a beautiful growing love-thunder that built and built, and then pounded, pounded, pounded, pounded.

Sort of like in those old Hitler movies. (*The Boys From Brazil*, 1977, pp. 237-38).

For most of its course, Levin's book is a clever exercise in reader-hoaxing. The mystery as to why a random selection of men are being simultaneously murdered around the world is sustained until well into the narrative. The truth of the Nazi comeback plot is revealed as an effective *coup de théâtre*. A less effective string of novels on Levin's pattern have followed up the best selling success of *The Boys From Brazil* (many inspired, as Levin seems to have been, by a prurient interest in SS eugenic experiments). In *Golden Girl*, the athlete heroine is 'a bright, beautiful manufactured monster, bred from Nazi stud-farm stock'. Her victories at Moscow will re-establish Aryan racial superiority. The link between the Moscow Olympics and Nazi Germany is similarly exploited in James Patterson's *The Jericho Commandment* (the fact that 1980 was the first setting of the games in a totalitarian state since 1936 clearly occurred to several novelists): 'A ghastly secret, born in the extermination camps of Nazi Germany . . . a mysterious need for vengeance . . . a horrifying ultimatum delivered at the 1980 Moscow Olympics.' *Spawn*, by Robert Holles, again takes the 'Nazi stud farm' idea (and treats it rather better than Lear did in *Golden Girl*):

Blue-eyed, blonde, and desperately anxious to have a child, Marianne has been impregnated at a fertility clinic with what she thinks is her lover's sperm. In reality, Nazi agents have substituted the semen from the contents of a hermetically-sealed canister over 30 years old. Unwittingly and unwillingly, Marianne's body has become an incubator for the Fourth Reich.

As well as cloned and implanted offspring, Hitler is fantasized in these novels as having natural and adoptive children. In Gus Weill's *The Führer Seed*:

Candidate for mayor of West Berlin, *protégé* of the aging

Chancellor, young Kurt Hauser looks like Germany's man of destiny. Then an astonishing revelation — verified in South America by Martin Bormann himself — shows Kurt and a stunned world just what that destiny is.

Kurt Hauser is really *Kurt Hitler*, the son of Adolph Hitler and Eva Braun . . . and he decides to risk all in the kind of deadly gamble his father took. With an inevitability that recalls the grim events of the 1930s, the name of Hitler begins its second incredible rise to power.

John Gardner's *The Werewolf Trace* ('stunning story of a nightmare that would never die') conceives a more apostolic relation between the old and new Hitler:

In the closing hours of the Third Reich Adolf Hitler emerged from his bunker and singled out for decoration one of the uniformed boys who were the last defenders of Berlin. . . . In 1977 Hitler's 'last hope' is a respectable British businessman, suspected by British Intelligence of being the key to the Nazi revival. But the man code-named 'Werewolf' is haunted by his past. And by something far more terrifying. . . . Was a boy smuggled out of the Führer's bunker? What did he grow into? What kind of political threat does he pose?

All these novels take as their *donnée* the idea that Nazism is waiting to hatch again; that the fight against it is never-ending. Typically, it is assumed that Nazism can survive its democratic opponent. This is expressed in a nice twist to the end of *The Valhalla Exchange* when Bormann — or possibly his *doppelgänger* — lives to send a flower 'as promised' to the funeral of the Wiesenthal-like American Nazi-hunter who has been tracking him down, and has died in a mysterious plane explosion. In *The Strasbourg Legacy*, while Nato has a 'top level conference' its great opposite 'the Brotherhood' confer with 'their hideous plans of a fourth Reich about to become reality'. Ben Stein's *The Croesus Conspiracy* has a reverse 'Protocols of Zionism' plot:

In the dying moments of Hitler's Reich, a sinister conspiracy is hatched and begins its relentless drive towards global domination. . . . As elections near, a vast network of hidden neo-Nazis tightens its grip on an unsuspecting America.

In *The Odessa File*, without the mass of the similarly unsuspecting West German population having the slightest inkling, the remnant of the SS has assumed sufficient power to start the Third World War (by means of rockets, equipped with bubonic plague bacillus and nuclear waste, launched against Israel). It typically requires only the slightest stimulus to galvanize the still existing frame of Nazism back to violent life. Thus in George Markstein's *The Goering Testament*:

What would happen if the last words of Nazi Hermann Goering, written before he committed suicide, were to be revealed? Here they are presumed to be capable of serving as a rallying point for all the fascist groups in the world.

In Ludlum's *The Holcroft Covenant* one signature is enough to release the $780 m. of Swiss-held Nazi booty, which will permit the *Neuaufbau* of the Reich.

In these novels the Nazis are frequently credited with supernatural powers: regeneration, invisibility, survival beyond death. In Herbert Lieberman's superior − but hideously violent − *Climate of Hell* this indestructability has a nice twist. At the end of the novel Dr Grigori − Mengele? − becomes an incarnation of the immortally wandering Jew. On the run in South America, or underground in the west, Nazis still have the awful omnipotence and the unrestrained opportunity for sadistic cruelty that they enjoyed in Auschwitz. In *Marathon Man*, for example (in my view the best of these 'nightmare that wouldn't die' novels), a young, jogging Columbia postgraduate is whisked off the streets of his hometown New York to be tortured with a dentist's drill by the ubiquitous Mengele fiend. Much of the direct inspiration for these novels arises from justified liberal indignation at reports of Mengele's flagrantly comfortable exile in Paraguay as an allegedly honoured guest of President Stroessner.

The notion of the continuous and endless struggle against Nazism is given a slightly different working in Frank de Felitta's *Oktoberfest*. In this novel (with an effective German setting) a Jewish survivor of Auschwitz − conveniently Herculean − comes out of a catatonic trance in 1973. He runs amuck in Munich's October beer festival, murdering Germans who remind him, in his dementia, of prominent Nazis. He blows up the municipal shower baths, for example, because they are reminiscent of extermination chambers. Running through the novel is the xenophobic allegation that the new Germany is still the old Germany. Inevitably a major war criminal is uncovered in the general mayhem, justifying the madman's paranoid delusions. *Oktoberfest* anticipates in its main idea George Fox's *Amok* in which a gigantic samurai-sword-wielding Japanese soldier, some thirty years after the war, terrorizes a Philippines community. As in de Felitta's novel, the continued and undiminished physical power of the necessarily ancient survivor boggles the imagination. We have, for example, to assume that the young superman was originally recruited into the Japanese army at the age of twelve. Generally, however, the survival of a few pathetic Japanese soldiers in the Pacific has not inspired the same paranoid energy in the popular novelist as the survival of gangs of unrepentant prominent Nazis in South America or rehabilitated in West Germany.

II

If there is one thing that links the 'nightmare that wouldn't die' kind of fiction with the 'secret history of the war' variety, it is a primitive suspiciousness; there is more, these novels allege, to the *real* events of 1939-45 than meets the eye, or than published historical accounts let us know. Germany was *not* de-Nazified: Nazidom merely regrouped itself underground. In many ways the vigorous and still-booming 'nightmare' genre of novel would seem to be a folk-reaction to the 'thinness' and undramatic quality of the historian's retrospective view of Nazi Germany's evil. A reaction, for example, to Hugh Trevor-Roper's comment in 1979 that 'the plain fact is that the real Bormann of history was much duller than the phantom of journalism'. The real Bormann was, Trevor-Roper asserts, 'too stupid, too inagile or too inebriated to escape'. None the less the world of the popular novel (as in Higgins's *The Valhalla Exchange*) obstinately retains a Bormann more resourceful, powerful and wily in his South American afterlife than even the *Daily Express* credits. Above all, these novels contradict the rational view of Hannah Arendt, contemplating Eichmann's trial in Jerusalem, that Nazi history merely teaches 'the lesson of the fearsome word- and thought-defying banality of evil'. In this fiction, evil — as it traditionally should be — is reinvested with its *mana*, its fascinating, superhuman dimension. The Nazi bureaucrat of history gives way to the emotionally satisfying Nazi demon of popular mythology.

Chapter Eighteen

Fashionable crime I: hijack

I

Popular fiction has kept up with the popular press in its attention to the more noteworthy crimes of recent times. Such masterworks as Kennedy's assassination, the Brink's payroll job, the Vienna OPEC raid and the Great Train Robbery are commemorated in innumerable bestsellers, or would-be bestsellers. But it is not merely the size of the haul or eminence of the target which makes certain crimes specially noteworthy. Some crimes (computer embezzlement, for example) have only recently been devised and are interesting for their novelty; others could only be committed given modern social-military-economic equipment and its capacity for spectacular misuse. Popular fiction (especially genre) is very quick on the uptake where criminal innovation is concerned; so much so that quite ordinary novels are regularly credited with leading the field and blueprinting the more imaginative crimes of the day. One recent example: among the FBI's suspects for the abduction of Patty Hearst was the author of an obscure pornographic adventure story of a year before which predicted the main outline of the actual kidnap. The novel was promptly reissued — as *Abduction* — and enjoyed some useful notoriety.

Two fashionable crime formulas are examined in the following chapters: hijack, together with the related hostage crimes of siege or kidnap, and the new, grander forms of larceny by which a white-collar criminal can burgle the world market.

Popular fiction and Hollywood caught on to the possibilities of the hijack very fast. Not only was this a topical form of crime with a 'natural' narrative to it (i.e. it had quick build-up, suspense and a usually prompt and bloody climax); it also had built-in mass-reader appeal since ordinary people (the hostages) were typically at the centre of things. Hijack was, moreover, easily adapted to the traditional 'Narrenschiff' structure by which a social panorama is involved on the 'all life is there' principle. Thus *The Taking of Pelham 123* (hijacked subway train) has a dual focus which switches from the gang to the motley cargo of passengers whom they hold captive: these include a plainclothes policeman, a hooker, a black radical, a wise old man, a querulous woman, a drunk and so on. In Robert Cawley's *Shockwave* the PLO, IRA, Japanese Red Army, Baader Meinhof and Tupamaros combine as a terrorist international to hijack a cruise liner, with a full complement of passengers. (They demand $500 m., or they will start killing the children on board, one by one.) In *Siege* by Peter Cave, a Spanish holiday resort is held to ransom with all its British holidaymakers. In these 'common experience' hijacks there is always a broad range of humanity at risk. No reader need lack a victim to identify with.

A number of ingenious hijack scenarios were invented in popular fiction of the 1970s; the writer's mind running wildly far ahead of the criminal's (though hijack is, in fact, one of the more imaginative and creative forms of crime). In *Rosebud*, Black September kidnap the beautiful daughters of five millionaires and hold them captive aboard a hijacked yacht against the release of Palestinian prisoners. In Bonne-carrère's *Ultimatum*:

A hijacked supertanker threatens mammoth ecological disaster . . . $50,000,000 and an immediate total ban on registering ships under flags of convenience or 32,000 tons of crude oil will be released . . . enough to ensure the destruction of all animal and vegetable life in the western Mediterranean.

(Forsyth uses this same threat to better effect in his *Devil's Alternative*.) In Stanley Cohen's *330 Park* a private army of desperadoes hold a New York tower block and its 500 occupants to ransom, exacting payment from every firm on every floor (total take around $20 m.). In *Pelham 123* a subway train is hijacked ('What the fuck would anyone want to hijack a subway train for?' is authority's first baffled response; $1 m. is what for, they are informed). In Patrick Mann's superior *Dog Day Afternoon* an incompetent band of robbers hit a New York bank, discover the vaults are empty and so decide to hijack the premises and its occupants instead. (Their ultimate, cloudy aim, is asylum in Algeria; they are wiped out at Kennedy airport.) In Gerald Green's *The Hostage Heart*:

> One of the world's richest and most powerful men lies on the operating table, undergoing arterial surgery. Behind the surgeon stands a man with a gun. He is a revolutionary terrorist, fanatical and megalomaniac. The terrorist group is demanding $10m in two hours.

Other rich and powerful targets have been hit on — even, in daring leaps of the authorial mind, the President of the US (*The Golden Gate*) and the Queen of England. The following is the publisher's come-on for Walter Nelson's *The Minstrel Code*:

> Never before has anyone dared to write about the unthinkable. . . . In this tense, fast-moving novel, a new terrorist organization, Bloody Christmas, launches a suicide mission against the most impossible target yet. Five desperate men, among them a fearsome martial arts master from the East, kill their way to Britain to seize the one person in the heart of London who must be protected at all costs.
>
> In a daring and ingenious assault, they take their victim hostage and demand a ransom which three nations have to pay. Nothing can stop them, for the life of the hostage they threaten cannot under any circumstances be endangered.

In *The Golden Gate* the Presidential motorcade is hijacked on the famous San Francisco bridge, and the great man and two oil-rich Arabian travelling companions are held up for $300 m. Another, more ingeniously devised hijack of a famous American is found in Godey's *The Talisman*, where a gang remove the unknown warrior from his Washington grave.

Nuclear-weapon heists were an obvious elaboration of what the papers were reporting. In Walter Wager's *Viper 3* (filmed as *Twilight's Last Gleaming*) five convicts take over

command of an ICBM launch site, intending to 'mug' the
country for $5 m. and safe conduct out of the country with
the President as hostage. In *The Triton Ultimatum* a nuclear
submarine is hijacked and its Poseidon missiles used to extort
$4 bn in gold (a record demand for this kind of novel, I think).

II

In the words of *330 Park*'s blurb, the novel offers 'the
essence of a modern nightmare'. The 'modernity' of the
hijack idea lies in its two-fold reliance on advanced technology.
The first reliance is on the address system by which its
demands are made and passed on. There is an essential
reliance from the beginning on hotlines, headlines, squawk
boxes, news agencies, telecommunications. Immediate
publicity is essential: 'the fucking media', complains Cohen's
gang-leader, 'they're not getting the story out fast enough'
(*330 Park*, 1979, p. 68). In *The Golden Gate* an all-party
press conference covered by the three main TV networks is
set up, minutes after the capture. It is in this media-reliance
that hijacks differ from the kidnap routines chronicled in
earlier bestsellers like *No Orchids for Miss Blandish*, with
their primitive snatches, ransom notes, hideouts, drops and
pickups.

The other reliance on advanced technology is where the
'threat' is concerned. In now-dated gangster melodramas a
gun was sometimes called an equalizer, in recognition of the
fact that it levelled chances between a big man and a small
one. Contemporary equalizers are vastly more efficient. One
man who breaks through an 'access control' to level a gun at
a pilot's head is now all powerful: a Palestinian, without a
state, can dictate terms to a superpower, its national airline
and its government. This is actually the plot of Nelson de
Mille's *By the Rivers of Babylon*, in which PLO terrorists
hijack a Concorde-load of Israeli peace negotiators. One
threatened bullet undoes years of shuttle diplomacy. Notion-
ally, at least, the single criminal has, via the hijack, come
within striking distance of the omnipotent fantasies of
Mabuse.

The arbitrary power of the irresponsible individual with his finger on the trigger or button is stressed in these works: 'It takes one man to kill the Mediterranean . . .'; 'He's going to wipe out the whole world. . . .' But, of course, this pressure cannot be profitably applied as extortion unless it is immediately relayed to the top, and ruthless government counter-action paralysed by the publicity which bluffs it into assuming a 'no loss of life' priority. (In the eastern bloc, where the 'eyes of the world' can be effectively blinkered, hijacks are rare and suicidal exercises: Forsyth makes the point effectively in *The Devil's Alternative*, where Migs shoot down any hijacked Russian plane before it can get to free air space.) Hence the attraction of the favourite hijack target — the inflight aeroplane — is not just that the pilot is vulnerable and the craft valuable, but that he and it have a communication system in the cockpit by which the outside world can be patched in as spectators. The telephone, television and tele-printer are as much the weapons of hijack as the gun or grenade. In *Rosebud*, within two pages (some three hours of narrative time) a couple of broadcasts and a dozen phone calls serve to involve four national intelligence agencies, Willy Brandt, Moshe Dayan and the news services of the world in the action. The hijackers choose flamboyantly, but logically, to transmit their demands on worldwide TV, with the five beautiful hostages displayed naked. 'You're going to be a star,' one of them is told, 'a great international star.' Hijacking makes stars of its victims, superstars of its criminals and voyeurs of the viewing world.

In life the most spectacular hijacks have had political motives. The practical reason for this is the need for a safe haven to which the successful hijacker can retreat with his ransom and the protective shield of hostages. A country without an extradition treaty for political crimes — or any extradition agreements at all — is the ideal choice. But, as Castro himself, and the Algerians later, insisted, there is no welcome for mere 'gangsters' in the otherwise puritanical revolutionary regimes which defy the US. The alternative is to do what some desperate apolitical American did: demand a parachute with the dollars and symbolically jump into the void a rich man. The survival rate does not seem to have been high. And a crime without getaway chances has little attraction for the professionally thoughtful criminal.

Although it figures prominently in actual hijacks, in fiction any political affiliation is, typically, stripped away. Often the criminals indicate that they will eventually need a plane, fuelled for an unknown destination; but since they seldom get even as far as the airport the novelist's bluff is rarely called. This disembarrassment leaves the more manageable elements to play with: the countdown, the vast ransom at hazard, the rebellion among the criminals, tense negotiation, the shoot out, the rescue. What is, in 'real life', typically a terrorist strike becomes in popular fiction a 'caper', a 'heist'. This simplification of aims brings with it a reduction of incomprehensible political motivation (incomprehensible, that is, in terms of the ideology of bestselling fiction) to comprehensible human motives. These motives can be categorized as: money, criminality, grudge and madness.

Money motives are predominant. In the best of the hijack novels considered here, *Pelham 123* (it also made the best film), the leader has a revealing conversation with an accomplice as they sound each other out for the forthcoming job:

'You're a soldier, soldier of fortune?' Longman read a great deal, adventure novels, and so the concept was not entirely alien to him.

'That's a fancy name for it. Mercenary is more accurate.'

'Meaning someone who fights for money?'

'Yes' (*The Taking of Pelham 123*, 1974, p. 66).

'I'm whatever I'm paid to be,' he adds a minute later. All the hijackers in *Pelham 123* are neutral, men without an institution or a cause: one is a retired railwayman, another has been fired from the Mafia for undue violence(!), the leader is a professional mercenary soldier. 'Money — what else is there?' one of them asks. In *330 Park* the planning genius conceives the job as a 'carefully planned operation which could bring him all the wealth and respect that the world had so far denied him.' He also has a grudge — the largest firm in the building fired him on his return from Vietnam; as he broods on this injustice, '*the plan* began to form in his mind' (p. 14). In MacLean's *The Golden Gate*, the President refuses to authorize the handover of the $300 m. without an assurance that it won't be used for 'any anti-American purposes'. 'What am I compared to America?' he asks. Branson replies, 'This money is required for purely apolitical purposes. It's for a private trust, in fact. Branson enterprises, Inc. Me' (*The Golden Gate*, 1978, p. 73).

The criminality of the hijacker is prominently stressed in the nuclear-blackmail novels. In *Viper 3* the hijackers are a half dozen military prisoners, who have escaped from Death Row. The criminal element is also prominent in *The Triton Ultimatum*. Only criminals or madmen, these novels imply, would want to aim a nuclear rocket at the US. That one could have any good reason for doing so is unthinkable. (The 2,000 or so Russian SS9s somehow get brought in here.) And the novel, in the largest sense, works a typical cold-war doublethink. In order to understand our 'defences' in terms of the 'terror weapons' which they latently are (Russian children with eyeballs dribbling down their cheeks) we must think of them in the possession of a madman/criminal/fanatic. Someone, that is, as unlike ourselves as possible. In this way, since we know that madmen do not, cannot, have their fingers on the button, we feel safe in the possession of our arsenal.

Wager's novel is at pains to stress the total alienation of the leader of the hijackers. He is many cuts above the scum he leads; but his unfair conviction for a justified passionate crime has given him a terrible grudge. (In the end, however, his better self comes through and he surrenders.) In *The Triton Ultimatum* the nuclear muggers are a mixed bunch of men with grudges and hang-ups. One, for example, takes part in the mission because he was too short to make the college football team; another has an unfaithful wife, etc. And they are all led by a fanatic, 'a megalomaniac of the most frightening kind'. As in all hijack novels, there is no comradeship between the hijackers (as there is, typically, between the police who oppose them). Camaraderie would imply that there was some cause, a unifying code or commonly held belief, by which men sharing hardship or risk move closer together. The hijackers, under stress, typically fall out among themselves. In Craig Thomas's *Rat Trap*, for instance, 'the Army of the Night' hold a British Airways 707 to ransom at Heathrow.

The band of hijackers, composed of fanatics, heroin addicts, psychotic heiresses and Palestinians end up destroying themselves. 'Liebestod,' the watching policeman comments — he, meanwhile, has forged closer bonds with his colleagues and with his wife who was, fortuitously, one of the captives. The message of these novels, taken together, is that hijackers are sick, deranged, criminal or downright mad. Given this generic simplification, *Rosebud* by Paul Bonnecarrère and Joan Hemingway warrants some notice as being exceptional. Written and set outside the Anglo-American bestseller axis (Bonnecarrère is French, Hemingway the famous novelist's daughter) this novel attempts something more subtle than the run of hijack fiction. The authors do, in fact, introduce a layer of political discussion around the action. Since they choose to do this by essayistic digression, it is not a graceful addition; but one is led to concede that the thought counts. Aimed primarily at a French readership, *Rosebud* is both more perceptive and ambivalent in its attitude to Arab discontent than what one would expect from a corresponding American bestseller (Harris's *Black Sunday*, for instance). Apart from the voyeurism (arguably as French a national characteristic as the Arabophilia), it is a superior novel in terms of construction and complexity. Yet, at the end, it makes exactly the same concession as the others make from the start. The anarchist Schrantz, his plans confounded, nevertheless taunts his captors with the inevitability of his propaganda victory:

'What counts is what the masses believe, and they've
swallowed my bait whole. You can try whatever you want,
my accomplices — as you call them — will nevertheless
remain martyrs to a noble cause in the eyes of the public.
Shoot them if you've got the balls. They'll face your firing
squads proudly, will refuse your blindfolds with contempt
and accept your bullets shouting. *"Vive la Liberté", "Vive
Palestine!"* And then you'll give in once more. Legally and
officially, you'll have to put their bodies on a plane at Le
Bourget in coffins draped with the Palestinian flag. The
television crews of the world will give live coverage to the
state funerals that will be held in Cairo, Beirut or Tripoli
where the coffins of the martyrs will be passed from hand

to hand above the heads of thousands of raving fanatics in the streets' (*Rosebud*, 1975, p. 265).

He is then finally demolished by the news that his accomplices have sold out: 'they're just two-bit crooks' he is informed, not martyrs. On hearing the news of their mercenary deal Schrantz relapses into madness: 'the flame that had lit the very depths of his eyes was dead and gone' (*ibid.*, p. 268). The familiar conversion had been made, the hijacker is reduced to a compendium of greed, criminality and lunacy.

It is conceivable that hijackers are depraved or deranged in the ways these novels suggest. Fiction, after all, could hardly embellish Mogadishu's 'Captain Mahmoud' or Teheran's 'students'. But what the novel does in all these cases is to make a folkloristic generalization. It leaves one with the same commonsense incontrovertibility of 'all coppers are bastards', 'all mothers-in-law nag', 'all car dealers lie about mileage', 'all bullies are cowards'. All hijackers, it is suggested, are nuts.

Chapter Nineteen

Fashionable crime II: embezzlement – the man with the briefcase

I

When Ian Fleming's magnificent villain Auric Goldfinger schemes to burgle Fort Knox of its $15 bn worth of gold, his plan of action is in essence hardly different from Ned Kelly's daring raid in the tin suit. To carry out Operation Grand Slam, Goldfinger intends first to poison the water supply with 'the most powerful of the Trilone group of nerve poisons' (*Goldfinger*, 1964, p. 186). Assisted by gangsters from the six main American Mafia families he will then smash down the vault doors with a stolen Corporal tactical nuclear missile, evacuate the many tons of gold by human chain, load it onto a hijacked train and thence to a waiting Russian cruiser off the coast of Virginia. The coup, of course, depends on a co-operative indifference by American authorities to daylight robbery of the national treasure.

Operation Grand Slam was rather too mind-boggling for the makers of the film *Goldfinger*. They toned down Fleming's plot by having Goldfinger ally himself with the Chinese, who supply a 'dirty' nuclear device, which, when exploded in the vault, will render its contents unusable for millennia and Goldfinger's hoard correspondingly more valuable by virtue of scarcity. Even so, this caper requires an air raid by Pussy Galore's lesbian squadron, the dropping of cannisters of poison gas, the searing away of the treasury gates with laser guns, pitched battles between Chinese and the 60,000 US military personnel stationed at the Fort, culminating in Connery/Bond's epic hand-to-hand struggle with Oddjob next to a ticking atom bomb.

In Paul Erdman's string of bestsellers the techniques of

massive, international larceny are modernized. So are the
social-moral typologies on which Fleming depends; his
reliance, for example, on the degenerate 'alien' arch-criminal
(directly descended from Fu Manchu, Mabuse and — remotely
— Wilkie Collins's 'Napoleon of Crime', Count Fosco). In
Erdman's fiction it is consortia of businessmen who plan
'billion dollar killings'. Erdman also dispenses with Fleming's
nationalistic obsessions. His heroes are jet setters, men
without country. And the Erdman master thief never needs a
weapon. He is the prime example of Don Corleone's maxim
that a man with a briefcase can outsteal the hood every time.

Erdman's are 'insider's' novels. They 'take the lid off'
international finance. His professional credentials for this
kind of exposé are impressive; the curriculum vitae given out
by his publisher dwells with almost maternal pride on the
strings of degrees and top jobs he has had:

Paul E. Erdman was born in 1932 in Stratford, Ontario,
and was educated at Georgetown University, at the School
of Foreign Service, Washington D.C. and at the University
of Basel, Switzerland, where he took his M.A. and PhD.
His occupations have included consulting economist to the
European Coal and Steel Community, Executive Vice
President of Electronics International Capital in Bermuda
and Vice Chairman of the United California Bank in Basel.

The blurbist doesn't mention what A.P. Hackett reports, that
Erdman wrote *Billion Dollar Killing* in a Swiss jail — which
may explain both his change of profession and his inveterate
hatred for that country.

Erdman's is 'researched' fiction at its flashy best — the
research coming not from intensive boning up (as with, for
example, Hailey's 'inside Detroit' novel, *Wheels*) but from
years of intimate professional experience in a highly specialized
occupation. Publishers have latched on to the 'educational'
aspect of his work as a good selling point. Arrow, for instance,
give pride of place on the cover of their edition of *Billion
Dollar Killing* to Len Deighton's encomium (Deighton is
another heavy researcher):

It has more information about economics, wealth and
investment than many textbooks offer. The author has
artfully blended the thriller with step-by-step lessons in

high finance. Even the uninitiated will come out the other end understanding 'dumping' 'selling short' and 'forward buying'.

There is something in this vision of a self-improving reader poring over Erdman's fiction as a kind of Samuelson without tears. But it does not account for the fact that his novels now sell in their millions. (*The Crash of '79* was a #1 seller in the US and had a good afterlife with the fall of the Shah, who it correctly predicted would come to a sticky end in that year.) Most readers probably skate over the economic expertise and are more taken with the scandalous and quite unpedagogic revelation that the Swiss secretly allied themselves with the Nazis in the Second World War, or, on a more domestic level, that Swiss businessmen all 'fuck their secretaries in the way of business' once a week, and that their technique is 'unimaginative' in the performance of this office chore (*The Crash of '79*, 1977, p. 67).

The really potent appeal of Erdman's novels is that they confirm deep, collective suspicions in the consumer-oriented western countries, where they principally sell. He successfully insinuates the idea that the world financial crisis, which has occupied the west's mind since 1973 (when Erdman came on the bestselling scene) originated in a gigantic conspiracy; that the public, indeed whole nations, are suckers in the hands of unscrupulous financiers. For all its surface technicality, its layers of 'research', Erdman's fiction gives an emotionally manageable folklore for the mysteries of macroeconomics. It is easy and natural to suppose if the 1975 pound in your pocket is only now worth 60p that someone (Gnomes of Zurich, Mafia, Sheiks) has taken the 40p, rather than trying to grasp the acronymic subtleties of MLR, IMF, OPEC, GNP etc.

Thus all Erdman's novels make a satisfying link between large economic problems and the simple explanations of greed and theft. As the cover to *Billion Dollar Killing* puts it: 'When the mighty dollar falls, unscrupulous speculators will make a killing, a billion dollar killing.' The rises and falls of currency and international commodities are similarly simplified into the machinery of the 'heist':

On May 16 1968 the international commodity market

witnessed the most spectacular upheaval in recent financial history. Against all odds, the price of silver began to plummet. By the time it hit rock bottom, thousands of small investors had lost their shirts — and a few really big speculators had made a fortune (plot synopsis of *The Silver Bears*).

This 'Gnomes of Zurich' reading of world events is based on a deep, reflexive xenophobia. Erdman's 1976 novel, *The Crash of '79*, focuses demonologically on the man who, via OPEC and with the connivance of the international financial market (i.e. loathed Switzerland), humiliated the US. That man, of course, was the Shah of Iran. Erdman's description of the Shah, then a potentate, would doubtless have earned him some close attention from SAVAK had the author extended his promotional tour to the Gulf in 1977:

Despite the grandiose title, he was actually nothing more than the son of an obscure Iranian colonel — a man who was actually illiterate until adulthood — who had lucked it out in a rebellion against the real Persian dynasty [there follows an extended description of how Pahlavi was kicked out by the west for supporting 'his fellow Aryan' Hitler, how Mohammed was restored after Mossadegh's overthrow by the CIA, and how he became a 'puppet of America' and 'the Playboy of the Eastern World'.] Nobody really took him seriously. Then came the 1973 bombshell. The Arabs put an embargo on oil exports to the West, and within months, in the most successful blackmail attempt in the history of the world, had forced through a quadrupling of the petroleum price. True to his past, the Shah contributed nothing to this coup. In fact, he despised the Arabs. But once the danger of possible Western military intervention subsided, he suddenly stepped front and center and became the self-appointed spokesman for OPEC. . . . He soon had Europe cringing at his feet. He was surrounded by delegations of bowing and scraping Japanese, desperate for Iran's petroleum. He was praised by Giscard D'Estaing, embraced by Harold Wilson, sumptuously entertained by Gerald Ford. . . . The King of Kings had arrived (*The Crash of '79*, pp. 26-9).

The Crash of '79 chronicles a conspiracy between the Shah

and Switzerland. He guarantees their oil supply (as earlier the Nazis had guaranteed their coal supplies) in return for the nuclear technology which they have clandestinely developed in their usual sneaky way. The Swiss scientist seconded to the Shah makes him the bombs he wants, which he intends to drop on Saudi Arabia. His strategic aim in this unprovoked act of war is to overrun the Saudi oil fields when the fallout from the 'clean' Swiss bombs clears, and so monopolize the world's energy supplies. But the Shah has been doublecrossed by the Swiss scientist, who once had a Jewish wife and who sees the danger to Israel in this megalomaniac plan. The bombs are 'dirty', thus rendering Saudi Arabia a thermonuclear desert. A US-led counterattack detonates some leftover nukes on the ground in Persia, killing the Shah and all his entourage. A new 'oil crisis', dwarfing that of 1973, is visited on the world for a decade at least. Fifty years after the Wall Street Crash, the US is thrown back to the horse-drawn pioneer era — and the Shah did it. (As prophesied, 1979 was the year of the crash for the Shah — though in a more banal way than Erdman's global apocalypse.)

The huge success of this novel (especially in America) feeds off a national resentment at the new 'unearned' power of Mickey Mouse states like Saudi Arabia, Iran and Switzerland; joke countries which never won a war and scarcely an Olympic bronze medal, yet who now dictate to superpowers. Only national, consensus rage could license a depiction such as Erdman's of the Shah, quoted above. (Imagine the reaction if he had done something similar for Golda Meir.) This recent oil crisis-linked xenophobia and anger at reverse imperialism by finance manipulation is to be found in Peter Tanous and Paul Rubinstein's *The Petrodollar Takeover*, to take another, less illustrious example. This novel closely resembles Erdman's, even down to the cited expertise of the 'Wall Street men':

> The time: tomorrow, or the day after. The war between Saudi Arabia and Iran is going badly for the Saudis; they need more and better tanks and they need them quickly. John Haddad, a young Wall Street banker, is chosen by the Saudis to undertake a deal so amazing that, at first, he can scarcely believe it himself. For Haddad's commission is to buy out General Motors. And all the Saudis need to make

that possible is the income of 18 weeks' oil production . . .
18 weeks' Petrodollars! Tanous and Rubinstein, both top
Wall Street men, have used their experience and inside
knowledge brilliantly to create tomorrow's story today.
'We have become an IMF colony,' Tony Benn declared in
May 1979. We have become an OPEC colony, Erdman and
the lesser Erdmans' novels declare. In this mood of national
resentment, the Shah, the man with his finger on the life-
blood tap, became a bogeyman, attracting powerfully mixed
and crude emotions in the west. While David Owen (then
Foreign Secretary) protested that he was a real friend, and
Jimmy Carter oozed about the Persian people's 'great love'
for their monarch, the bookstalls of the English-speaking
world carried such fictions as Peter Ritner's *Red Carpet for
the Shah* (1975):

> Blinded by the vision of an all-powerful Islam, the Shah of
> Iran aims the sleek warheads of his American missiles at
> the heart of Russia, thus forcing the two superpowers to
> the point of a third world war. Secretary of State Kalldorf
> advises caution, but the decision rests with President
> George Arnold, to order an act so horrifying in its
> implications that only the forestalling of a global nuclear
> holocaust can justify it. ASSASSINATION.

One can make the obvious connection here with traditional
anti-semitic paranoias, which in periods of economic distress
have made scapegoats of international Jewish finance. But
the familiar pathology of Erdman's novels is less interesting
than the innovative assimilation he makes between financial
dealing, theft and gambling. In his fiction these become one
morally neutral praxis. There is a similar assimilation in his
dramatis personae. In the coups which his novels chronicle
(and which, we are led to believe, have their origin in historical
'fact') the Mafia, European aristocracy, oriental potentates
and international bankers join their forces. In so doing they
transcend their social and national selves, becoming 'citizens
of the world'. Thus, in *The Crash of '79*, the hero is a Swiss-
based American economist, in the employ of the Saudi
Arabians, negotiating with the Iranians. Significantly, Erdman's favourite fictional setting is the nationally neutral
Switzerland: a country which is less a sovereign state than a

world trade centre, a modern Venice.

II

Thomas Gifford's *The Man From Lisbon* comes with appropriately warm endorsements from Paul Erdman ('explodes with financial intrigue and irresistible romance') and *Business News*. An apparently remote story, it tells of financial crime in another place (Portugal) and a long time ago (the 1920s). Just over 50 years ago, a wealthy Portuguese business man pulled off the most astonishing confidence trick the world has ever known. So ingenious was it that even his partners-in-crime believed what they were doing to be perfectly legal. So cleverly constructed, that the Portuguese criminal code had to be rewritten to deal with it. It netted him over $5m. Toppled a government.

Yet for all its historicity and foreignness, *The Man From Lisbon* resonates powerfully with events of here and now. Its narrative centres on a lone criminal of no great personal interest, who engineers national inflation by means of an obscure financial loophole. (The Bank of Portugal does not check on the issue of notes with duplicate serial numbers.) By exploiting this, Alves Reis succeeds in quietly debauching the escudo; he ruins his country's economy and gets away with it. He remains invisible, insignificant, as Portugal wallows in the slumpflation that will eventually lead to fascism. Reis evades this disaster by emigrating with his wealth to Brazil.

Reis is one of the soft-faced men who traditionally make personal fortunes out of national misfortunes; ruin, war, financial crash. Like Greene's Harry Lime, the aim of such men is always to obliterate themselves, to become invisible. Reis, we are led to believe, succeeds in this divestiture of presence, he negates his historical existence.

Like Erdman's novels, *The Man From Lisbon* voices two myths current in the popular mind. The first is that when currency goes mad (as it did in the period 1973-5) someone, somewhere, is making a lot of money. The second, that there is a top-division of crime in which the master criminal is invincible, and above judgment. Historically there is some evidence for this belief. Nixon survives a millionaire in California; Vesco a multi-millionaire in Costa Rica; the Shah allegedly a billionaire in Panama or Egypt. Their crime is not theft or embezzlement — but astute financial dealing. As Alves observes at the crucial moment of his career:

> The point was, it was the petty crimes that were punished — the small crimes, the small men — not the important men who manipulated the large amounts of currency, who toyed with the banking rules and did business as it suited them (*The Man From Lisbon*, 1978, p. 82).

It is, manifestly, envy at the privileged nature of this super-crime (which by its grandeur becomes non-crime) that has inspired some of the preposterous hijack claims. With one coup the hijacker hopes to become a member of the super-league of crime. Thus in *Dog Day Afternoon* Littlejoe, who started with a planned $50,000 bank robbery, announces his hijack claim of $1 m. in Nixonian terms:

> One of the cameramen atop a TV van yelled: 'Wave to us, Joe.' Joe held out both arms at shoulder height and gave a V sign with both hands. 'I want to make one thing perfectly clear,' he yelled. 'After this is over I'm retiring to San Clemente and gonna live off my pension of seventy-five grand a year. And you're gonna keep paying it till the day I die.' The crowd went wild (*Dog Day Afternoon*, 1975, pp. 165-6).

Novels like Erdman's and Gifford's express a canny, peasant distrust of *politics* — the democratic system by which power is, allegedly, extended to 'little men'. As Alves puts it: 'Politics is a waste of time . . . money is what makes the difference, not politics' (*The Man From Lisbon*, p. 417).

Chapter Twenty

QB VII and the bestselling novel after Auschwitz

To write poetry after Auschwitz is barbarous.

(T. Adorno)

I

Leon Uris has a string of bestsellers to his credit. His two supersellers, *Exodus* (#1 title in 1975, later an internationally successful film) and *Trinity* (seventy appearances in the NYT list as a hardback), take the familiar 'making of a nation' theme. It is mainly an American subject matter, America being the country which has been most spectacularly made in recent history. But the mode is transferable. As Uris puts it: 'You can write westerns in any part of the world' (*Publishers Weekly*, 29 March 1976). *Exodus* (Israel) and *Trinity* (Ireland) centre on epic historical moments — 1947 and 1916. They celebrate the contribution of personal heroism to the forging of new supra-personal national identity, maximizing the role of the individual while glorifying the collectivity of the new-born state. It is only at such dramatic moments as national genesis, and usually only in the imaginary past, that the tension between state and individual can be thus dissolved. Novels such as Uris's (and Michener's) allow the luxury of a good wallow in a paradoxical condition of absolute heroic individualism and selfless devotion to a common cause. Classically, and tediously, this therapeutic drama has been set in the American west. Uris has profitably varied the formula by exporting it to worldwide relocations.

Taken against *Exodus* and *Trinity*, *QB VII* represents something of a low point in Uris's career. It only made sixth place in the 1970 bestsellers list, though it had a useful boost as a paperback five years later when American and British television screened it as one of the first TV 'bestseller' blockbusters.

The televisation of *QB VII*, like the original novel, is of great length and tedium. But it has an indirect interest in that it contains a revealing self-portrait of the bestselling novelist as Uris apparently conceives the role. The hero, Abe Cady, is a Jewish veteran of Jewish veteran Uris's generation. Cady is made to write an epic bestseller about the founding of Israel, called *The Holocaust*, as Uris in life had written *Exodus*. *Exodus*, as is well known, provoked a trial (Dering *vs* Uris) in 1964, in which a surviving concentration-camp doctor sued the novelist for libel; the offensive passage in *Exodus* claiming that Dering had 'performed 17,000 experiments in surgery without anaesthetic' for the Germans in Auschwitz. Dering won his case (the number of operations accredited to him was grossly exaggerated), but he was awarded derisive damages of one halfpenny, the lowest-value coin of the realm. The impression made by victims Dering *had* operated on (some for the removal of sexual or reproductive organs) was sensational, as was the evidence of a French lady doctor (Dering was by birth Polish), Dr Hautval, who had nobly refused to take part in medical experiments while imprisoned at Auschwitz. Dering, who had been awarded the OBE for his medical services in postwar Britain, died shortly after his judicial humiliation, a broken man. The Dering *vs* Uris trial, heavily melodramatized, forms the main plot of *QB VII*. And since the dead cannot be libelled, the novel does something of a dance on the Polish doctor's grave. (Nevertheless, Uris prudently takes conventional refuge behind the 'any resemblance . . . is coincidental' formula.)

II

Some authors, like Hailey or MacLean, are engagingly modest about what they do for a living. They conceive themselves merely as employees of the public's entertainment industry: 'I don't write for myself,' declares MacLean, 'I write for my public.' Or at worst they affect a 'crying all the way to the bank' manner, as does Hailey sometimes when pressed on the subject. No great claim to literary significance is entered by such writers. Other bestselling novelists display more ego and exact more tribute. An example of signal self-conceit is Irving Wallace, who has gone so far as to publish a workbook for one of his novels; this record brings to the operations of the Wallace sensibility a Gidean degree of artistic introspection.

On the face of things, Uris would seem, like Wallace, an immodest and narcissistic author, at least as he projects himself in *QB VII*.

The narrative of *QB VII* is divided into two separate strands, corresponding to the adversaries who finally confront in the courtroom, Queen's Bench Seven. The 'plaintiff', Adam Kelno (i.e. Dering), is a Polish Catholic doctor who has survived Nazi imprisonment. He is either a hero, a saint of the camps or an anti-semitic butcher who willingly carried out the SS's hideous experimental surgery. The truth of his background and nature is not divulged until the courtroom climax. Before arriving at this revelation of the 'real' (anti-semitic) Kelno, we follow him through twenty years of his successful postwar life, during which he achieves distinction in his adoptive country's empire and is finally rewarded with a knighthood for services to medicine.

The opposing 'defendant' is Abraham Cady. We follow him as a rough and tumble all-American kid, 'handy with his dukes', who can't wait to get at the Germans and join the RCAF to become a Battle of Britain pilot. A devil-may-care sort of fellow, fond of the bottle, Cady (the name conflates honest Abe Lincoln and Buffalo Bill Cody) beds and weds a beautiful English aristocrat who can't resist his Yankee macho. Having helped win the war, Cady turns to writing and his career, in which he excels, takes him to Hollywood and a series of domestic and artistic crises. In Hollywood, Abe's 'art' becomes 'polished' and 'glib' and 'plastic'. He produces 'dishonest' bestsellers and cheats on his wife. Finally, through the revival of a mystical bond with his orthodox father and his 'people', Cady finds himself, redeems his art and discovers what his mission in life is to be. He will write an 'honest' Zionist saga. On his father's grave in Israel he vows to 'write a book to shake the conscience of the human race' (*QB VII*, p. 145). This involves an arduous investigative 'Odyssey' tracing the Jewish bondage in Europe and the Exodus to Palestine/Israel. The discovered tragedy and heroism behind the Jewish war of independence results in a bestseller prophetically (for a bestseller) called *The Holocaust*, and quite patently *Exodus*.

On receiving the manuscript of *The Holocaust*, Cady's London publisher, David Shawcross, telegrams heartfelt congratulations:

I HAVE READ YOUR MANUSCRIPT STOP I BELIEVE THAT
YOU HAVE ACHIEVED WHAT EVERY WRITER ASPIRES TO
AND FEW REALIZE STOP YOU HAVE WRITTEN A BOOK
THAT WILL LIVE NOT ONLY BEYOND YOUR MORTAL TIME
ON EARTH BUT FOR ALL TIMES(*ibid.*, p. 169).

To write poetry after Auschwitz is, according to Adorno, barbarous. But not, apparently, bestsellers. *The Holocaust* is 'an overnight success'. Cady is now born into his new life as national chronicler, Jehovah's PR man. In *The Holocaust* Abe slanders Kelno with the same allegation as to camp experiments which Uris levelled at Dering. A libel trial ensues, in which the mighty apparatus of British civil jurisprudence is invoked to determine the rights of the argument. It is touch and go until Abe contrives, by dogged sleuthing, to get the camp operating register which shows Kelno to be all that *The Holocaust* alleged. The process results in derisory compensation for the shattered plaintiff, and moral victory for the author. His 'fiction' is now officially certified as the truth.

All this, of course, mirrors the actual *Exodus*-Dering affair. And in the light of the correspondence, Uris's depiction of Cady implies a self-portraiture which is to be recognized by the reader. (Dering *vs* Uris was given huge newspaper publicity, and in the early 1970s would be assumed to be popular knowledge.) If so, Uris clearly does not hate himself. Cady, as he emerges from *QB VII*, is a whole gallery of fantasy figures: he is a baseball star in his young manhood (minor league professional), an ace fighter pilot, he is irresistibly attractive to women and — before he finds his 'mission' — a hell-raising playboy (his writing is customarily interrupted for a therapeutic 'roaring drunk' to clear the artistic tubes). Above all, he is a genius. His genius is evident long before he undertakes the epic *Holocaust*. His wife looks on humbly at the young novelist in full flow:

Samantha became the silent partner and privileged observer to one of the unique [*sic*] of all human experiences, the writing of a novel. She saw him detach himself from the first world of reality and submerge into the second world of his own creation. There was no magic. There was no inspiration that people always look for and imagine in the writer. What there was was a relentless plodding requiring a special kind of stamina that makes the profession so limited. Of course there came those moments when things suddenly fell into a natural rhythm and even more rare, that instant of pure flying through creative exhilaration (*ibid.*, p. 130).

Witnessing this creative agony, Shawcross concludes that Cady has 'within him the key to greatness'. But to realize his greatness he must face the terrible and risky solitude of the artist: 'When a young man sets sail on the sea of authorship, he is alone with little knowledge of the winds and tides and swells and storms' (*ibid.*, p. 113). At his best, Abe's novels strike 'at the heart'. But, possessed as he is of immense talent, the temptation to misuse it is correspondingly immense. He is constantly in danger of sacrificing his 'art' to the mercenary values of Sodom/commerce, symbolized in *QB VII* as Hollywood. Yet, in his triumph with *The Holocaust*, Cady scales the twin peaks of literary greatness and international bestsellerdom.

II

One is invited to do so, but there is a problem in assimilating Abraham Cady with Leon Uris. In life Uris presents a thoroughly professional and no-nonsense personality. He cheerfully admits that 'a crash course in history' sets up his novels which – as previously quoted – he conceives as transported westerns. His description of how he came to write *Trinity* suggests opportunism and professional prudence, rather than Cady's messianic sense of mission:

Uris first became deeply interested in Ireland when he and his wife, the photographer Jill Uris, were in London watching events across the way on British television. It was spring 1972, and he thought he saw an opportunity for Jill to do a stint of photojournalism. They spent Easter reconnoitring Ireland, then went back in June and stayed until November. Then they went back again, just to be sure (*Publishers Weekly*, 29 March, 1976).

It would be impossible, however, for Uris to inscribe this competent writing personality into *QB VII*. The reason is to be deduced from Adorno's maxim about poetry and Auschwitz. In the face of such suffering, literature should be silent. And if 'literature', how much more popular literature? But the bestseller will not be silent. It wants the gigantic toys of history to play with. So long, that is, that they are not so historically near as to be personally painful – witness the absence of any popular fiction about Vietnam during that war.

This impertinence of popular narrative was debated with considerable heat immediately after the TV screening of *Holocaust*. (It had the highest-ever viewing figures in the US: the BBC paid a quarter of a million pounds for the right to transmit it; despite the coincidence of titles, Uris had nothing to do with it.) Dennis Potter, for example, reacted with a review in the *Sunday Times* which was practically demented in its indignation. *Holocaust* he found to be:

a Book of the Dead written in the style of the Bestseller Yuk which now and intermittently fills spaces on the TV screens like soft plaster pressed into a badly cracked wall. The case against 'Holocaust' is not that it is bad soap opera, but worse – much worse – that it is very good soap opera. It was well made, often well acted, skilfully mounted, beautifully shot, and the scores of naked extras quivering above the already open graves were sufficiently accomplished not to show their genitals to the cameras. Prime-time codes of behaviour, praise be, are still strong enough to over-ride Nazi edicts. It also meant – and pardon me if I splash you with my vomit – that not all the extras needed to be circumcised (*Sunday Times*, 10 September, 1978).

Potter's outrage is magnificent. And clearly it is inspired

by the conviction that some subjects are not decently dealt with by the 'bestseller'. They must be generally proscribed and licensed for use only to the artist who has earned the right to them. Bestsellerdom defies such edicts, enforced as they are with nothing more than canons of taste and the bad temper of high-minded critics. On the other hand, works like *Holocaust* and *QB VII* do have a conscience, and, at a deep level are permeated with a certain shame. *QB VII*'s unease is evident in two main aspects of the book. First in the narrative, which takes as its main event a trial which legitimates bestselling fiction about the holocaust. If the majesty of English law endorses such novels, even against one of its ennobled citizens, *QB VII* declares, who are you to look down your nose? *QB VII*'s unease is secondly witnessed by the overblown conception of Cady. Uris clearly sensed that only a special kind of author could honestly write 'a book to shake the conscience of the world'. Ironically, it was the kind of author Uris patently isn't — subtle, commercially disinterested, artistic. Uris got round this by fabricating a surrogate Uris (Cady) of Promethean stature and creative intensity. It is preposterous, but one can see why it is done.

The segmental narrative and televisation

QB VII was one of the trail blazers for 'bestseller televisation'. It is noticeable that, of all Uris's novels, it is the one which most obviously divides into separate narrative strands (corresponding to Kelno and Cady's pre-trial careers). Another pioneering television bestseller — one which, thanks to its media tie-in made the decade's ten bestsellers — was Irwin Shaw's *Rich Man, Poor Man* (the first of ABC's 'Novels for television' in February 1976):

> the story of two brothers whose contrasting natures reflect the turmoil of post-war America. Rudy is the rich man — a romantic who would let no one stand between him and success. Tom is the poor man — the black sheep of the family on the run from his violent past.

Shaw retained the segmented story lines in his follow up, specifically designed for television and entitled, inevitably,

Beggarman, Thief: 'a worthy successor', as the advertisers put it, 'to the greatest paperback and television event of the seventies'. The biggest television event was, in actual fact, *Holocaust*. And this television serial-cum-novelization also adopted a split narrative, moving between the fortunes of a Jewish and a German family.

It is not hard to understand why television should have manifested this clear preference for segmented narrative. It works in shorter units, and can rely on a shorter attention span from its consumers than can the bestselling novel. But just as the cinema's increasing reliance on special effects in the 1970s brought a lateral pressure to bear on fiction, so too television's appetite for 'bestsellers' to process can be expected to inspire novelists to produce many more segmented narratives in the 1980s.

Graham Greene, the popular novel and twentieth-century horror

Novelists more able and more artistically conscientious than Uris have dealt with the 'popular novels after Auschwitz' problem. Graham Greene's *The Third Man* (an early novelized screenplay) takes as its historical subject not concentration but postwar refugee camps in Austria. The hero, Rollo Martins, is confronted with this overwhelming human catastrophe in his search for his 'friend', the Judas mastercriminal Harry Lime. Lime, as Rollo eventually discovers, has been trading in adulterated penicillin on the medical black market, a peculiarly vile form of profiteering which produces meningeal damage in children. A guided tour through the 'reality' of the children's hospital wards is the climax of the story.

Rollo is a novelist with two professional characters, both hopelessly inadequate to deal with his Viennese experience. He makes his living writing genre westerns in which the complexities of life are reduced to the simple formulas of frontier fiction — shootouts, standing tall, posse justice (ironically his pulps are favourite reading matter of the NCOs and other ranks on duty in Vienna). Rollo is persecuted by a second novelistic personality. He is constantly mistaken for a namesake novelist of fine Forsterian sensibility. There is a hilarious British Council meeting in which he answers *in propria persona* (as a disciple of Zane Grey) questions put to him by earnest culture-hounds who address him in his other persona as a Bloomsbury lion.

This play with novelist's role has the status of a comic subplot to the search for Lime. It is also, presumably, something of a private joke; critics are always assuming that Greene — the writer of 'entertainments' — is 'really' a portentous, serious artist. But in the larger context of the story we can take *The Third Man* as a kind of Jamesian 'critical parable'.

Neither of the novelistic personae of Rollo can connect with the reality of Vienna. Its quantum of human wretchedness eludes the formulas of the western as completely as it defies the sensibility of the traditional liberal novel. There is no literary equipment adequate to the task. At the conclusion of the novella the writer leaves Vienna, having lost everything — friend, girl and occupation.

Chapter Twenty-one

Nightmare and medicare: *Coma*

I

Probably one of the most useful social functions of bestselling fiction is to make collective anxieties manageable by embedding them in heavily stereotyped, and therefore comfortably familiar, narrative forms. *Coma* is an illuminating case in point. This 'shock packed chiller' by Robin Cook did well as a paperback, selling 2 m. copies in 1979, and even better as a 'terrifying' film from MGM. (Screenplay and direction were by 'movelist' Michael Crichton.) Pan's synopsis indicates the kinds of thrill *Coma* offers, the blurb writer half opening the door on the horrors within:

It began with two patients undergoing routine minor
surgery in Boston's greatest hospital. Under the anaesthetic
in Operating Room 8 they became the victims of an
inexplicable mishap. They never regained consciousness.
Up against the scorn of the medics, and the hostility of the
establishment, one girl medical student starts to probe the
coma cases, steadily uncovering something unbelievably
hideous.

A commentator in *American Bookseller*, noting the sales success of *Coma* in its two carefully tied-in forms, advanced a shrewd market analysis:

A statistical profile on *Coma* would probably show that
the audience for both book and movie was largely female
and under thirty. Essentially, the story is gothic, with a
beautiful female doctor in jeopardy. It plays on deep
seated hostilities many of us feel towards hospitals and
their staff (*American Bookseller*, August 1978).

At a very basic level, then, *Coma* seems to conform to the

familiar cultural practice by which anxiety-rousing objects bifurcate into starkly opposed images — what might be called the fairy godmother/wicked stepmother dualism. *Coma*'s 'nightmare' coexists with popular soap operas of the Dr Kildare or *Emergency Ward 10* kind, which deal with 'deep seated hostilities' by cosy reassurance. *Coma*, and works like it, deal with these hostilities in an opposite way, by playing them out in heavily conventionalized and stereotyped horror fiction designed to terrorize the reader (potential patient).

At the level of its literary formation, *Coma* is clichéd gothic. In the novel's *scène à faire*, the intrepid young heroine discovers that 'This was no ordinary hospital'. The hospital with its secret chamber is a modernized version of the abbey, castle or mysterious house of gothic tradition. Robin Cook's heroine, Susan Wheeler, has as her respectable ancestors the similarly inquisitive Catherine Morland and Jane Eyre. Her less respectable ancestors are the swooning heroines of Mrs Radcliffe. In reading *Coma* one hears distantly Isabella Thorpe's twittering 'horrid . . . delightfully horrid', as a tribute to a form of silly novel that not even Jane Austen's satire could put down. So common is *Coma*'s 'Bluebeard's chamber' theme nowadays that the modern paperback gothics have a standard cover illustration which shows a young girl (often barefoot, always dishevelled) running from a threatening castle/mansion within whose walls we *know* she has seen something very nasty indeed.

At what might be taken as its surface level, *Coma* alludes to current anxieties about medical treatment which preoccupy the thinking American. In a preview, *Publishers Weekly* (7 February, 1977) advertised it as containing 'horrifying revelations about present day hospital scandals'. 'Indirect allusion to' rather than 'revelations of' is the correct formulation; but the present-day scandals or anxieties clearly in *Coma*'s frame of reference are:

1 the prevalence of iatrogenic or doctor-induced illness.
2 the ethics of transplant operations.
3 the 'legal definition of death' controversy, especially as it focused on such cases as Karen Quinlan, brain but not body-dead. Quinlan, a comatose young girl on a life

support system, attended by what were in the popular mind vampiric — because money-making — doctors, who might or might not throw the switch, clearly was a direct inspiration for *Coma*, and helped create its main appeal with women of Quinlan's age group.

4   the malpractice suits and the vast damages increasingly awarded by American courts to patients who could prove faulty or incompetent treatment.

5   the crippling cost of medical treatment in the US, and the successful resistance to medicare by the AMA and interested lobbies. As a result the first conscious thought of most postoperative American patients is, supposedly, not 'Am I cured?' but 'How am I going to pay for all this?'

These issues are 'discussed' at the level of debate or intellectual controversy by such as Susan Sontag, Michel Foucault, Szasz and Illich. Newspapers will take up the subjects according to their readership's capacity and tastes. Thus the occasional 'drama' like Quinlan's will occupy the whole spectrum of the press, eliciting high-sounding editorials in the *New York Times* and human interest coverage by the tabloids. The dramatic and usually short-lived organ-transplant stories (as short-lived, that is, as the luckless patients) also interest the whole range of British and American newspapers, on those occasions when they are headline news (Barnard rather overdid it). Malpractice suits are protracted civil cases; usually they make big headlines only when the case comes up and when the 'record breaking' award is made. But they are in the air, fostering hostility. Papers often invoke the mythical American doctor who sees an auto accident on the freeway and un-Hippocratically puts his foot down so as not to get legally involved.

In popular fiction and entertainment such anxieties are not intellectually examined or articulated, even as sketchily as in sensational journalism. But the issues protrude here, as in other areas of popular consciousness. One of the great supersellers of the 1970s was a revived novel of the 1960s, *One Flew Over the Cuckoo's Nest*. Its phenomenal success (five Oscars, millions of book-sales) was due at least partly to the 1970s climate of suspicion against the medical profession – a profession which in the novel and film (particularly the film) takes healthy people and iatrogenically turns them into sick people.

The organ-transplant and definition-of-death questions brought new social relevance to the crudely conventional Frankenstein (spare-parts man) and Dracula (undead man) formulas. These are old favourites in popular entertainment and are reprocessed every few years. But what is notable in the 1970s is how many respectable writers and film makers were suddenly interested (Herzog, Polanski, Warhol, Mirisch) and how they provided the inspiration for 'sophisticated' comedy (e.g. *Young Frankenstein, Love at First Bite*.)

Coma is not, in fact, a terribly respectable or sophisticated venture (though Crichton's connection gives the film a certain superiority over what Hammer does with the theme). Essentially *Coma* uses the whole box of gothic tricks in a competent but unimaginative way. The largest of these is to take a collectively disturbed state of mind (disturbed in this instance by the cluster of medical problems presented to the American public in the 1970s), and convert this disturbance into 'excitement'; that is to say a purely literary effect. Once converted, excitement can be controlled by the practised mechanisms of literary response. We can deal with the 'terrifying', the 'unbelievably hideous' and the 'chilling'. Paradoxically, it is harder for us to deal with the lower-key 'disturbing' or 'worrying' social problem.

Coma starts, as did the earlier hit *Carrie*, with a closely observed and traumatic menstruation in a young girl whom we automatically identify as the heroine. If nothing else, her description cues us to this assessment; 'a delicately angular and attractive girl with an aristocratic appearance' (*Coma*, 1979, p. 8). She has a heavy period, which develops into haemorrhage. Discomfort intensifies to pain, to humiliation (under the hospital examination), to nightmare and, finally, to unconsciousness as she is taken into the operating theatre. At this point Cook jolts his reader: 'Nancy Greenly fell asleep at 7:24 on February 14, 1976, for the last time' (*ibid.*, p. 14).

This is the trick which Hitchcock used in *Psycho*, with the stabbing of Janet Leigh. The narrative creates a false sense of security by suggesting that the audience has a heroine in view (we know that heroines in gothic fiction are always at risk — but they never die). Cook's motives are different from Hitchcock's, however. *Coma* has another 'real' heroine lined up who will be properly protected. As it is, the sudden extinction of Greenly creates the most significant *frisson* in the novel — that of having consciousness switched off, never to be regained.

The plot which follows is less successful than the opening episode. Daring detective work by the real heroine, an intern, uncovers what it is that is 'unbelievably hideous' at the mysterious Jefferson Institute. In a secret, heavily guarded part of the hospital she finds a ward containing life-supported, brain-murdered victims; an organ bank. The Institute (connected, remember, with 'Boston's greatest hospital') is 'a clearing house for black market transplant organs'. It provides spare body parts — but only for those who can pay extortionate rates. Having broken into this Bluebeard's chamber, the young girl overhears two surgeons chatting at their work:

'I wonder where that heart's going from that previous case?'

'San Fran', said the second surgeon, running down a knot, pulling it tight. 'I think it's only bringing seventy-five thousand dollars. It was a poor match, only two out of four, but it was a rush order.'

'Can't win 'em all,' said the first surgeon, 'but this kidney is a four-tissue match, and I understand it's going for almost two hundred thousand. Besides, they might want the other one in a few days.'

'Well, we don't let it go until we find a market for the heart,' added the other, tying another rapid knot.

'The real problem is finding a tissue match for Dallas. The offer is a million dollars for a four-match. The kid's father is in oil' (*ibid.*, p. 218).

Here we have the nucleus of the novel. The super-rich enjoy a super-effective medical service which the poor don't. Worse, the rich get their better treatment not just at the cost of corresponding neglect for the less rich majority, but by means of actual exploitation. When it comes to medicine, the rich are cannibals, the medical profession are their chefs and the poor are fodder.

A gothic novel cannot stay with its theme thus nakedly exposed. (Satire, incidentally, can; see, for example, Mordecai Richler's *Cocksure*.) Quickly we are back to the world of the chase, and the mad scientist with his usual megalomaniac self-defence: 'we need people like myself, indeed like Leonardo da Vinci, willing to step beyond restrictive laws in order to insure progress. What if Leonardo da Vinci had not dug up his bodies for dissection? What if Copernicus had knuckled under to the laws and dogma of the church?'.

And finally *Coma* offers a twist on Poe's 'buried alive' horror; conscious, but speechless through paralyzing drugs, Susan is wheeled into the theatre for the operation which she knows will leave her brain-dead, so much meat for the organ supermarket upstairs. Last minute rescue, led by her square-jawed doctor lover, saves her at brain-death's door.

Of the aspects it might have taken, *Coma* fixes most powerfully on the economic and class-discriminatory aspects of medical treatment. It shadows, inarticulately, the medicare debate; the fact that only the very poor, for example, are forced to sell blood in the US; or that the Quinlan parents were conceivably facing ruin from the expense of day-round intensive care to keep their daughter 'alive'. More distantly, we recall that Barnard's donors were often black, his beneficiaries white, and the relative infant-mortality statistics for black and white populations in South Africa.

II

With some ingenuity, it is possible to discern a running concern with social problems in many, perhaps most, bestsellers. Rarely, however, do they meet them straight on. There are, of course, those novels which, like Hailey's or Michener's, go through a show of setting up a 'debate' on weighty questions of the day. Thus, for example, Michener's *Sayonara* furrows its brow at what we are led to believe is an issue: '*Sayonara:* The challenging novel which probes unflinchingly into the question of why so many American men prefer the tender and submissive women of the exotic east.' Because they are tender, submissive, exotic and not offensively coloured is the answer to this pseudo-question. For its time (the mid-1950s) a really challenging novel might have asked why so many American men were prepared to lynch or castrate any black American who dared prefer the tender and submissive women of caucasian descent.

An opposite technique, which has the virtue of avoiding Michener-style cant, is Erich Segal's. *Love Story* and *Oliver's Story* simply blank out all socially charged material. (Susan Sontag in *Illness as Metaphor* points out that the disease which kills the girl in *Love Story* is artfully chosen for its symptomlessness: like the consumption of Victorian fiction it kills without disfiguring, merely rendering its victim interestingly pale.) Segal's conscious ideological evacuation of his material is unusual, as, indeed, are most aspects of *Love Story* other than its banal love story. A more common mode of evasion is what Freud, discussing dreams, calls 'condensation'; that is to say the radical simplification of the complex into manageable, symbolic units. With a little indulgence of the imagination we can read the two *Towering Inferno* novels (*The Tower*, *Glass Inferno*) or see the film as a malevolent allusion to the urban renewal programmes which have ravaged city centres, replacing human habitation with offices. The tower stands for all arrogant new architecture and the fire for what we would like to happen to it. Following this line of attack, a novel like George Fox's *Amok* can be read as an exasperated Occidental response (matching a popular mood) to Japan's refusal to lose the war. Thirty years after being thrown back in the Pacific, and atom-bombed into the stone age, they have come back to dominate their victors economically. The yellow peril will not, it seems, surrender. Its invincibility is condensed into one gigantic Jap:

> When the Japanese occupation forces evacuated the Philippines in the last bloody months of the war, one man was left behind. A renegade giant capable of nightmare violence and terrifying brutality. He was armed with a razor-edged samurai blade and ordered to delay the enemy advance for as long as possible. Three decades later that man is still killing.

A clearer-cut example of fictional condensation is Ira Levin's *The Stepford Wives*. This bestselling romance (by a man, though the name is usefully ambiguous) is commonly sold on women's liberation bookstalls among all the fierce tracts, treatises and protest pamphlets. The Stepford wives are small-town Americans transmuted into obedient androids by their husbands, under the evil mastermind of an engineer supposedly trained in such arts at Disneyland. On the face of it Levin's novel is, like *Coma*, a gothic chiller. But women, at least, have discerned its core allusion and promoted it as a socially aware *exposé* of man's inhumanity to woman, and it is displayed in company with Millett, Greer and Friedan.

The most common technique of all is to incorporate a social problem into the *mise en scène*, and then dump it behind as the narrative turns to some 'caper', or adventure with no social resonance whatsoever. Thus in Wambaugh's *The Black Marble* (a sardonic, tough-cop novel) a Pasadena socialite has her prizewinning schnauzer dognapped. The thief demands $85,000 ransom. Besotted as she is with the animal, Madeline would pay; but she hasn't got the money — her trust fund has been depleted by her mother's falling ill a year before it matured:

The medical bills had been truly unbelievable. That was the word. Until you'd been visited by a relentless cancer and all it entailed — chemotherapy, radiotherapy, *four* years of extensive hospitalization, outpatient nursing — the expense was not to be believed. It was legally difficult, hence expensive, even to break the trust so that the money could be used. Lawyers had to be paid so that Madeline could pay doctors. . . . Toward the end, Madeline's lawyer tried to persuade her to apply, on her mother's behalf, for Medi-Cal. *Welfare*. A word used in Old Pasadena with words like *leftist* and *Socialist*. It was so unthinkable it would have killed the old woman swifter than the disease (*The Black Marble*, 1978, pp. 59-60).

Statistically, the chances of incurring financially ruinous cancer are greater than being extorted for a similar sum by a dognapper — even in California. But *The Black Marble*, as it must, follows the crisis of the stolen dog, the material cause for its non-return (Madeline's poverty) being left as a parenthesis.

In the interest of pseudo-realism or pseudo-profundity,

bestsellers (especially thrillers) often allude thus, in passing, to urgent social matters — only to leave them hanging. In *The Taking of Pelham 123*, for example, the hero muses on a Levy's rye bread ad, as he waits for the subway train he will hijack:

It pictured a black child eating Levy's bread, and the caption read YOU DON'T HAVE TO BE JEWISH TO LOVE LEVY'S. This was followed by an angry scrawl in red ballpoint ink: BUT YOU HAVE TO BE A NIGGER TO CHEAT ON WELFARE AND SUPPORT YOUR LITTLE BLACK BASTARDS. Beneath that, in block letters, as if to cancel out bitterness with the simple antidote of piety, were the words JESUS SAVES. But still another hand, neither raging nor sweet, perhaps above the battle, had added, PLAID STAMPS (*The Taking of Pelham 123*, 1974, pp. 9-10).

'Such as it was,' Ryder muses, 'it was the true voice of the people.' The narrative then goes on to its main business — the 'taking' of the train, the demand for $1 m., the internecine struggle within the gang and their ultimate downfall.

In *The Taking of Pelham 123* racial tension is introduced at various points — but merely as a prop; realistic detail to validate the tough New York location and its hardboiled etiquette ('You say something to me spic?', 'Up your black ass!'). At the same time such props serve to reassure us that the novel is not really ignoring anything — not putting important matters out of mind. This reduction of social problems to so much local colour and authenticating detail is one of the more offensive aspects of much popular fiction.

Chapter Twenty-two

Documentary, superdocumentary and technology

I

Thomas Gifford's 1977 novel, *The Man From Lisbon*, has a bold, three-word preface: 'It really happened.' Since the novel would have us believe that every single modern history of Portugal is wrong about what really happened, we may beg to disbelieve. Nevertheless, much modern bestselling fiction is devoted to a similarly quixotic attempt to authenticate the fantastic, and either strains or wins over our credulity. (There is a large fund of credulity to strain: the author of the *Flashman* series, George Macdonald Fraser, reports that he regularly gets letters — mainly American — from readers who honestly believe that his Victorian bounder's confessions are genuine.) A number of tricks are used to pull off the hoped-for illusion. One trick is to encrust the narrative with a surplus of researched information; this has the incidental and therapeutic function of reassuring the reader that he is not merely enjoying himself, he is learning something. Another trick is the recruitment of a novelist who is a privileged insider (e.g. the former Vice President of the United States) or who has knowledgeable connections that are prominently disclosed by the publisher. One might note the vogue in the late 1970s for novels written by front performers in news-media. Television in Britain furnished such newscasters-turned-novelists as Michael Nicholson, Sandy Gall, John Snow and Gerald Seymour. In America, CBS and ABC collaborated in the authorial persons of Marvin Kalb and Ted Koppel on *In the National Interest*, a saga of middle-east shuttle diplomacy enigmatically endorsed by Dr Kissinger as 'A great work of fiction'. The association of novels with newscasters tends, of course, in the opposite direction — to validate them, that is, as 'great works of fact'. And the subjects chosen by such novelists — political intrigues, coups, international crises — are carefully consonant with their familiar broadcast messages to us.

A third trick is the transparently close shadowing of recent celebrated news events. J. Kwitny's *Shakedown* advertises itself as: 'the true story, almost, of a $4.5bn phoney check heist'. So are many modern novels 'true stories, almost.' And the wide-awake novelist is very quick off the mark — thus only months after the Harrisburg disaster James N. Rowe brought out *The Judas Squad* with its banner headline — 'What happened at Three Mile Island was a warning. What happens in this novel is a threat.' It took the ever resourceful Scortia and Robinson only a little longer to rush out their 'Legionnaires' disease' novel, *The Nightmare Factor*.

A fourth trick is the elaborate use of authenticating devices. Most of these are familiar in the history of the novel, but the graphics of the electronic media and science bring new verve to their employment. It is this fourth kind of authentication which is considered in this chapter.

II

The 1970s have been marked by a series of superficially far-fetched thrillers which have none the less made impudent claims to historical veracity. Forsyth is the leader in this fact-fiction school. One of the refrains of his Hutchinson publicity machine is that it takes him as little as six weeks to write a book — 'but the research takes years'. The synopsis for *The Odessa File* and its final question reflect the novel and its veridical pretensions fairly enough:

The life-and-death hunt for a notorious Nazi criminal
unfolds against a background of international espionage
and clandestine arms deals, involving rockets designed in
Germany, built in Egypt, and equipped with warheads of
nuclear waste and bubonic plague. Mossad, the Israeli
intelligence service, is locked in a struggle with Odessa, the
organization of former SS men in Germany. As the story

leads to its final dramatic confrontation on a bleak
winter's hill-top, the question that every reader asked at
the end of THE DAY OF THE JACKAL will inevitably be
asked again: CAN this be fiction?
If it weren't, one may ask, would any sane man — and he an
ex-Reuter's correspondent — tell the secret in a mass-market
novel of which everyone inevitably asks: CAN this be fact?
Forsyth uses all the above-listed devices. *The Odessa File* has
a liberal supply of pedagogic scenes in which the researching
reporter-hero has to play the *ingénu* to — among others —
Simon Wiesenthal. The narrative claims to be informed with
privileged information by virtue of Forsyth's contacts, who
must be kept anonymous for their own safety, as he tells us
in a preface. It shadows recent reported assassinations by
Israeli intelligence services abroad. And the text is interrupted
by owlish editorial footnotes, as if one were reading a monograph on the resurgence of fascism, rather than a romance.
    Of course, there *is* a venerable romantic tradition to which
the most modern fact/fiction can be attached. Graham
Greene, for example, noted of Wallace's early twentieth-
century thrillers that they 'tell an almost incredible story
with very precise realistic details' (Greene, 1970, p. 172).
Curiosity can trace authenticating gimmickry like Forsyth's
back to the eighteenth-century gothic novel, and its convention of the editorial preface asserting that the following
narrative is based on a found manuscript. We still encounter
such prefaces in a form which would have been familiar to
Mrs Radcliffe. In Brian Garfield's *Kolchak's Gold* the traditional foreword is embellished by typography which simulates
a typewritten letter from historian to literary agent. Publicity
labours to create a rich mystification, as in the following
blurb to Ludlum's *The Scarlatti Inheritance*. (Ludlum it is,
incidentally, who seems to have made fashionable and largely
helped do to death the vogue for pseudo-objective titles:
The Rhinemann Exchange, *The Matarese Circle*, *The Ipcress
File*, *The Anderson Tapes* etc.):
Fact or Fiction?
That's the question Americans have been hotly debating
since this extraordinary book was published. The original
publishers, World Publishing of New York, stated that 'In

response to announcements of the book's forthcoming publication, certain persons contacted us to offer private knowledge of the novel's origins. Curiously, their several versions all agreed . . .' What is certain is that an American multi-millionaire, Chandler Douglas, an associate of pro-Nazi Americans, *did* disappear in that crucial year of 1926 and was never heard of again — at least, not under his American name.

Finally and just prior to the bestselling publication of *The Scarlatti Inheritance*, World Publishing contacted America's Defense Intelligence Agency and was referred to Lt. Cmd. Van Fergus. He replied that 'Army History has no information to confirm the Scarlatti premise.' When asked if records other than Army History were also clear of evidence he replied, 'I cannot answer that question.'

So there you have it — fact or fiction?

III

Subtlety is not much prized by the contemporary bestseller or its reader; but authentication is one area in which popular novelists can achieve a near-Nabokovian *trompe-l'oeil*. Patrick Mann's *Steal Big*, for example, chronicles an alliance between the 'mob' and the 'outfit' (Mafia and CIA) to fix the European elections to keep the reds out. This is how the blurb presents Patrick Mann to us:

Patrick Mann is the pseudonym of a former US Army Intelligence agent who has for many years been a crime reporter for a nationwide American newspaper syndicate. He has worldwide contacts with the underworld and with law enforcement authorities. He is the author of *The Vacancy* and *Dog Day Afternoon* — the award winning film starring Al Pacino.

The hero of *Steal Big* is one Max Patrick (NB 'Patrick'), a former intelligence agent who knows too much and who has insured himself against 'Uncle' (i.e. an ungrateful government) bumping him off by 'notoriety'. He has put himself safely in the limelight by writing superselling novels about — of course — the sinister alliance between the Mafia and CIA.

In *Steal Big*, Max Patrick's last novel is being turned into a film with Al Pacino in the lead.

Documentary authenticism of Mann's kind is embedded into the text as a teasing parenthesis to the main narrative, a half-given, half-withheld warranty of the accuracy of the story. Such subtlety is, presumably, overlooked by many readers without any great loss to enjoyment. Similarly, Forsyth's validating prefaces and footnotes or Ludlum's 'Fact or Fiction' advertisements stand decently at the edges of the narrative. In this the Ludlum-Forsyth style of authentication device mimics the apparatus of historical-scholarly discourse, legal presentation or the report. The fabric of thrillers such as *The Odessa File* is not disturbed or violated by such exterior packaging.

In the 1970s, however, there emerged a fashionable genre of fiction in which authentication was flagrant, and calculatedly designed to rupture the surface of the narrative. In this modish fiction the discreet self-effacement of the pseudo-scholarly preface, or footnote of the 'file' or 'dossier' kind, gave way to something much more exhibitionistic and aggressive. The name coined and widely publicized for these newly fashionable novels was 'superdocumentary'. Superdocumentaries were applauded by their publicists as something entirely new. Thus in endorsement for *The Anderson Tapes* Arthur Hailey enthused over the novel as 'Frightening. . . . A completely new kind of novel . . . fascinating, exciting, fast-moving.' There had, of course, been frightening novels before, and novels which moved fast and could legitimately claim to be exciting. What made novels like *The Anderson Tapes* 'completely new' was their form. Narrative, in this case, was given as unprocessed or raw tape transcription. Such narration totally in the language of electronic printout was startling; but the general principle was not quite as brand new in 1970 (when Sanders published *The Anderson Tapes*) as Hailey suggests. By this date Michael Crichton had already put out his very successful *The Andromeda Strain*, which made the bestseller lists for thirty weeks in 1969. (Crichton was later to publish the less successful *The Terminal Man* in 1972). *The Andromeda Strain* opens with a facsimile first page which does literally what *The Odessa File* did allusively, that is, it presents itself as an actual file:

THIS FILE IS CLASSIFIED TOP SECRET

Examination by unauthorized persons
is a criminal offense punishable
by fines and imprisonment up to
20 years and $20,000.

DO NOT ACCEPT FROM COURIER
IF SEAL IS BROKEN

The courier is required by law
to demand your card 7592. He
is not permitted to relinquish
this file without such proof of
identity.

Thus the Dell paperback, which the reader has bought from his drugstore for $1.25, is a top-secret dossier. The isomorphic hoax is carried on with a straightfaced preface by 'MC' which announces that 'This book recounts the five-day history of a major American scientific crisis' ('recounts' not 'invents'). The preface is accompanied by an impressive list of political and scientific debts of gratitude, and the mock-humble apology, 'this is a rather technical narrative, centering on complex issues of science'. In fact the ideas of *Andromeda* (plague from space) are threadbare sf. What gives it new life is that the story is done throughout in the modish super-documentary manner, with a bizarre profusion of printouts, transcripts, buzz words, graphs. *The Andromeda Strain* finishes with a long bibliography of 'unclassified documents and references that formed the background to the book' ('unclassified' is a nice touch). This cites such sources as:

> 4. Twombley, E.R., et al. 'Tissue Thromboplastin in Timed Release from Graded Intimal Destruction,' *Path. Res.* 19: 1-53.

5. Ingersoll, H.G. 'Basal Metabolism and Thyroid Indices in Bird Metabolic Stress Contexts,' *J. Zool.* 50: 223-304.

Having begun as a file, the novel signs off as a thesis. Of course, it is all mystification, so much mumbo-jumbo. The idea that Crichton's five million or so readers will gravely turn up *'Path. Res.'* (*Pathological Research?*) is comical. The bibliography is just one of *The Andromeda Strain*'s technogrammatic devices, and contributes to its *poésie concrète* appearance and deliberate formal barbarousness.

IV

Crichton's performances in the superdocumentary mode are artificial and have not stood up well. (Not as well, for example, as the early work of Len Deighton, whose *Ipcress File* Crichton acknowledges to have been an inspiration.) His plots strike anyone familiar with sf as hand-me-down, and his ability to pep them up with *appliqué* documentary facsimile palls after a while. One simply skips the hardware and is left with a thin story line.

A more subtle and thoroughly satisfying use of the mode is achieved by Lawrence Sanders in his 1970 superseller, *The Anderson Tapes*. (Without the narrative trickery it was converted into a goodish film, with Sean Connery in the lead.) Sanders's novel is told virtually entirely through tape transcripts. The hero, 'Duke' Anderson, is a specialist thief of the old school, planning a heist on a whole apartment block on New York's plush East Side. Although he never guesses it (and dies without realizing), his preparations and his whole private life are bugged at every point by a battery of snooping agencies: Peace of Mind Inc. (they furnish divorce evidence), the New York Police Department, the New York State Income Tax Bureau, the Narcotics Board, the Internal Revenue Service and so on. There are about a dozen in all, some too sensitive to be named, even by acronym. The abortive robbery itself is documented via District Attorneys' depositions, police reports, newspaper stories etc. All this espionage and reportage is not concerted and purposeful —

Anderson is usually on the periphery of some other target
under investigation. The narrative of the crime is knit together
by 'the author' — a newspaper reporter on the Newark (NJ)
Post Ledger, and, as a final documentary touch, this is
alleged to be Sanders himself. In fact, before his novel-
writing career got going late in life, Sanders was editor of
Mechanix Illustrated among other technology-concerned
trade papers; hence, presumably, his ease with specialized
knowledge. Crichton studied medicine at Harvard, which
clearly stands him in good stead.

There is more to *The Anderson Tapes* than a new wrinkle
in thriller narration. The plot, of course, is familiar enough —
the super-heist undertaken by a motley criminal band (homosexual connoisseur, 'Professor', hip black, trigger-happy
mafioso etc.). Presiding over this gang is Duke Anderson,
whose personality is, as we indirectly piece it together, a
centre of unusual interest. Anderson is a tragic figure; a
skilled professional and a charismatic leader: 'If you can't
trust a man like Duke, who can you trust?' asks one of the
criminals later under investigation (*The Anderson Tapes*,
1979, p. 231). The allusion to John Wayne — that other
Duke — seems conscious. Anderson is defeated, appropriately
enough, not by crime's traditional human opposition (the
detective or law enforcer), but by the new technology and
the new police organization into highly efficient assault
squads ('Tactical Patrol Units'). As he dies, the implicit
conclusion is that of Wells's *The Invasion of the Ironclads* —
'Machinery defeats humankind'. With Watergate two years
ahead, the point of Sanders's prophetic novel is that, potentially, every private sector of life is now public. It is Orwell's
thought-policed *1984* removed from the realm of dystopian
future to documented present.

The Anderson Tapes achieves a sustained and stimulating
oddity of narration. The pathetic and passionate story of the
hero is relayed obliquely through the indifferent voice-
operated recorders for whose supervisors Anderson is a
cipher. 'You become part of the eavesdropping apparatus,'
as the *New York Times* observed. And, as with any act of
eavesdropping, the information exacts a toll of human
degradation. The tie-in movie is somewhat handicapped in

this respect, since it narrates rather than eavesdrops. Sanders himself makes the point that a story which is all playback and never visual would have come over better as a radio play — but, of course, as a medium, radio can no longer raise the capital to purchase rights in bestsellers. The film is further damaged in that it sacrifices the complexity of Anderson's motivation which might, loosely, be termed Dostoevskyan; 'Crime is the truth, law is the hypocrisy' (*ibid.*, p. 253) he confides to his diary. Anderson's sexual predilection for flagellation is also removed from the film — presumably so as not to compromise the star Connery's 'straight' image.

Sanders makes no great claim for *The Anderson Tapes*, and affects a bewilderment at such commendatory reviews as that in the *New York Times* — 'I don't take myself seriously, so why should anyone else? I'm writing entertainment — I hope intelligent entertainment, but that's all' (*Publishers Weekly*, 2 August, 1976). None the less his novel stands out from the debased run of bestsellers as something superior. But, in general, superdocumentary seems to have had a short vogue. Sanders, Crichton and, in England, Len Deighton made something of it — but all moved on to other things. (Crichton became a versatile 'movelist', Anderson wrote straight crime and political thrillers like *The Tangent Factor* and *The Second Commandment* — something of a comedown in my opinion — while Deighton went in for military history.) Superdocumentary continued to be written, but no longer made the bestseller lists: only modest success attended such works as Leo Clancy's *The Fix* ('The story is told through recordings of an interrogation conducted under drugs — drugs that provoke total recall') or James Mills's *Report to the Commissioner*, a police story related as if it were an actual confidential report prepared by the Internal Affairs Division of the NYCPD. The novel is allegedly based on 'real documents' which Mills — a former *Life* reporter — does 'not choose to disclose'. By the mid-1970s the gimmick would seem to have been largely played out, and it came to be just one of many devices used to pep up the formula crime novel.

V

Why did the superdocumentary have its vogue when it did? Latently, of course, the idea is present in the novels of writers like Dos Passos, and in various works of sf. But until 1969 the superdocumentary had never figured in the best-seller lists. Commentators were quick to tie in the smash success of *The Andromeda Strain* with the moonshot of 1969, in which man first set foot on extraterrestrial soil. The barbarous technologism of Crichton's novel mirrored the current drama of American life. As Houston's scientific communications invaded the TV screen, driving off the police serial, soap opera and western, so Crichton's printouts and scientific hardware ruptured the narrative of his novel, enacting the violent encounter of popular culture with advanced technology.

In comparison with the 'literary' novel, the bestseller is often very quick on the uptake where technological innovation and new machinery is concerned. An early example of this pre-, or early, cognition of revolutionary technology is to be found in Edgar Wallace. Wallace was well behind his contemporaries Conrad and Lawrence in literary terms; but he did appreciate the significance of the telephone, telegraph and modern journalism. Many of his plots hinge on newspaper scoops, phonecalls, rapid *modern* communications.

Contemporary bestsellers — especially thrillers and spy stories — show a similar interest in the latest technological innovation, and reflect the tempo and perspectives of new communication. The novels of Alfred Coppel, for example, move, chapter by chapter, from one superpower capital to another, one war zone to another. The plots of *The Dragon* and *34 East* (brink-of-unthinkable-war themes) centre on jet aircraft, communications satellites, early-warning stations, war rooms. Coppel was himself once a jet pilot, and the mobility of his narratives, their wideranging reach, reflect a worldview in which global space is shrunk to a strategic theatre with headquarters in constant linked communication to all points. A favourite Coppel scene is that of the President of the US talking by hot line to the USSR Secretary of State.

It is evident that the bestseller serves to digest new technology and reduce its alien configurations to familiarity, for the easier consumption of a non-technocratic reading public. The fascination of superdocumentary writers like Crichton or Sanders is that they take something strangely new (computer analysis, electronic surveillance) and incorporate it into the familiar and controllable setting of the bestselling novel. They domesticate the buzz words of the new technology and put them into circulation. They don't actually *teach* us anything. No one can learn how to programme a computer from *The Andromeda Strain*, how to bug or debug from *The Anderson Tapes*. Such novels serve, rather, to add a new range to the common man's frame of reference, to put these scientific innovations in the same known but not fully understood terms as the jet engine, the TV set and the transistor radio.

Chapter Twenty-three

Disaster

'Perhaps someone up there is trying to tell you that he's still number one.'
(Old Indian to young scientist in *A Fire in the Sky*; NBC TV-movie, teleplay by Dennis Nemec and Michael Blankford, novelized by Walter Kendrick, based upon a story by Paul Gallico.)

I

The mid-1970s vogue for disasters was principally a Hollywood phenomenon. But given the advancingly tied-in nature of the media, the book trade could only profit from the boom with novelizations, original scenarios, *à la mode* potboilers. Such was Hollywood's appetite for this fashionable material that when Hailey put out *The Moneychangers* for film rights in 1974 the word came back, 'Tell Hailey we want disasters' (Sheila Hailey, 1978, p. 177). Hailey managed to sell his novel as a successful TV mini-series. But he clearly heard the industry's call, as any alert bestselling novelist should, and he responded with his next novel, the duly catastrophic *Overload*. That lesser writers had an eye to Hollywood as they wrote can be inferred from the fact that over half the envisaged disasters in fiction afflict the handy film location of California. (Los Angeles, for example, is ravaged by earthquake twice, burned down, visited by an Ice Age, polluted by a power station gone China syndrome, inundated by flood.)

The big films in the disaster genre were *Earthquake*, *Airports '75, '77* and *'79* (all based on Hailey's original, disasterless melodrama), *The Poseidon Adventure* (devised by novelist Paul Gallico), *Towering Inferno* ('partly based' on Stern's *The Tower*, 'largely based' on Scortia and Robinson's *Glass Inferno*), *Juggernaut* and the remake of *King Kong*. These were blockbusters to end all blockbusters — all-or-nothing films which cost huge amounts in special effects. Their multiple narratives involved whole troupes of overpaid stars and hordes of extras. *Towering Inferno*, for example, had Steve McQueen, William Holden, Fred Astaire, Paul Newman, Richard Chamberlain; apart from anything else, satisfying all those egos' needs for top billing must have been an advertising man's nightmare. No expense was spared. *Earthquake* actually necessitated re-equipping cinemas with the vibrating 'sensurround' sound system. That these were the most lavish films ever made, and that they employed the most up-to-date media technology, was a main part of the sales pitch.

The novelist, whose special effects cost nothing, could stagger the mind on a smaller budget. Imagination soared with a string of astonishing disaster scenarios. In *Hermes Fall*, *A Fire in the Sky* and *Fireball* the earth is threatened by asteroids or comets which men vainly try to shoot down or run from. Worlds colliding has always had a minor currency as a favourite sf theme; Niven and Pournelle's *Lucifer's Hammer* did extraordinarily well for genre at this period, boosted as a small bestseller in the open market by the current fad. Climatic disasters were a rich vein; they included Herzog's *Heat* ('the long-feared "greenhouse effect" which can swiftly put an end to all higher life forms and turn our planet into a self-generating inferno'), Jack Bickham's *Twister* ('no life touched by the Twister, as it wreaks a billion dollars worth of damage, will ever be the same again'), Jon Cleary's *Vortex*, Richard Doyle's *Deluge* ('freak winds and driving rain had created a thirty-foot surge in the Thames and London was facing the worst disaster in its history'), *Blizzard* by Thom Racina ('Los Angeles, Sun City, became a City of Ice'), *Freeze* by George Stone ('worst blizzard in history buries the Eastern United States'), *Ice Quake* by Crawford Killian (this novel also deals with a second Ice Age. I suspect that these 'chillers', which provided more than their share of disaster scenarios, were inspired by the 1977 American domestic oil shortages, when thermostats went down all over the continent). In addition to *Poseidon* (and the ludicrously entitled *Beyond the Poseidon Adventure*) and *Juggernaut*, novelists provided such disasters at sea as *Firespill* (600 m. gallons of high-octane fuel poured out on the windswept waters off British Columbia) and *Liner* ('a world cruise ship, heading for a typhoon, with metal fatigue in the engine room and lifeboats corroded to davits'). *Juggernaut*'s gimmick of the multiple hidden bombs was taken up in *Rollercoaster*, where explosives are similarly planted randomly in amusement parks. A bizarre combination of air and sea disasters in *Airport '77* produced a Boeing 747 (custom-built for a millionaire) which goes submarine, and requires underwater rescue. Earthquakes elicited *Earthsound* from the indefatigable Herzog ('the earth's crust splits open like the jaws of hell'), Alistair MacLean's *Goodbye California*, Gerald A. Browne's *Slide* and *Superman*. Technology disasters, of which the film *The China Syndrome* was the most effective representative, inspired novels such as Hailey's *Overload* (Californian power failure) and Scortia and Robinson's *The Prometheus Project*:

> Prometheus is the largest nuclear power plant in the world. Pressure from the White House puts it on stream before the safety checks are complete. . . . The coolant system fails and Prometheus becomes a holocaust of molten debris and exploding hydrogen. A huge radioactive cloud drifts slowly towards Los Angeles.

II

A number of commentators observed that the disaster movie/novel performed a useful therapeutic function. As one film producer, John Calley, put it: 'Disaster films help relieve social tensions by giving people the feeling that we're all in it together.' (*Evening Standard*, 23 October, 1976). Typically, disaster is a shared experience. This, I suspect, is why it goes down so well in the cinema, where large numbers of people are congregated. Disaster narratives tend to be made up of an ensemble of little subnarratives, loosely linked as collective experience. Thus in the *Inferno* novels and film, for instance, the centre of interest switches from architect, to fire chief, to hotel manager, to janitor, to confidence-trickster guest, to VIP, to average family group, to child, to mayor, to old couple etc. This redundancy creates intractable narrative problems, since the reader/audience is never with any one set or dominant character long enough to become inward with them. Hence the casting preference for actors like Charlton Heston, whose simple virtues are recognizably inscribed on their rugged faces.

Although it dissipates narrative energy, the wide range of characters and plots creates the desired 'all life is there' plenary cross section. And, characteristically, the formulators of the disaster film/novel fall back on what Brian Aldiss calls the 'cosy catastrophe'. That is to say, within the disaster area there are discovered close-knit groups — little communities, families, husbands and wives — all brought into even closer intimacy by the catastrophic events that overtake them. And in the larger sense, community is affirmed, and the complexities of social life dissolved. Officers of law and practical, simple, good men take command. Public servants (nurses, firemen, pilots etc.) are glorified in their competence to handle emergency, and a new social solidarity between previously antagonistic groups is forged. This congealing process ('the diverse population sink their differences') and the way in which loners are brought back into the social fold are apparent in the publisher's synopsis for Richard Stern's *Flood*:

Jay Harper was a loner. A brilliant young geophysicist, he had worked in Alaska, Saudi Arabia and on a North Sea oil rig. Between jobs he decides to scuba dive in the artificial lake which drowned the village his ancestors had settled. While looking for family tombstones he notices some disturbing features in the enormous dam which supplies water and electric power to the city on the plains. The local senator is an 'Anglo': the mayor of Mexican origin. The richest and most influential local businessman is self-made and a widower with a spoilt and beautiful daughter. The powerful, in their large and comfortable houses, live on a hill protected by a massive wall and a storm drain. The Chicanos live in caravans and shanties on the banks of the sluggish river. For the last ten years there have been no flood problems because the dam controls the melted snow from the mountains that loom over the city. During the tense days after it is accepted that the dam may not stand up to the freak weather which is moving inexorably towards the area, the diverse population sink their differences in a fight to avert a cataclysmic disaster. One of the comforts of disaster fiction is suggested by the wildly improbable plot of *Wild Card*, by Hawkey and Bingham. There the authorities in the US are conceived as fabricating an alien invasion to defuse the political and social tensions which are tearing the country apart ('the restoration of social cohesion is now wholly dependent on the appearance of an overwhelming alternative enemy'; *Wild Card*, 1976, p. 74).

While it devastates and inflicts suffering of a physical kind, the disaster (especially when it is a 'natural' crisis like fire, flood, quake or storm) relaxes political and social strain, 'bringing people together' and releasing simple and noble virtues in otherwise ordinary or alienated men and women. At the same time the disaster is a valuable test, showing up weak or corrupt members of society. Thus in *The Tower*, the two cowards who try to escape — one, for example, by stealing the lift which is to take the women to safety — die horribly and prematurely. Those remaining 'good ones' (invariably a healthy majority, incidentally; the mass of humanity always emerges creditably in the disaster ordeal) are purified — literally tested by fire. And most are saved; although a few are allowed nobly to lay down their lives for others.

Typically the disaster simplifies by converting economic, political and socially ordered existence into a state of nature where instinctive or natural codes take precedence. This is apprehended by the blurb writers of Gerald A. Browne's *Slide* ('more thrilling than *The Towering Inferno*, more horrific than *Earthquake*'):

Friday May 4th. The fourteenth consecutive day of rain on once sun-scorched California. Over 300 hours of continuous drizzle soaking into the loose topsoil, saturating the uplands along the coast, flushing trees and houses down into the valley. Turning Sheep Hill into a

1300 foot mountain of mud now sliding down into the
ocean – and the Seaside Supermarket which stands in its
path. . . . And inside the store, amid the wreckage of the
most sophisticated selling operation of our age, men and
women battle for life. With only their most basic instincts
to guide them, the survivors take part in an epic of
endurance.

Browne has, for my money, created the best of the disaster
novels in his vision of a supermarket becoming a killing
ground. But his main device is the standard one in the genre:
the sudden regression from high civilization to savagery. The
'most sophisticated selling operation of the age' becomes a
slimy pit, in which 'the most basic instincts' are all that the
characters have to guide them. (There is a nice scene where
trapped shoppers have to dive into the mud to fetch up
tinned oysters.) In this regression, economic order and social
hierarchy are done away with. Natural leaders and honest
men stand revealed; evil men are similarly stripped and shown
up. 'Real' selves and 'real' relations (love, hate, envy) are
free to emerge in the common crisis.

It is one of the laws of the disaster novel/film that the
blow should fall where it will do most damage; not, however,
to the human population but to the social formation and to
the sophisticated technological apparatus of modern society.
An imagined flood in London (in *Deluge* on the day that
the American President is visiting the capital) is more 'disastrous' than the floods which regularly ravage Bangladesh,
killing hundreds of thousands. (But how could 'billions of
dollars worth of damage' be done there? They haven't got
billions of dollars worth of anything; even life is uninsured.)
An imaginary earthquake in California is infinitely more
disastrous than the frequent actual earthquakes in Turkey
or Iran. If all the lights and lifesupport systems went off in
India, as they do in *Overload*'s California, what difference
would it make? The Indians already live in a state of nature.
If a boat peoples' craft capsizes, killing hundreds, what is
that compared to the capsizing of a luxury liner (*Poseidon*,
Liner, *Juggernaut*)? In Guy N. Smith's *The Thirst*, a herbicide
is accidentally dropped in a reservoir serving the British
home counties ('the most deadly weedkiller ever invented').

Deadly herbicides *were* cunningly invented and dropped to the peril of the native population of South Vietnam — but that wasn't a disaster worthy of bestselling fiction. Another *Thirst* (1977, an opportunistic re-release of C.E. Maine's *The Tide Went Out* to tie in with the 1976 English drought) is set not in actually parched Ethiopia, but in London. Such is the geopolitical lottery that the inhabitants of actual disaster areas with no 'civilization' to separate them from their 'basic instinctive selves' are not conceived as really capable of experiencing catastrophe.

For all their ingenious *données* and variations, the disasters considered here, involve a natural violation of a highly sophisticated community or artefact. The Poseidon is 'the first of the giant Ocean liners'; the planetoid or Ice Age, when they strike, strike New York or Los Angeles. The underlying emotion on which these novels seem to draw is a primitive anxiety lurking under an assertive pride in progress; a sense that western civilization may be guilty of hubris in thinking that it has finally pacified nature. It is noticeable, for example, how often these works draw on archaic and non-scientific cosmogony in their titles — Inferno, Poseidon, Deluge, Prometheus. The recurrent message of these narratives is that the highest shall be brought calamitously low, that pride goes before a fall. Two final synopses — with their emphasis on millionaires and VIPs, on the 'most luxurious plane in history' and the 'world's newest skyscraper', bring the basic *de casibus* theme out clearly enough:

Michael Scheff and David Spector
Airport 77
Millionaire Philip Stevens had built the most luxurious
plane in history. Filled with his art treasures, crowded with
friends and family, its maiden flight was a triumph of pride
and expensive engineering. Nothing could go wrong. And
then without warning, the 747 swerved off course. In a
few seconds, the magnificent craft was a shattered hulk,
trapped in the most inaccessible place on earth. Struggling
with panic and treachery, a few brave men fought to save
the lives that depended on them.

Richard Martin Stern
The Tower
For 125 floors the world's newest skyscraper rises tall and clean and shining. In its highest room film stars, celebrities, politicians, diplomats, tycoons and their wives celebrate the official opening. Suddenly, an explosion rocks the building. The electrical system is sabotaged. Fire rages upwards from the fourth floor. Totally isolated, the VIP guests are trapped. Who can escape, and how . . . and who must be left to die . . .?

Chapter Twenty-four

British pessimism: the 'as if' narratives

James Michener's *Centennial* was a bestseller cunningly designed to ride on a crest of American bicentennial celebrations. The 1,100-page saga monotonously chronicles the American spirit's victory over all adversaries from the primeval rocks of some three billion years ago through the first 'inhabitants' — diplodocus and allosaurus — to the great Depression of the 1920s and 1930s. *Centennial* serenely took its place at the top of America's bestseller lists: the hardback came out in 1974, the more lucrative paperback came out in the centennial year, 1976, and the most lucrative television tie-in edition appeared in 1979. At the same period in Britain, Len Deighton's *SS-GB* was a superseller that did unusually well. The hardback sold over 100,000 in 1978; the paperback headed the British bestseller lists in early 1980. This work, together with other successful British 'as if' narratives (*The Alteration*, *An Englishman's Castle*) bespoke a curious sense of national defeat and exhaustion, directly opposite to America's (admittedly whipped-up) buoyancy and centennial pride. (*Centennial* had its companion novels as well, eager to cash in on the appetite for epic 'making of America' themes in the mid-1970s: such blockbusters as Howard Fast's *The Immigrants* and John Jakes's 'The Kent Family Chronicles' — subtitled the 'American Bicentennial Series'. All share *Centennial*'s national optimism and narcissistic self-satisfaction.)

Len Deighton's *SS-GB* is clearly spun off, in one sense, from his historical fiction and history *tout court* of the Second World War (*Bomber* and *Fighter*). The novel portrays a 1941 England whose empire has imploded like a white dwarf:

In February 1941 British Command surrendered to the Nazis. Churchill had been executed, the King is in the

Tower and the SS are in Whitehall. For nine months
Britain had been occupied – a blitzed, depressed and dingy
country. The plot of *SS-GB* is that of a murder hunt by Scotland Yard
('business as usual') in the transformed Nazi colony. This
eventually becomes mixed up with the 'secret weapon' (the
atom bomb – more potent than historical Germany's V2)
which will perhaps one day lead to liberation. All this is
exciting enough, but the really powerful element in *SS-GB*
is its setting and its atmosphere of national enervation. The
forms of English society, its jurisprudence and police procedure are much the same as ever. But they rest on an alien
ideological base – the base that elsewhere in fiction, Deighton's
fighters and bombers helped defeat forever in 1945. Deighton's
novel is experienced by the British reader as an assemblage of
'effects', a making-strange or defamiliarization of 'our'
country. It presents a London, for example, in which the
shells of the imperial past horribly survive the national
energy that once created and informed them:

It was a big BMW motor-cycle, with an airship-shaped side-
car, and an axle that connected the two rear wheels. With a
machine like that, he could climb a mountain. It had SS
registration plates and a London SS HQ recognition device.
Douglas climbed into the side-car and gave the rider a nod.
Then he had to hang on tight to the machine-gun
mounting, as they roared down Grosvenor Place with noise
enough to wake half London.
In the air there was the green, sooty fog typical of those
that London suffered, but the rider did not slacken speed.
A Gendarmerie foot patrol was marching through the
Victoria railway station forecourt but they ignored the SS
motor-cycle. The fog was worse as they neared the river,
and Douglas caught the ugly smell of it. After Vauxhall
Bridge, the motor-cyclist turned right, into a street of
squat little houses and high brick walls, and advertisement
hoardings, upon which appeals for volunteers to work in
German factories, announcements about rationing and a
freshly pasted German-Soviet Friendship Week poster
shone rain-wet through the fog (*SS-GB*, 1979, p. 136).

Victoria, Victory and Victorian achievement are all confounded in such descriptions. Even the cosy rituals that got the British through the dark nights of the blitz ('We can take it!') are ruined; the 'nice cup of tea', for instance, offered the policeman hero by his landlady:

'More tea?'

'No thanks.'

'It's the German ersatz. They say it's made for them to have with lemon. It's not very nice with milk is it?' (*ibid.*, p. 69).

There is nothing in *SS-GB* of the 'grim warning' school of fiction. It strikes very differently from, for example, Sinclair Lewis's impassioned vision of fascist takeover in the US, *It Can't Happen Here*, or Constantine Fitzgibbon's equally urgent fantasy of Soviet takeover in the UK, *When the Kissing Had to Stop*. But Deighton's novel is, of course, generically different. These other works are 'awful prophecies'; they foretell a possible future and strike a loud-mouthed Cassandra pose. Deighton's quieter work belongs to a new and ingenious form of historical fiction known in sf (where it originated) as the 'alternative universe' novel. The most famous example is Philip K. Dick's 'classic' of 1962, *The Man in the High Castle*, which portrays an America defeated and occupied by the Second World War Axis powers. Following Dick's breakthrough, alternative universe fiction has had a good run in sf, but before the mid-1970s had made no impact on the British bestseller lists. Nor was *SS-GB* a single exception. At the same time that it was selling its hundreds of thousands many of its readers must also have watched the BBC's serial *An Englishman's Castle* (BBC-2 early 1979, BBC-1 late 1979), and some must have already taken in an unusual novel of Kingsley Amis's, *The Alteration*, which made the 1976 bestseller lists, if not as spectacularly as Deighton did two years after.

An Englishman's Castle is set in a more-or-less contemporary 1970s England. The country which is discovered is in many ways recognizably the here and now; prosperous, affluent, massively apathetic — Orwell's 'gentle' England, your England — but with the difference that it is part of the victorious Nazi-German world empire. This produces subtle rather than gross discrepancies; the 1960s haven't swung, for example, and a range of American cultural influences are absent (oddly enough, this serves to make the setting more 'English', in a way). The Reich, having eliminated English Jewry and rendered the economy 'sound as a bell' (a nice irony) has withdrawn. There are no gauleiters, no garrison commanders, no *SS-GB*. Occupation is felt only as a self-discipline among the British administrative class, who retain all their traditional icy charm and 'impartiality'.

The plot of *An Englishman's Castle* is regrettably melo-dramatic, given the excellent *mise en scène* and leading performance by Kenneth More. It concerns a BBC television producer, Peter Ingram, who has devised a new television soap opera (*An Englishman's Castle*) to capitalize on the nostalgia boom of the 1970s. The narrative Ingram invents re-creates the gallant but doomed British resistance to invasion in 1940. It is, after thirty years, a neutral enough subject until Ingram, who is relying largely on personal wartime recollection, introduces a Jewish corporal. One thing leads to another, and eventually the hero finds himself at the head of a liberation struggle against the (still invisible) Germans.

The popularity of *SS-GB* and *An Englishman's Castle* seems to draw on a dim national awareness that despite VE and VJ, Britain has nonetheless 'lost'. These narratives answer to a suspicion of ultimate non-victory. An unnoticed invasion, they imply, has gradually achieved everything that the dramatically thwarted invasion of 1940 would have intended. We have lost the war which the chronicles claim we won. The casting of More, stiff-upper-lipped hero of so many how-we-won-the-war films, was a brilliant stroke.

Amis is a slightly different case from either Deighton or Philip Mackie, who wrote *An Englishman's Castle*, though the shared 'as if' device is clear enough. Amis is the cleverer novelist, and *The Alteration* is more consciously contrived as a homage to sf. There is also a longer and more complex historical perspective. The novel is set in a contemporary Britain for which the Reformation has never occurred:

It is 1976, but things are not the same. Due to a slight alteration in history involving Catherine of Aragon, Martin Luther, Thomas More and others, a Holy Victory was won in an event called the War of the English Succession, and today England, like most of the world, is virtually ruled by a Macchiavellian Pope who hails from Yorkshire. Piety is rampant, science is a forbidden word and New England is a wild abode of exile for Schismatics and common criminals. Amis's altered England is a world in which an ostensibly benevolent but totalitarian ideology has removed all subordinate ideological difference. We are inside the whale, in Orwell's superstate where, for example, one cannot commit the individualistic act of reading or writing novels. (The schoolboy hero with his mates defies Catholic totalitarian discipline by devouring such bootlegged sf novels as *Pavane*, *The Man in the High Castle* and *Bring the Jubilee* — all alternative universe fictions.) Officially there are no alternative views any more. This social neutering or castration is signalled clearly in the funeral service for King Stephen III of England, which opens the action. There are, among the massed visiting church dignitaries:

two . . . aged representatives of the Holy Office in their black vestments symbolically piped in scarlet: Monsignor Henricus and Monsignor Lavrentius, or to give them the familiar names by which they were known in their native Almaigne and Muscovy, Himmler and Beria (*The Alteration*, 1976, pp. 8-9).

The great oppositions and separations which shaped the modern world have never happened in Amis's fable.

Each has its individual points of interest, but there is one feature that *SS-GB*, *An Englishman's Castle* and *The Alteration* share which is pertinent to British history of the 1970s, the period in which their alternate worlds are set. In all three Britain belongs to (not in, but to) a European superstate whose centre is Berlin or Rome, depending on the 'as if'. It is not difficult to relate this to the great event of the decade, namely the entering of the Common Market. These novels would seem to express a sense (clearly a widespread sense, given their bestselling success) that the initial EEC decision and the corroborative mid-1970s vote of assent was a surrender, not a great historic step. However the crosses were made on the ballot papers, there is a lingering resentment that the national separateness of England, preserved for so long and at such expense of blood and sacrifice, has finally been ceded without a struggle. We might as well have lost the war, or not bothered to fight it.

Epilogue

According to Walter Bagehot, it is only by a certain firmly held and widespread idiocy that modern society keeps itself going:

> I fear you will laugh when I tell you that what I conceive to be about the most essential quality for a free people, whose liberty is to be progressive, permanent, and on a large scale; it is much *stupidity*. . . . In fact, what we opprobriously call stupidity, though not an enlivening quality in common society, is nature's favourite resource for preserving steadiness of conduct and consistency of opinion (quoted in Barzun, 1959, p. 148).

A whole range of sustaining and (largely) amiable Anglo-Saxon stupidity is openly displayed in its bestselling fiction. We are daily bombarded with gloomy news, and most of the population live lives of quiet desperation. Nevertheless, bestsellers invariably have upliftingly happy or providential endings. The enemy may be at the gate, but in our novels the shark is killed, the hijack foiled, the plague narrowly averted, the demon exorcized, civilization as we know it saved from innumerable close-run things. There are two million unemployed in Britain, but novels like Arthur Hailey's resolutely continue to celebrate the noble fulfilments and unbounded opportunities of the 'little man'.

'Frighteners' and 'Nazism resurgent' fantasies (a few of which deviate by having ominous or ambiguous endings) perform a subtler and less blatantly escapist trick. So do the disaster scenarios and Erdman's international finance melodramas. In these bestselling works the complex social and economic technicalities of the world are converted into the comfortably primitive formulations of human motivation (greed and will to power, in Erdman's case) or demonology. Since 1945 the western world has lived only four minutes away from the nuclear annihilation which man has prepared for himself. But the disasters with which bestsellerdom terrifies us are typically 'natural', not of our making: flood, fire, earthquake.

Even where they touch on 'real' social problems in an 'enlightened' frame of mind, the tendency is for bestsellers to be safely behind the times. The muck they rake is never fresh, the causes they espouse never genuinely new. Thus a work like Marilyn French's *The Woman's Room* comes in, fists flailing, when the fight for female emancipation has moved to other arenas. Novels such as hers and Erica Jong's do not, as advertisements impudently claim, 'change lives'. In so far as they have a useful function it is in serving to domesticate alien, life-changing social ideas for the mass of the population, just as Michael Crichton's superdocumentaries domesticate new and life-changing technology. Essentially these works have much the same appeal as the pure romance which they affect to oppose (bodice rippers and westerns, for instance). They are anodynes. They soothe. No one could guide their life by the codes, awareness and information which bestsellers furnish. But they clearly make lives more livable for millions of British and American consumers.

Potentially, the bestseller is a powerful instrument for social change, instruction or enlightenment. In the past some popular novels have undoubtedly realized that potential. One thinks automatically of *Uncle Tom's Cabin*, *The Jungle*, *The Grapes of Wrath*. But there are few recent cases where a bestseller has led, rather than followed, progressive thought. And in the supersellers of the 1970s there are no exceptions to record. These pre-eminently successful novels provide much in the way of thrills and excitement, but nothing in the way of serious intellectual, moral or social disturbance of received stupidity.

Potentially, too, the bestseller is a huge resource for the student — whether his discipline is history, literature or sociology. But nor have they here been exploited as they might have been. As the latest guide to research ruefully observes:

No comprehensive work on bestsellers has been published since Hart's *The Popular Book* came out in 1950. No good anthologies exist. In short, although they were read by more people than other books at a particular time, bestsellers have been neglected as a tool for studying American culture (Inge, 1980, p. 47).

At least in America, cultural critics have got to the stage of setting up the board with a guide to research. In Britain, academic ignorance and incuriosity about bestsellers seems complete and self-willed. I have been surprised, for instance, to discover that the British Library, the major research facility of the nation, does not apparently exercise its copyright deposit options on many 'ephemeral' novels of the day (notably, as far as I can discern, on 'paperback originals'). One charitably assumes that this is an institutional form of Bagehot's benign 'stupidity'. But if prejudices change, much of the surrounding undergrowth of our current bestsellerdom will be very hard to come by in fifty years time.

Prejudices will change, I think. Attention will surely be drawn to the bestseller if only because of the extraordinary commercial dynamism it has recently manifested. The gross increase in the consumption of novels, and the emergence of 10 m. sellers in the US and 2 m. sellers in the UK, indicate a new and rather terrifying mature phase of the paperback revolution. The sales apparatus of bestsellerdom (lists, hype, tie-ins) is now enormously rationalized. Bestsellers are produced with consummate efficiency, and on scales which we have never witnessed before. Such efficiency and magnitude will be hard to ignore for much longer.

Checklist of fiction

(Where novels are quoted from, the edition used is indicated.)

Abduction, Harrison James, 1974
The Adventurers, Harold Robbins, 1969 (London, New English Library, 1977)
Airport, Arthur Hailey, 1968
Airport '77, M. Scheff and D. Spector, 1977
Airport '79, Kerry Stewart, 1979
Albion! Albion!, Dick Morland, 1974
Alien, Alan Dean Foster, 1979
The Alteration, Kingsley Amis, 1976 (London, Cape, 1976)
The Amityville Horror, Jay Anson, 1978
Amok, George Fox, 1978
The Anderson Tapes, Lawrence Sanders, 1979 (London, Granada, 1979)
The Andromeda Strain, Michael Crichton, 1969
Apache Squaw, John J. McLaglen, 1977 (London, Corgi, 1977)
Audrey Rose, Frank de Felitta, 1975
August 1914, Alexander Solzhenitsyn, 1972
A Badge for a Badman, Jonas Ward (Brian Garfield), 1967
Battlestar Galactica, Glen A. Larson and Robin Thurston, 1979
Bear Island, Alistair MacLean, 1971
Beggarman, Thief, Irwin Shaw, 1977
The Billion Dollar Killing, Paul E. Erdman, 1973
Black Camelot, Duncan Kyle, 1978
The Black Death, Gwyneth Cravens and John S. Marr, 1977
The Black Marble, Joseph Wambaugh, 1977 (London, Futura, 1978)
The Black Orchestra, Robert Vacha, 1979
Black Sunday, Thomas Harris, 1975
The Black Widow, John J. McLaglen, 1977 (London, Corgi, 1977)
Blizzard, Thom Racina, 1977
Blood Secrets, Craig Jones, 1978
The Blue Knight, Joseph Wambaugh, 1973
Bomber, Len Deighton, 1970

The Bormann Receipt, Madelaine Duke, 1979
The Boys From Brazil, Ira Levin, 1976 (London, Pan, 1977)
Brass Target, Frederick Nolan, 1974
Breakheart Pass, Alistair MacLean, 1974
Bring the Jubilee, Ward Moore, 1955
By the Rivers of Babylon, Nelson de Mille, 1978
The Caine Mutiny, Herman Wouk, 1951
The Canfield Decision, Spiro T. Agnew, 1976
Caravan to Vaccarès, Alistair MacLean, 1970
The Carpetbaggers, Harold Robbins, 1961
Carrie, Stephen King, 1974
Cashelmara, Susan Howatch, 1974
The Cats, Berton Roueché, 1975
The Cats, Nick Sharman, 1977
Centennial, James A. Michener, 1974
Children of the Dark, Charles Veley, 1978
The Chilian Club, George Shipway, 1972
The Choirboys, Joseph Wambaugh, 1975
Circus, Alistair MacLean, 1975
City of the Dead, Herbert Lieberman, 1976
Clara Reeve, Leonie Hargrave, 1975
The Climate of Hell, Herbert Lieberman, 1978
A Clockwork Orange, Anthony Burgess, 1962
Close Encounters of the Third Kind, Steven Spielberg, 1977
Cocksure, Mordecai Richler, 1968
Coma, Robin Cook, 1977 (London, Pan, 1979)
The Company, John Ehrlichman, 1976 (London, Fontana, 1976)
Condominium, John D. MacDonald, 1977
Conflict of Interest, Les Whitten, 1976
The Crash of '79, Paul E. Erdman, 1976 (London, Secker & Warburg, 1977)
The Croesus Conspiracy, Ben Stein, 1978
The Crowd Pleasers, Rosemary Rogers, 1978
The Cruel Sea, Nicholas Monsarrat, 1951
Csardas, Diane Pearson, 1975
The Cult, Max Ehrlich, 1978
Damon, C. Terry Cline, 1975 (London, Futura, 1976)
Dare to Love, Jennifer Wilde, 1977
Dark Fires, Rosemary Rogers, 1975
The Day of the Jackal, Frederick Forsyth, 1971
Death Dreams, W. Katz, 1978
Death Knell, C. Terry Cline, 1977
Death List, R. McKew and R. de Rouen, 1979
Death Rites, John J. McLaglen, 1978 (London, Corgi, 1978)

Death Sentence, Brian Garfield, 1976 (London, Pan, 1977)
Death Wish, Brian Garfield, 1972 (London, Coronet, 1974)
Deluge, Richard Doyle, 1976
Demon Seed, Dean Koontz, 1973
The Devil's Alternative, Frederick Forsyth, 1979
Dog Day Afternoon, Patrick Mann, 1974 (New York, Dell, 1975)
The Dogs of War, Frederick Forsyth, 1974
Dolores, Jacqueline Susann, 1976
Do With Me What You Will, Joyce Carol Oates, 1973
The Dragon, Alfred Coppel, 1977
Dragon Spoor, Jack H. Crisp, 1978
Dreams Die First, Harold Robbins, 1977
The Dream Merchants, Harold Robbins, 1949
Dress Gray, Lucian K. Truscott IV, 1978
The Eagle Has Landed, Jack Higgins, 1975
Earthsound, Arthur Herzog, 1975
Elizabeth, Jessica Hamilton, 1977
The Empire Strikes Back, Donald F. Glut, 1980
An Exchange of Eagles, Owen Sela, 1977
Exodus, Leon Uris, 1959
The Exorcist, Peter Blatty, 1971 (London, Corgi, 1977)
Eye of the Needle (*Storm Island*), Ken Follett, 1978
Falling Angel, William Hjortsberg, 1978
The Far Pavilions, M.M. Kaye, 1978
Father Pig, Burt Hirschfeld, 1972
Fear is the Key, Alistair MacLean, 1977
Fear of Flying, Erica Jong, 1973
The Final Diagnosis, Arthur Hailey, 1959
Fireball, V. Mayhew and D. Long, 1977
Firespill, Ian Slater, 1977
A Fire in the Sky, Walter Kendrick, 1978
Five Hours from Isfahan, William Copeland, 1975
The Fix, Leo Clancy, 1979
Flashman, George Macdonald Fraser, 1969
Flight Into Danger, Arthur Hailey and 'John Castle', 1958
Flood, Richard Martin Stern, 1979
Fools Die, Mario Puzo, 1978
Force 10 From Navarone, Alistair MacLean, 1968
Four Days, Harold King, 1976
Four Just Men, Edgar Wallace, 1905
Freeze, George Stone, 1977
The French Connection, Robin Moore, 1969
The Führer Seed, Gus Weill, 1979
Full Disclosure, William Safire, 1977

The Fury, John Farris, 1976
The Gang, Herbert Kastle, 1978
The Glass Inferno, T.N. Scortia and F.M. Robinson, 1974
The Godfather, Mario Puzo, 1969 (London, Pan, 1977)
The Godsend, Bernard Taylor, 1976
God Told Me To, C.K. Chandler, 1976
The Goering Testament, George Markstein, 1978
The Golden Gate, Alistair MacLean, 1976 (London, Fontana, 1978)
Golden Girl, Peter Lear, 1977
The Golden Rendezvous, Alistair MacLean, 1962
Goldfinger, Ian Fleming, 1959 (London, Pan, 1964)
Gone With the Wind, M. Mitchell, 1936
Goodbye California, Alistair MacLean, 1977
The Greek, Pierre Rey, 1973 (London, Coronet, 1975)
The Green Berets, Robin Moore, 1965
Green Ice, Gerald A. Browne, 1978
The Guns of Navarone, Alistair MacLean, 1957 (London, Fontana, 1976)
The Hab Theory, Allan W. Eckert, 1976
The Haunting of Hill House, Shirley Jackson, 1959
Heat, Arthur Herzog, 1977
Hell House, Richard Matheson, 1971
The Hermes Fall, John Baxter, 1978
The Hess Cross, J.S. Thayer, 1977
HMS Ulysses, Alistair MacLean, 1955 (London, Fontana, 1977)
The Holcroft Covenant, Robert Ludlum, 1978
Holocaust, Gerald Green, 1978
Holocaust 2000, Michael Robson, 1978
The Hostage Heart, Gerald Green, 1976
Hotel, Arthur Hailey, 1965
The House on the Hill, J. Black, 1978
How to Save Your Own Life, Erica Jong, 1977
Ice, James Follett, 1978
Icequake, Crawford Killian, 1979
Ice Station Zebra, Alistair MacLean, 1963 (London, Fontana, 1969)
The Immigrants, Howard Fast, 1977
In High Places, Arthur Hailey, 1962
In the National Interest, M. Kalb and T. Koppel, 1978
The Investigation, Dorothy Uhnak, 1977 (London, Pan, 1979)
The Ipcress File, Len Deighton, 1962
It Can't Happen Here, Sinclair Lewis, 1936
It's Alive, Richard Woodley, 1977
I the Jury, Mickey Spillane, 1947
Jaws, Peter Benchley, 1974 (New York, Bantam, 1975)

Jaws 2, Hank Searls, 1978
The Jericho Commandment, James Patterson, 1979
Jonathan Livingston Seagull, Richard Bach, 1970
The Judas Squad, James N. Rowe, 1975
Julia (Full Circle), Peter Straub, 1975
Keeper of the Children, William H. Hallahan, 1978
K.G. 200, J.D. Gilman and John Clive, 1977
The Killing Gift, Bari Wood, 1975 (London, Pan, 1977)
King Rat, James Clavell, 1962
Kiss Me, Deadly, Mickey Spillane, 1952 (London, Corgi, 1967)
Kolchak's Gold, Brian Garfield, 1973
Lady Chatterley's Lover, D.H. Lawrence, 1928
Landslide, Desmond Bagley, 1967
Leviathan, John G. Davis, 1977
Liner, James Barlow, 1972
The Lonely Lady, Harold Robbins, 1976 (London, New English Library, 1977)
Looking for Mr Goodbar, Judith Rossner, 1975
The Looking Glass War, John le Carré, 1975
Lord of the Rings, J.R.R. Tolkien, 1954-5
Love All, Molly Parkin, 1974
Lovers and Gamblers, Jackie Collins, 1977
Love's Tender Fury, Jennifer Wilde, 1976
Love Story, Erich Segal, 1970
Love's Wild Desire, Jennifer Blake, 1977
Lucifer's Hammer, Larry Niven and Jerry Pournelle, 1977
Lupe, Gene Thompson, 1977
Lynch Law Canyon, Brian Wynne (Brian Garfield), 1965
Magic, William Goldman, 1976
The Man From Lisbon, Thomas Gifford, 1977 (London, Futura 1978)
The Man in the High Castle, Philip K. Dick, 1962
The Manitou, Graham Masterton, 1977
The Man With the President's Mind, Ted Allbeury, 1977
Marathon Man, William Goldman, 1974
The Matarese Circle, Robert Ludlum, 1979
Memoirs of an Ex-Prom Queen, Alix Kates Shulman, 1972
Memories of Another Day, Harold Robbins, 1979 (London, New English Library, 1979)
Mendaga's Morning, David Ferran, 1979
Meteor, E.H. North and F. Coen, 1979
The Minotaur Factor, Stuart Stern, 1977
The Minstrel Code, Walter Nelson, 1979
The Mittenwald Syndicate, Frederick Nolan, 1976
The Moneychangers, Arthur Hailey, 1975

The Moonchild, K. McKenney, 1978
The Multiple Man, Ben Bova, 1976
The Naked and the Dead, Norman Mailer, 1948
The New Centurions, Joseph Wambaugh, 1970
The Nightmare Factor, T.N. Scortia and F.M. Robinson, 1978
No Orchids for Miss Blandish, James Hadley Chase, 1939
North Dallas Forty, Peter Gent, 1972
The October Plot, Clive Egleton, 1974
The Odessa File, Frederick Forsyth, 1972
Oktoberfest, Frank de Felitta, 1974
Oliver's Story, Erich Segal, 1977
The Omen, David Seltzer, 1976
Omen II (Damien), Joseph Howard, 1978
One Flew Over the Cuckoo's Nest, Ken Kesey, 1962
Orca, Arthur Herzog, 1977
The Other Side of Midnight, Sidney Sheldon, 1973
Out of Control, G. Gordon Liddy, 1979
Overload, Arthur Hailey, 1979
The Paladin, Brian Garfield, 1980
Pavane, Keith Roberts, 1966
Perdido, Jill Robinson, 1978
The Petrodollar Takeover, P. Tanous and P. Rubinstein, 1975
Phoenix, A. Aicha and E. Landau, 1979
The Phoenix Assault, John Kerrigan, 1980
The Pirate, Harold Robbins, 1974
Portnoy's Complaint, Philip Roth, 1969
The Poseidon Adventure, Paul Gallico, 1972
Presidential Emergency, Walter Stovall, 1978
The President's Mistress, Patrick Anderson, 1976
Princess Daisy, Judith Krantz, 1980
The Prometheus Project, T.N. Scortia and F.M. Robinson, 1975
Puppet on a Chain, Alistair MacLean, 1969 (London, Fontana, 1971)
QB VII, Leon Uris, 1970 (London, Corgi, 1979)
Ragtime, E.L. Doctorow, 1975
The Rainbow, D.H. Lawrence, 1915
The Rats, James Herbert, 1974
Rat Trap, Craig Thomas, 1976
Red Carpet for the Shah, Peter Ritner, 1975
The Reincarnation of Peter Proud, Max Ehrlich, 1974
Report to the Commissioner, James Mills, 1972
The Rhinemann Exchange, Robert Ludlum, 1974
Rich Man, Poor Man, Irwin Shaw, 1970
River of Blood, John J. McLaglen, 1976 (London, Corgi, 1976)
Rollercoaster, Burton Wohl, 1979

The Romanov Succession, Brian Garfield, 1974
The Rommel Plot, John Tarrant, 1977
Rosebud, J. Hemingway and P. Bonnecarrère, 1973 (Harmondsworth, Penguin, 1975)
Rosemary's Baby, Ira Levin, 1967
Salem's Lot, Stephen King, 1975
The Satan Bug, Alistair MacLean, 1962 (London, Fontana, 1968)
Savage Eden, Constance Gluyas, 1976
Sayonara, James A. Michener, 1954
The Scarlatti Inheritance, Robert Ludlum, 1971
Sea Witch, Alistair MacLean, 1977
The Sentinel, Jeffrey Konvitz, 1974
Sentinel II, Jeffrey Konvitz, 1978
The Set Up, Robin Moore and Milt Machlin, 1975
Shadow of the Vulture, John J. McLaglen, 1977 (London, Corgi, 1977)
Shadow of the Wolf, James Barwick, 1978
Shakedown, J. Kwitny, 1977
Shall We Tell the President?, Jeffrey Archer, 1977
The Shining, Stephen King, 1977
Shockwave, Robert Cawley, 1980
Shōgun, James Clavell, 1975
The Shrewsdale Exit, John Buell, 1972
Side Effect, Raymond Hawkey, 1979
Siege, Peter Cave, 1980
The Silver Bears, Paul E. Erdman, 1974
Slide, Gerald A. Browne, 1977
Small Changes, Marge Piercy, 1973
The Snake, John Godey, 1978 (New York, Berkley, 1979)
The Snow Tiger, Desmond Bagley, 1974
The Soul of Anna Klane, Terrel Miedaner, 1977
South by Java Head, Alistair MacLean, 1958
Spawn, Robert Holles, 1978
SS-GB, Len Deighton, 1978 (London, Panther, 1979)
Star Wars, George Lucas, 1976 (London, Sphere, 1977)
Steal Big, Patrick Mann, 1978
The Stepford Wives, Ira Levin, 1972
The Strasbourg Legacy, W. Craig, 1979
Such Good Friends, Lois Gould, 1970
Suffer the Children, John Saul, 1976
The Swarm, Arthur Herzog, 1974
Sweet Savage Love, Rosemary Rogers, 1974
Tai-Pan, James Clavell, 1966
The Taking of Pelham 123, John Godey, 1973 (London, Coronet, 1974)
The Talisman, John Godey, 1976

The Tangent Factor, Lawrence Sanders, 1978
The Tangent Objective, Lawrence Sanders, 1976
Ten Little Niggers, Agatha Christie, 1939
The Terminal Man, Michael Crichton, 1972
Testament, David Morrell, 1976
The Third Man, Graham Greene, 1950
34 East, Alfred Coppel, 1974
Thirst, Charles E. Maine, 1977
Thirst, Guy N. Smith, 1980
The Thorn Birds, Colleen McCullough, 1977 (London, Futura, 1978)
330 Park, Stanley Cohen, 1977 (London, New English Library, 1979)
Tim, Colleen McCullough, 1975
Tinker, Tailor, Soldier, Spy, John le Carré, 1974
Tinsel, William Goldman, 1979
To Catch a King, Harry Patterson, 1979
To Kill a Cop, Robert Daley, 1976
The Tower, Richard Martin Stern, 1973
Trinity, Leon Uris, 1976
Triple, Ken Follett, 1979
The Triton Ultimatum, Laurence Delaney, 1977
Twister, Jack Bickham, 1978
Ultimatum, Paul Bonnecarrère, 1975
The Users, Joyce Haber, 1976
The Valhalla Exchange, Harry Patterson, 1976
The Valkyrie Encounter, Stephen Marlowe, 1978
Viper 3, Walter Wager, 1973
Vortex, Jon Cleary, 1978
The Warriors, Sol Yurick, 1965
Watership Down, Richard Adams, 1972
The Werewolf Trace, John Gardner, 1975
Wheels, Arthur Hailey, 1971 (London, Pan, 1973)
When Eight Bells Toll, Alistair MacLean, 1966 (London, Fontana, 1970)
When the Kissing Had to Stop, Constantine Fitzgibbon, 1960
Where Eagles Dare, Alistair MacLean, 1967
White House, Patrick Anderson, 1978
The Whole Truth, John Ehrlichman, 1979
Wicked Loving Lies, Rosemary Rogers, 1974
Wild Card, R. Hawkey and R. Bingham, 1974 (London, Panther, 1976)
The Wildest Heart, Rosemary Rogers, 1974
Wolfsbane, Craig Thomas, 1978
The Woman's Room, Marilyn French, 1977
Women in Love, D.H. Lawrence, 1921
The World According to Garp, John Irving, 1976
The Young Lions, Irwin Shaw, 1949

Bibliography of non-fiction

Adorno, T. (1967), *Prisms*, London, Neville Spearman.
Aldiss, Brian W. (1973), *Billion Year Spree*, London, Weidenfeld & Nicolson.
Arendt, H. (1964), *Eichmann in Jerusalem*, London, Faber & Faber.
Barzun, J. (1959, repr. 1962), *The House of Intellect*, London, Mercury.
Barzun, J. and Taylor, W.H. (1971), *A Catalogue of Crime*, New York, Harper & Row.
Blair, Joan and Clay (1976), *The Search for J.F.K.*, New York, Berkley.
Blond, A. (1971), *The Publishing Game*, London, Cape.
Burgess, A. (1968, repr. 1971), *The Novel Now*, London, Faber & Faber.
Cawelti, J. (1970), *Six Gun Mystique*, Ohio, Bowling Green University Popular Press.
Cheney, O.H. (1932), *Economic Survey of the Book Industry, 1930-31*, New York, Bowker.
Contemporary Novelists (1976), London and New York, St James Press and St Martin's Press.
Daley, R. (1978), *Prince of the City*, London, MacGibbon & Kee.
Deighton, L. (1977), *Fighter*, London, Cape.
Enzensberger, H.M. (1962, repr. 1973), *Einzelheiten I*, Frankfurt, Suhrkamp.
Escarpit, R. (1966), *The Book Revolution*, London, Harrap.
Exner, J. (1977), *My Story*, New York, Grove Press.
Fischer, E. (1959, repr. 1978), *The Necessity of Art*, Harmondsworth, Penguin.
Friedan, B. (1963), *The Feminine Mystique*, London, Gollancz.
Gedin, P. (1977), *Literature in the Market Place*, London, Faber & Faber.
Goulden, M. (1978), *Mark My Words*, London, W.H. Allen.
Greene, G. (1969, repr. 1970), *Collected Essays*, Harmondsworth, Penguin.
Greer, G. (1971), *The Female Eunuch*, London, MacGibbon & Kee.
Hackett, A.P. and Burke, J.H. (1977), *80 Years of Best-Sellers*, New York, Bowker.

Hailey, S. (1978), *I Married a Best Seller*, London, Michael Joseph.
Hodges, S. (1978), *Gollancz: The Story of a Publishing House*, London, Gollancz.
Hoggart, R. (1957), *The Uses of Literacy*, London, Chatto & Windus.
Howard, M. (1971), *Jonathan Cape, Publisher*, London, Cape.
Inge, M.T. (1980), *Handbook of American Popular Culture*, Connecticut, Greenwood Press.
James, H. (1962), 'The Future of the Novel', in L. Edel (ed.), *The House of Fiction*, London, Mercury, pp. 48-59.
Johnson, B. (1978), *The Secret War*, London, BBC Publications.
Jones, R.V. (1978), *The Most Secret War*, London, Hamish Hamilton.
Kael, P. (1973), *Deeper Into Movies*, Boston, Atlantic Monthly Press.
Kahn, D. (1978), *Hitler's Spies: German Military Intelligence in World War II*, New York, Macmillan.
Leavis, Q.D. (1932), *Fiction and the Reading Public*, London, Chatto & Windus.
Lewin, D. (1978), *Ultra Goes to War*, London, Hutchinson.
Loynd, R. (1978), *The Jaws 2 Log*, London, W.H. Allen.
Madison, C.A. (1974), *Irving to Irving*, New York, Bowker.
Mailer, N. (1975), *Marilyn*, New York, Warner Books.
Mills, C. Wright (1956), *The Power Elite*, New York, Oxford University Press.
Morgan, T. (1978), 'Sharks: The Making of a Best Seller', in R. Atway, *American Mass Media*, ed. B. Orton and W. Vesterman, New York, Random House, pp. 140-50.
Mott, F.L. (1947), *Golden Multitudes*, New York, Macmillan.
Nuttal, J. (1968), *Bomb Culture*, London, MacGibbon & Kee.
Orwell, G. (1968), *The Collected Essays, Journalism and Letters of George Orwell*, vol. 3, ed. Sonia Orwell and Ian Angus, London, Secker & Warburg.
Peters, J. (1976), 'Kleiner Versuch über den grossen Erfolg', in A. Rucktäschel (ed.), *Trivialliteratur*, Munich, Wilhem Fink, pp. 139-68.
Puzo, M. (1972), *The Godfather Papers*, London, Heinemann.
Rolph, C.H. (1961), *The Trial of Lady Chatterley*, Harmondsworth, Penguin.
Sontag, S. (1978), *Illness as Metaphor*, New York, Farrar, Strauss & Giroux.
Spock, B. (1946, repr. 1974), *Baby and Child Care*, New York, Pocket Books.
Thomas, H. (1978), *The Murder of Rudolf Hess*, London, Hodder & Stoughton.
Tolstoy, N. (1978), *Victims of Yalta*, London, Hodder & Stoughton.
Tompkins, J.M.S. (1932), *The Popular Novel in England, 1770-1800*, London, Constable.

Van Nostrand, A.D. (1960), *The Denatured Novel*, New York, Bobbs-Merril.
Wambaugh, J. (1974), *The Onion Field*, London, Weidenfeld & Nicolson.
Watson, C. (1979), *Snobbery With Violence*, London, Methuen.
The White House Transcripts (1974), New York, Bantam.
Whitney, S. (1975, repr. 1978), *Charles Bronson: Superstar*, London, Robert Hale.
Williams, R. (1977), 'Literature in Society', in H. Schiff (ed.), *Contemporary Approaches to English Studies*, London, Heinemann, pp. 24-37.
Williams, R. (1961), *The Long Revolution*, London, Chatto & Windus.

Index